THE MORMON CHURCHES
a comparison from within

THE
MORMON
CHURCHES

a comparison from within

Francis W. Holm, Sr.

This book is dedicated
to the memory of my
Father

PREFACE

Why would a man write a book on as moth-eaten a subject as Mormonism? Doesn't he know that for more than a hundred years scores of volumes have been published on the subject and that nobody is interested today? Moreover, isn't this the age of ecumenism when old differences in religions have been forgotten? At a time when rockets are transporting men to the moon, why does he ride a dead horse?

If the above even roughly approximates the reader's reaction on discovering this volume, he should be prepared for a surprise.

Francis Holm has written a book which differs from other books about Mormons in the following ways:

(1) He is not a disgruntled dissident looking for a literary vehicle in which to carry his grievances to a wider public.

(2) He is not a "Gentile" writing another expose of the alleged weaknesses of Mormonism.

(3) He is not a Mormon zealot seeking to prove that one church is better than the other.

(4) He is not a graduate student whose approach to the history of the Mormons may be influenced as much by the need to impress a committee responsible for granting him a degree as by the need for fairness to persons involved in that history.

(5) He is not a sensualist relishing the authorship of one more book on polygamy.

(6) He is, instead, an honest man who sees an important present-day need with which no other book has dealt, and he has sought to meet that need squarely and sensibly.

What need does he see?

Francis Holm believes that there was once an American prophet who had great ideas for our time—ideas which ought to be shared now with a world that sorely needs a prophet. Francis Holm is convinced that neither one of the principal churches which claim Joseph Smith as their founder is following exactly the direction given through the prophet and that the needy world is suffering as a result. Francis Holm feels that each of the churches can profit from burying the hatchet and adopting as its own those good practices which are scripturally sound and have proven themselves for the other church, that each church may improve further by changing, or dropping those traditions which are not in harmony with what God intended as seen in the revelations quoted in this book.

And Francis Holm feels that *every* Christian will profit from an examination of a church which claims to have been established in our time by divine command.

The reader may not agree with the author's point of view on every item he covers in the book. The reader may even challenge some matters which the author presents as historical facts. But if the reader approaches the book with an open mind and a desire for fairness, he will discover many suggestions about which he may find himself commenting: "Yes, that is a good recommendation; the Church of Jesus Christ in the latter-days (latter days?) ought to do it that way."

The book can easily become for the reader a test of his own objectivity. If he feels the hackles rising because the author seems to be taking the member's church to task for departing from what the author views as a sound scriptural position, the reader could be well advised to read on. Soon he will feel that he is in good company as the writer takes the other church to task for what he sees as that church's failure to follow sound doctrine.

The honest investigator who is not a member of the church (churches?) founded by Joseph Smith ought to know why the author considers the Restoration prophet such an important figure.

One contemporary evaluated him this way:

"It is by no means improbable that some future textbook, for the use of generations yet unborn, will contain a question something like this: What historical American of the nineteenth century has exerted the most powerful influence upon the destinies of his countrymen: And it is by no means impossible that the answer to that interrogatory may be thus written: Joseph Smith, the Mormon prophet."

Thus did Josiah Quincy, the former president of the Massachusetts Senate and mayor of Boston and himself the son of an illustrious American pioneer, assess the worth of Joseph

Smith, Jr., in his book *Figures of the Past* published in 1882 almost forty years after the Bostonian had visited the American prophet.

Whether or not one agrees with Senator Quincy, the accomplishments of Joseph Smith—as seen both in the fifteen years of his ministry before his death in 1844, and in the subsequent growth of the movement he started—when compared with the treatment he has received at the hands of numerous writers, suggests that America may not have given appropriate recognition to one of its authentic heroes.

Perhaps historians have discarded angels and revelation, and therefore cannot accept a "prophet, seer, and revelator." Undoubtedly religious bigotry prevents many persons from accepting the notion that any but biblical times could produce a genuine prophet.

Anyway, as has been said, "In our times we have scientists, so who needs prophets?"

Yet most observers would agree that the 1970's are a time of sad harvest, a day of reaping the consequences of a century of material "progress" made possible because of scientists who were more interested in pure research than the moral consequences which would follow the release of the monsters developed in their laboratories. Polution of the air, the soil, and the waters of the earth have provided a bitter cornucopia for the descendants of Adam who were supposed to have subdued their environment. The latest news is that even the protective envelope of oxygen on which life on earth depends is in jeopardy.

This is the legacy of a people who worshiped science and technology but forgot that scientists and technologists can make mistakes—awesome mistakes.

And the most bitter harvest of all is the pollution of the human soul by pride, lust, violence, and greed—realities which we can blame only on ourselves.

Obviously something hasn't been working for the best of mankind as we have followed the old ways of doing business on planet earth. Something new is needed under the sun.

The disenchanted, seeking a way out, could well ask, "If God loves us, isn't it time that He made Himself known?"

In the view of Francis Holm He has done so, and He continues to make His will known through the prophets who have succeeded Joseph Smith as leaders of the church. God speaks to us in the twentieth century through the prophet of the nineteenth century.

What kind of man was this modern prophet?

Joseph Smith may have been a preacher, but the profession which describes him best is Social Innovator, or to use a more conventional word, builder.

He was not a builder in the usual sense of one who erects a house or constructs a subdivision. His kind of building went to the heart of the matter. He recognized that religion had to do with all of the activities in which men are engaged. He knew that men gather in cities to do their work. He understood that the institutions in which men labor in their cities mold the laborers. He sought nothing less than the establishment of communities conceived in righteousness by righteous men who would labor together with God for purposes which originated in God. He sought to build a New Jerusalem in the "Center Place" of the American continent.

In this, he was not unlike the founding fathers of the land, which Joseph Smith called "the promised land," who came to this continent to find freedom and to build a new world.

He knew that if men were to live in safety and joy in cities, they needed a model city.

His followers today are still engaged in the unfinished task, begun by the founding fathers and advanced by the prophet—the divine assignment of building the City of God.

But if Joseph was not primarily a minister in the traditional sense, one could not accuse him of failing to leave a great body of religious literature upon which future generations could judge the worth of his contribution. Consider the following highlights from the literary record of the American prophet:

In response to instructions received from an angel he was led to discover a notebook of golden leaves bearing an inscription in a language unknown to him, by divine power was enabled to translate the ancient message into English, eventually offered the work in printed form for the scrutiny of a critical public, calling the final product *The Book of Mormon* and identifying it as new scripture worthy to be placed next to the Bible as a standard reference for Christian conduct.

Recognizing imperfections in the Bible itself, and making another application of his gifts as a "prophet, seer, and revelator," he proceeded not only to revise sentences and paragraphs in the sacred record but to add whole new sections based on information which had been lost through the machinations of lesser men centuries before, thus giving to the world a corrected edition of the *Holy Scriptures* identified today as the *Inspired Version*.

Responding to needs for enlightenment to govern the affairs of the kingdom which he sought to help the Lord establish, the prophet received numerous revelations, enough to fill a small book; revelations representing God directing —often in great detail—the conduct of His people, including instructions on what to eat, what to wear, the need for a temple (with specific instructions concerning size and other details of construction), the duties of church officers, the curriculum to be studied, and many other matters, the whole to be published as law to the people of God and bearing the title, *Book of Doctrine and Covenants*.

And literature was not the sum of his legacy.

In harmony with commandments of God, he established a church, known today, depending on what you believe as the Church of Jesus Christ of Latter-day Saints (world headquarters: Salt Lake City, Utah) or the Reorganized Church of Jesus Christ of Latter Day Saints (world headquarters: Independence, Missouri).

On a swampy bend in the Mississippi River, he built a magnificently planned community which became the largest city in Illinois. In that city he established what was probably America's first public school system in which learning was coordinated from the first grades through the university; he gave the leadership which led to the publication of the first newspaper and the establishment of the first school in Independence, which was about to become the "Queen City of the Trails," the embarkation point for wagon trains being fitted for the building of the West.

No mean record for fifteen years of ministry!

So Francis Holm has written a sympathetic book. It is sympathetic toward Joseph Smith, and toward the churches which claim him as their founder.

But he has also written a hard-hitting book in which he calls it, right or wrong, as he sees it.

Obviously such a book could cause embarrassment for the publishing house of either of the churches. So a corporation was formed to make the book available to members of all churches and to anyone else interested in that "historical American of the nineteenth century [who] has exerted the most powerful influence upon the destinies of his countrymen."

Contributing to the timeliness of the book is recognition of the fact that the winds of change are sweeping through the churches. Some observers are predicting the death of the church. Others who have known the joy of fellowship within the church and have committed themselves to the mission of the church are more apt to opt for a revival within the church based on a clearer understanding of the objectives of the church and the elimination of practices which do not contribute to those objectives as well as the adoption of those practices which do contribute.

This book should help in the determination of both objectives and practices as the reader is encouraged to view the matter from the perspective of the founding prophet.

The undersigned has worked for many years in the ecumenical movement, most recently serving as President of the Board of the Kansas School of Religion, the agency by which the University of Kansas offers credit for religious courses taught to its students. This experience has taught him that all churches can use new truth. It has also taught him that cooperation by religious leaders across denominational lines can replace arrogance with humility, turn animosity into appreciation, suspicion into respect, ignorance into understanding, and provincialism into brotherhood—at no cost to individual identity and with reinforcement to faith.

This book has become for him another tool to these ends.

R. Edwin Browne
Independence, Missouri

FOREWORD

The reader should keep in mind that the church that was established by Christ while on his sojourn on earth, after his death was subjected to many persecutions both from within the church and outside. However, persecutions were not the real danger confronting the followers of Christ. The real danger existed in the desire of men to improve upon that which had been given to them. This is first demonstrated by the Apostle Paul and his elaboration of the teachings of Christ. His teachings are not necessarily contrary to those of Christ but his attitude toward women was far less tolerant when he advocated "Let the women keep silent in the church."

As the church began to grow many different individuals of strong character began to influence the teachings of the church and led the innovation of changes in the sacraments, introduction of new doctrines such as the adoration of Mary, the mother of Christ.

All of these innovations have resulted in the various "Christian" denominations as they exist today. Some of these false ideas came about when efforts were made to promulgate the infallibility of the man selected to head the church. The rise of the Protestant movement was a recognition of the errors that had entered the organization and man's attempt to correct the errors.

The Restoration actually being the re-establishment of the church of Christ, was also subject to the same vicissitudes of the early church. Strong men had united with the church and began to make their presence felt and especially so during the period just preceding the prophet's death and immediately thereafter. Innovations began to appear in the church in various ways and there began to grow an attempt to make the prophet appear infallible. This feeling grew very rapidly after the death of the prophet and has led to much that has fed the differences existing between the two major factions of the Restoration.

The paralleling of the history of the primitive church of Christ and the history of the Restoration should serve as a warning to all true believers in the message Christ brought to mankind. The many efforts that have been made to complicate the simplicity of Christ's message should serve to alert man in his search for the truth.

The author has attempted to present the position of the church as it was initially given to the prophet. Any elaborations or innovations should be apparent to the student.

The author has studiously avoided the use of "hearsay" testimony and the supporting of any traditions because these are usually the end result of misapplication of teachings given through inspiration.

If the Prophet Joseph Smith was responsible for any of the errors that entered the Restoration, it can be attributed to the humanness that is dominant in all men. Any error he may have committed certainly should not affect that which is true because God has given to all mankind the opportunity to know the truth independent of what any man has said. This is an inherent right of all men and if what has been presented in this book will be of assistance, then the inspiration that accompanied its writing will be recognized.

ACKNOWLEDGMENTS

The author is indebted to a number of individuals who have been of great assistance by reading and commenting on the manuscripts, by supplying information and historical data and many books of reference.

The first to read the manuscript and offer encouragement was a very dear friend and associate in the priesthood, Bill Harper.

Among the most influential in supplying information and books was a very close friend, Elder James B. Keysor of Burbank, California. Brother Keysor was the mission president at Independence, Missouri, when the first contact was made. He is a member of the Mormon church and is, at present, a member of the presidency of the Los Angeles Temple. He both stimulated and aided the author by raising many questions and supplying many books and authentic information on his church.

Paul A. Wellington, editor of the *Saints' Herald* of the Reorganized Church, read and commented on the manuscript and made many helpful suggestions. Others of the Reorganized Church who have read and commented are Richard P. Howard, Historian for the Reorganized Church; L. Wayne Updike, president of the Denver Stake; Wayne Ham, editor of youth material; John Conway, president of Santa Fe Stake. Several others also read the manuscript.

Among Mormons who have read the manuscript and commented along with Brother Keysor was Jewel Pope while he was president of the Kansas City Stake.

One of the most outstanding and qualified readers was T. Edgar Lyon of Salt Lake City. He is the historian of the Nauvoo Restoration Corporation. He did an extensive and extremely helpful analysis of the book that has aided in the preparation for publication.

Eugene England, managing editor of *Dialogue* magazine, also read the manuscript and made some very complimentary remarks. He also offered to use some of the material in *Dialogue*.

CONTENTS

INTRODUCTION

Having been a member of each of the major organizations of the Restoration movement for over fifty years (explained later) namely the Church of Jesus Christ of Latter-Day Saints, commonly known as the "Mormon" church with headquarters in Salt Lake City, Utah, and the Reorganized Church of Jesus Christ of Latter Day Saints with headquarters in Independence, Missouri, commonly referred to as RLDS, I have had a strong impulse to put on record the conclusions I have formed from the experiences and observations of the two organizations. For the information to be of any real value, it is necessary for the reader to have some knowledge of my background and the reasons why I feel competent to make the observations contained in this book.

Due to the great influence my father had in the formation of my thinking and the extensive library I inherited from him, it is necessary that some facts about him should be made known. His name was Soren Sorensen Holm and he was born in Langemark, Denmark, on April 27, 1866. He was confirmed in the Lutheran Church on April 4, 1880.

While serving his apprenticeship as a baker, he learned of the Restoration and on August 12, 1887, was baptized a member of the Mormon Church. On October 5, 1887, he was ordained a Teacher and later was ordained a Priest. On September 29, 1889, he was ordained to the office of Elder and called to go on a mission for the church. His diary contains many very interesting experiences while on this assignment. On the completion of his mission he emigrated to Salt Lake City, Utah, where he became very active in the church.

On June 9, 1892, he was married to Christine F. Larsen in the temple at Logan, Utah, and to this marriage was born seven sons and one daughter. The writer is the sole survivor of this large family.

May 18, 1902, the Thirty-second Ward was organized in the Pioneer Stake and Robert Sherwood was selected as Bishop and my father was his first counselor and James E. Tregeagle his second counselor. This gave him the opportunity to continue his active service to the church that began with his mission in Denmark.

To be able to serve the church more effectively required much study and research which led to the accumulation of the many books which have proven of much value to the writer. These books also proved a source of information that led to a great change in my father's life. He spent many years of devoted activity to the church both in a local capacity as counselor in the bishopric and also doing a great deal of Temple work. As a result of this devotion to the church he was the recipient of a special blessing in the Temple which was known as the "Second Anointing." Recently the writer has been informed that this blessing is no longer given. To the best of my knowledge, my father is the only man having received this anointing that ever joined with the Reorganized Church. It may also be of interest to note that, even though my father remained in Utah and was the presiding elder over the Provo Branch of the Reorganized Church, at the time of his death the Bishop of the Third Ward in Provo, Utah, offered the use of their tabernacle for his funeral. This does indicate the respect in which he was held by those who knew him.

As a result of his study and investigation coupled with some very unusual incidents involving polygamy, many serious questions arose and he began a very intensive study that led to his leaving the Mormon Church and uniting with the Reorganized Church. After joining the Reorganization he endeavored to persuade his family to join with him. My mother, younger brother, and sister did unite with the church. The writer was somewhat more reluctant to join with the Reorganization. Most of my friends and associates were members of the Mormon Church and all of my social activities were centered in the various ward activities. I had no desire to give up those friends to join a small group that was looked upon with disdain. However, my deep respect and love for my father caused me to listen and study the many points he presented in reference to both churches. It was in these many sessions with my father that he revealed to me much of the inner workings and the experiences he had with the several leaders of the Mormon Church and some of the incidents that led to his dissatisfaction and ultimate membership in the Reorganization. For several years he was an appointee missionary for the Reorganized Church in the Utah-Idaho District.

While vital statistics are not always an important or

interesting factor in the presentation of material, some of the following data will be of interest and will also explain the statement made at the beginning. When the writing of this book began the author contacted the Central States Mission Office of the Mormon Church and there met a man who has proven of great assistance in verifying what has been written about his church. He wished to verify my previous membership in the church and he wrote to church headquarters in Salt Lake City, Utah, for information. He received the following: My birth date was Sunday, February 13, 1898, in Salt Lake City and I was blessed by Robert Sherwood on March 6, 1898. I was baptized on February 1, 1906, in the Tabernacle in Salt Lake City by my father (note that baptism occurred thirteen days prior to the age of eight). I was confirmed on February 4, 1906, by my father. On April 23, 1908, I was ordained a Deacon by Bishop Robert Sherwood (note that the ordination took place at the age of ten).

After my father left the Mormon Church my activities as a member of the church were lessened and I was always confronted with questions from those with whom I associated to answer why he had made the change. It was embarrassing not to be in a position to give intelligent answers in defense of my father and in order to avoid this embarrassment, it was necessary to learn his reasons. This was the beginning of my search for information that has continued over the years. It also led to my making a decision to join the Reorganization. On January 13, 1918, I was baptized by Elder Willard Parkes, an appointee missionary assigned to the Utah-Idaho District. Later I was ordained to the office of Priest by Apostle Gomer T. Griffiths and was assigned as a missionary to the district in 1920. I served as an associate of Elder R. L. Fulk, a missionary also assigned to the Utah-Idaho District. For a year we worked out of Malad, Idaho, and were quite successful in our efforts. In 1921 it was decided to transfer me to Independence, Missouri, to work in the office of the Presiding Bishop because I had specialized in the study of accounting.

When the statistical information was received from Salt Lake City by the mission president it was apparent that my membership in the Mormon Church was still a part of their records. This accounts for the statement made earlier that I was a member of both churches for more than fifty years. At the suggestion of the Mission President, a letter was written to the bishop of the ward in which I resided, requesting that my name be removed from their records. The Bishop visited my home to verify the request and then advised that it would be necessary to hold a Bishop's Court so the action could be done properly.

Later two elders called upon me and advised that the court would be held on the twenty-fifth of March, 1968, and an invitation to attend was extended. At this court many questions were asked and explanations given. One of the questions asked was in reference to whether or not I accepted David O. McKay as a prophet. My reply was that inasmuch as I have never had any contact or dealings with him, I was not in a position to either affirm or deny.

I requested the privilege of making a statement and this was granted. I then stated that I knew the Restoration was true and that Joseph Smith was a prophet of God and that the Book of Mormon was translated by the gift and power of God through Joseph Smith. Having borne my testimony, I then inquired what they were going to excommunicate from. Up to this writing no official notification has been received as to the action of the court. I may still technically be a member of both churches.

This privilege of membership in both churches and the fact that I was an adult when the decision was made to change, and the fact that I was ordained to the priesthood in both churches and the experiences in each, do qualify me to make comparisons of both which is to be the objective of this book. It will not be for propaganda purposes or to prove any certain beliefs because there are many books written from both churches to prove their individual positions. The major purpose of this book will be to compare the two organizations with that of the original church in the days of Joseph Smith, the martyr; especially in reference to organization and teachings.

To forestall any quick judgment as to my purpose or the depth of my conviction, it would be well to reaffirm my testimony as given at the Bishop's Court. I am thoroughly convinced of the truthfulness of the Restoration and the prophetic mission of Joseph Smith as a prophet of God and that the Book of Mormon was translated by the power of God.

It is also important to present my attitude toward the Mormon Church since I was once a member. It is notably true that the feelings of animosity and resentment are generally a result of conditions that are responsible for changing a person's outlook. There has been and still is a tremendous amount of bitterness between members of each of the churches because of the feeling that each has been wronged by the other. I sincerely disclaim any such animosity toward the Mormon Church, even though I have met many of the elders in discussion over the years. I have been severely criticized by members of the Reorganization because of my tolerance toward the members of the Mormon Church. Having lived among them and participated in services with them, it is impossible not to appreciate their sincerity and devotion. I have always sought out the literature of the Mormon Church, and have found some of the most vital information in their books. This has led to a broadening of my outlook and has put me in a position to fairly compare the position of each of the churches. I shall endeavor to compare the position of each church with the least amount of bias humanly possible. I do realize that a completely unbiased comparison is not possible due to the frailties of each individual, and because of this, I do implore the reader to weigh deeply those things that are presented.

CHAPTER I

THE RESTORATION

For those who may read this book there is a very real possibility there are some not familiar with the terms used, especially when reference is made to the term "Restoration." To clarify this for the benefit of those readers, a condensed resume of the history of this movement will follow.

After the establishment of the early church approximately two thousand years ago by Christ, it has been believed by many that as the church expanded and grew to ultimately become the state religion of Rome many changes in doctrine and belief took place. These changes were the cause of the "Reformation" that developed during the Middle Ages and was emphasized by the actions of Martin Luther. This movement led to the formation of many "Protestant" churches such as the Methodists, Presbyterians, Baptists and others. The development of many different churches resulted in much competition between them in seeking converts to their cause. Along with this competition came much confusion among the potential members because all of them professed to base their creeds and doctrines on the Bible. In fact many of them began to promulgate the theory that the Bible was the last revealed word and will of God and was infallible. With this doctrine or belief the adherents actually became "Bible Worshipers" rather than recognizing the real import of the message of Christ which was to "Love God with all your heart."

Among the many who were confused by the "preaching" of the various organizations was the family of Joseph Smith, Sr., who was living in the state of New York. The member of this family important to this narrative was the son, Joseph.

In the early 1800's there was much revivalism being conducted in the vicinity of the home of this family, and this had resulted in the family becoming divided as to the church they should join. Joseph's mother, two brothers and a sister had united with the Presbyterian church and were endeavoring to encourage him to unite with them in order that they could attend church together. It had developed that Joseph had become very friendly to a Methodist minister and had been inclined to unite with them.

One of the outstanding characteristics of families at this period was the devotion to the reading of the scriptures in the homes and the regular home devotionals. This characteristic was primarily responsible for the future events that transpired.

In the confusion between the desire to be with his mother and other members of the family in their church affiliation, and the impressive effect upon him by the Methodist minister, came the light which later proved so important in his life. On one occasion during the fifteenth year of his life he was reading the Bible and came across the epistle of James 1:5.

"If any of you lack wisdom, let him ask of God, that giveth to all men liberally, and upbraideth not; and it shall be given him."

As a result, this youth in his simple understanding and belief in God, decided to put his problem before God in prayer. Early in the spring of 1820 he went into the woods near the family home and there knelt in prayer. In his own words is the experience he had:

"After I had retired into the place where I had previously designed to go, having looked around me and finding myself alone, I kneeled down and began to offer up the desires of my heart to God. I had scarcely done so when immediately I was seized upon by some power which entirely overcame me, and had such astonishing influence over me as to bind my tongue so that I could not speak. Thick darkness gathered around me, and it seemed for a time as if I were doomed to sudden destruction. But exerting all my powers to call upon God to deliver me out of the power of this enemy which had seized upon me, and at the very moment when I was ready to sink into despair and abandon myself to destruction, (not to an imaginary ruin, but to the power of some actual being from the unseen world who had such marvelous power as I had never before felt in my being.) just at this moment of great alarm, I saw a pillar of light exactly over my head, above the brightness of the sun; which descended gradually until it fell upon me. It no sooner appeared than I found myself delivered from the enemy which held me bound. When the light rested upon me I saw two personages (whose brightness and glory defy all description) standing above me in the air. One of them spake unto me, calling me by name, and said, (pointing to the other) 'This is my beloved Son, hear him'

. "My object in going to inquire of the Lord was to know which of all the sects was right, that I might know which to join. No sooner therefore did I get possession of myself, so as to be able to speak, than I asked the personages who stood above me in the light, which of all the sects was right, (for at this time it had never entered into my heart that all were wrong,) and which should I join. I was answered that I must join none of them, for they were all wrong, and the personage who addressed me said that all their creeds were an abomination in his sight; that those professors were all corrupt; 'they draw near me with their lips, but their hearts are far from me; they teach for doctrine the commandments of men, having a form of Godliness, but they deny the power thereof.' He again forbade me to join with any of them: and many other things did he say unto me which I cannot write at this time. When I came to myself again I found myself lying on my back, looking up into heaven." (RLDS Church History Volume 1, pages 9 and 10)

It is from this young boy's experience that a new organization and church was established based upon the belief that the early church had so changed the principles and doctrines as taught by Christ that it had completely apostatized, that its authority, given by Christ, had been taken from the earth. For mankind to again enjoy the teachings of Christ would necessitate a restoration of the authority to function for him. In other words, the church of Christ had to be restored. This is the Restoration movement referred to in this book. This restoration movement believes in the continued revelation by God to His people as given in previous ages. They believe God has not changed in His concern for the welfare of His creation and that it was never His intention to imply, as in many churches, that the Bible was to be his last will and testament but that he would continually guide and direct those who loved Him and would allow Him to do so.

The Restoration believes in the same organization as established by Christ with power and authority given by Him for the benefit of mankind. It was through this power that Joseph Smith was permitted to translate the Book of Mormon which is a biblical record of early inhabitants of the Western Hemisphere.

We can only say to the reader that we realize much of what has been presented above may sound fantastic and unbelievable and from a pragmatic point of view, very hard to believe. However, when it is recalled that most of the Christian world accepts the belief in the Virgin Birth of Christ, there should be no doubt that God in His infinite wisdom and love for His creation would continually guide and direct them as in the past.

This new church organization was formed on April 6, 1830 with six men as the organizing group. It made such rapid growth that in fourteen years up to the time Joseph Smith was killed in Carthage, Illinois, it has been estimated that the membership consisted of from thirty thousand up to as high as two hundred thousand. It is impossible to document and set totals but it is generally estimated that there was a membership of approximately fifty thousand.

It is a distinctive organization and does not consider itself as a part of the "protestant" group.

After the death of Joseph Smith in June of 1844, a division occurred among the leaders of the church and resulted in the formation of several groups. Most of the smaller groups have passed into extinction leaving two major factions. One of which is headquartered in Salt Lake City, Utah, and is known as the Church of Jesus Christ of Latter Day Saints and is to be referred to in this book as the "Mormon" Church. The other faction is headquartered in Independence, Missouri, and is known as the Reorganized Church of Jesus Christ of Latter Day Saints and will be referred to as the Reorganized or RLDS church.

The comparison of these two organizations relative to the introduction or omission of doctrine that has taken place since the martyrdom of the founder is the purpose of this book. Also to analyze each organization in the light of the mechanics of organization and the success or lack of success resulting therefrom.

27

CHAPTER II

PROPHETIC SUCCESSION

One of the areas of interest and of much concern chosen for comparison is the manner in which each organization selects its leadership. During the lifetime of Joseph Smith, he was never called upon to make a decision on the question of succession of leadership but in his functioning as a prophet, he did receive some revelations that do have a bearing on the subject.

During the first year of the organization of the church, some of the men close to the prophet speculated much about the gift of revelation to the church. Hiram Page came into possession of a stone through which he claimed to receive some revelations for the church. Several were deceived by this and among them was Oliver Cowdery. This puzzled the prophet and he sought light from God as to the truthfullness of those revelations. In answer he received a revelation that is found in the Doctrine and Covenants of both churches. It reads as follows:

"But, behold, verily, verily I say unto thee, no one shall be appointed to receive commandments and revelations in this church excepting my servant Joseph Smith, Jr., for he receiveth them even as Moses; and thou shalt be obedient unto the things which I shall give unto him, even as Aaron, to declare faithfully the commandments and revelations, with power and authority unto the church. And if thou art led at any time by the Comforter to speak or teach, or at all times by the way of commandment unto the church, thou mayest do it. But thou shalt not write by way of commandment, but by wisdom; and thou shalt not command him who is at thy head, and at the head of the church, for I have given him the keys of the mysteries and the revelations, which are sealed, until *I shall appoint* unto them another in his stead."
(RLDS D & C 27:2; Mormon D & C 28:2-7)

This revelation was directed to Oliver Cowdery.

In December of 1830 another revelation was given through

the prophet that also pertains to this subject and it reads:

".. . and I have sent forth the fullness of my gospel by the hand of my servant Joseph; and in weakness have I blessed him, and I have given unto him the keys of the mystery of those things which have been sealed, even the things which were from the foundation of the world, and the things which shall come from this time until the time of my coming, if he abide in me, and if not, another *will I plant in his stead.*" (RLDS D & C 34:4; Mormon D & C 35:17, 18)

In this quotation and also in the previous one, the author has italicized for emphasis the statements that will be referred to in succeeding material.

One other statement appears in the Doctrine and Covenants of each church pertaining to this subject; it is as follows and was given in February of 1831:

"O hearken, ye elders of my church, and give ear to the words which I shall speak unto you: for, behold, verily, verily I say unto you, that ye have received a commandment for a law unto my church, through him *whom I have appointed* unto you, to receive commandments and revelations from my hand. And this ye shall know assuredly, that there is none other appointed unto you to receive commandments and revelations until he be taken, if he abide in me. But verily, verily I say unto you, that none else shall be appointed unto this gift except it be through him, for if it be taken from him he shall not have power, except to appoint another in his stead; and this shall be a law unto you, that ye receive not the teachings of any that shall come before you as revelations, or commandments; and this I give unto you that you may not be deceived, that you may know they are not of me. For verily I say unto you, that he that is ordained of me, shall come in at the gate and be ordained as I have told you before, to teach those revelations which you have received, and shall receive through him *whom I have appointed.*" (RLDS D & C 43:1-3; Mormon D & C 43:1-7)

From the above quotations it has been made extremely clear that God has reserved to himself the sole right of selection and appointment of the prophet to the church.

This then precludes the right of any church to assume the responsibility of selection or to set up any precedents or requirements that would presume to advise God as to whom He should select. As a comparison is made between the churches and the procedures that have been followed by each, it will be observed which of the organizations had adhered more closely to the above given instructions.

The first real confrontation of the church to the question of succession in leadership came out of the death of Joseph Smith at Carthage, Illinois, on June 27, 1844. Up to this time the prophet had not revealed by revelation on whom the responsibility of leadership should fall in the case of his death. There has been much written by both churches to justify the positions they have taken that is available to the reader if more information is desired. However, after the death of Joseph Smith, Sidney Rigdon, who had been counselor to the prophet for many years and was technically so at the time of the death, felt that the responsibility rested upon him to guide the church until God selected a new prophet. His claim was rejected in a public meeting in Nauvoo in August of 1844. At this meeting the Twelve were sustained "in their office and calling" and as the second quorum in the church, the responsibility to lead was theirs at least until God appointed a new prophet. Up to this time no precedents had been established.

At this point it will be of interest to learn what transpired in history that led to the succession by Brigham Young as president of the Mormon Church. Brigham Young was the president of the Quorum of Twelve at the time of the death of the prophet and in this office he was the leader of the group. The Twelve then led the church as the presiding quorum until January of 1848. In the meantime a number of events transpired that are highly questionable. Brigham Young and several of the Twelve traveled to Utah in 1847 having been driven out of Nauvoo. They arrived in the Salt Lake Valley, on July 24, 1847 and immediately set about laying out the city of Great Salt Lake. Reading from Wilford Woodruff's recording of the events we have the following:

"About this time President Young felt impressed that he and the brethren of the camp should renew their covenants by baptism. August the sixth, the Twelve were rebaptized by President Young. Elder Kimball baptized President Young and the latter confirmed his brethren and re-sealed upon them all their former blessings. Following this, the brethren selected their inheritances. Brother Woodruff's was the corner diagonally across the street from the southwest corner of the Temple Block, facing east and north. In the evening Elder Kimball baptized fifty-five members of the camp. Elder Woodruff assisted in their confirmation. August the eighth the general work of rebaptizing continued. Elders Kimball, Snow, Lewis, Goddard, Everett, and Shumway did the baptizing, while President Young and the Twelve confirmed. . . . The practice of the Saints coming into the Valley to renew their covenants by baptism was followed for many years, but later, when organization abroad became more perfect, and the Saints came with speedy and direct transportation from their native lands to the stakes of Zion, this practice has been discontinued as not being of the same necessity as in the early pioneer days." (*Wilford Woodruff* by Matthias F. Cowley, page 319)

For the benefit of those readers not familiar with the doctrines and practices of the Restoration Movement, the ordinance of baptism is for entrance into the church and for the remission of sins. For the renewal of covenants they partake of the Lord's Supper at Sacrament or Communion services.

Brigham Young and members of the Twelve left Salt Lake Valley to return to Winter Quarters on the Missouri River near what is now, Council Bluffs, where the Saints had gathered in preparation for the journey west. They arrived there on October 31, 1847 and shortly afterward began the rebaptism of all the members in camp. They also began the construction of a log cabin in which to hold a conference. In the meantime, the Twelve that were present, met at the home of Orson Hyde and selected Brigham Young to be president of the church with power to choose his counselors. This action was presented to the conference held on December 27, 1847 at which time they sustained the action of the Twelve.

It should be noted that at no time in all of the above procedures has there been a reference to God's participation in the selection of the prophet, the right he had reserved to himself in all of the quotations made at the beginning of this chapter.

No emphasis was made by the author to the matter of reordination when quoting from Wilford Woodruff. The statement, "President Young . . . confirmed his brethren and resealed upon them all their former blessings," does indicate that not only baptism and confirmation took place but also the reordination of each. The question arises as to the necessity for this action. Was it a requirement of God or was it the beginning of a new church organization?

Up to this time no precedent had been established pertaining to the selection of leadership but they did begin a recognition of seniority within the quorum of Twelve. The senior apostle succeeded Brigham Young as the president of the quorum and this practice has continued. The succession of the senior apostle as the president of the church did not become established as a precedent until later. This is shown in the delay that occurred in the selection of a successor to Brigham Young. A listing of the presidents of the Mormon Church and the date they were sustained is found in the *Essentials of Church History* by Joseph Fielding Smith on page 686. They are as shown below but not in this form:

PRESIDENT	DATE SUSTAINED	AGE	DATE OF DEATH	YEARS SERVED
Joseph Smith	Jan. 25, 1832	26	June 27, 1844	14+
Brigham Young	Dec. 27, 1847	46	Aug. 29, 1877	29+
John Taylor	Oct. 10, 1880	72	July 25, 1887	6+
Wilford Woodruff	April 7, 1889	82	Sept. 2, 1898	9+
Lorenzo Snow	Sept. 13, 1898	84	Oct. 10, 1901	3+
Joseph F. Smith	Oct. 17, 1901	63	Nov. 19, 1918	17+
Heber J. Grant	Nov. 23, 1918	62	May 14, 1945	26+
George A. Smith	May 21, 1945	75	April 4, 1951	5+
David O. McKay	April 9, 1951	77	January 18, 1970	18+

In the above listing it will be noted that a lapse of more than three years occurred between the time of death of Brigham Young and the selection of John Taylor as his successor. There is also a period of nearly two years elapsing before Wilford Woodruff was selected to succeed John Taylor. These lapses indicate that the precedent had not yet been fully accepted. However, starting with the selection of Lorenzo Snow and from that period on, no delays took place in selecting the senior apostle to the position. There has not been a precedent established which presumes to tell God whom he shall select.

There is an unfortunate situation that arises when precedents are established and especially so when the future is not taken into the evaluation, and this pertains to the age of the men involved. When seniority becomes a dominating factor in the selection of leadership rather than the qualifications of the individual, the dilemma of age will arise. This is shown in the above listing of the various men chosen, the youngest man selected after Brigham Young was Heber J. Grant who was 62 at the time he became president. It is not the intention to disparage the factor of age in leadership because in age there is wisdom. However, the problem of senility is apotential.

As a further commentary on the above procedure of succession as demonstrated by the Mormon Church, it should be noted that at no time has there been a revelation presented to the church by God indicating His choice. The membership are expected to believe that the action taken by the Twelve is God's will.

The approach of the Reorganized Church to the succession of leadership is quite different from that explained above in the Mormon Church. They have given much more consideration to the lineal rights in matters of succession.

Joseph Smith III was born in Kirtland, Ohio, on November 7, 1832, and was the eldest son of the prophet. It was the thinking of many that his was the right to succeed his father because of the law of lineage as practiced in Bible days. We find in the Reorganized Church history, the testimony of several individuals who claim to have been present at different periods when the prophet had blessed his son. One of these occasions took place while the prophet was incarcerated in the jail at Liberty, Missouri. Another occasion was in the grove at Nauvoo, Illinois, a short time before the prophet's death. However, it is not found in any of the official records as kept by the prophet nor did Young Joseph accept the responsibilities based upon those statements.

A little of the history of the beginning of the Reorganization is important at this point and the reader should be reminded to refer to the quotations made at the beginning of this chapter pertaining to the selection of a prophet. After the death of the prophet Joseph Smith in 1844 and after the Twelve had assumed direction of the church, many members were not as certain nor satisfied with many of the policies instituted by the Twelve. One of the major causes of resentment was the excommunication of members simply because of disagreement with the Twelve. It became a matter of test of fellowship if one was not obedient to the instructions issued by the Twelve. This situation had much to do with the rise of many aspirants to the claim of right of leadership. Among these were Sidney Rigdon, James J. Strang, William Smith and several others which resulted in much confusion among the members. Because of this confusion and growth of the animosity toward the church, they were forced to leave Nauvoo as an organization and the Twelve with Brigham Young leading, took the majority of the members to the West. Those that remained are those who formed the nucleus of the Reorganization.

For several years there was no organization other than those started by claimants like J. J. Strang that provided opportunities for the Saints that remained of getting together. It should be remembered that many of the men who were ordained to the priesthood during the days of the prophet, were with these people and attempted to guide them in their search for the truth. Among these men were Jason W. Briggs, Zenas H. Gurley, and W. W. Marks.

In 1852 a number of the Saints met in conference under the direction of some of these men and the first real effort ensued to bring together all of the scattered Saints into one organization. Many of these people were those that believed the son of the prophet should succeed his father. Some spiritual manifestations to several individuals tended to confirm this thinking. As a result, deputations were sent to Joseph Smith III, requesting him to join with them and to come and take his rightful place in the church. These pleas were rejected by him on several occasions as were also requests he received from officials of the Mormon Church that visited with him during this period. It was always his position that God would make it known to him if this was to be his task. In this he was in direct harmony with the revelations pertaining to the selection of the prophet.

In the Reorganized Church history, volume 3, page 254, is a lengthy article that was written by Joseph Smith III, that very completely outlines his viewpoint and the incidents that led up to his acceptance of the position. It is much too lengthy to incorporate here but the main theme all through the article was that until it was made known to him by God, he would join none of the factions. He made it a matter of prayer in the same manner his father did. When the testimony did come to him, it was then he presented himself to the conference held at Amboy, Illinois, in April of 1860 and offered his services. It was at that time he stated:

"I would say to you, brethren, as I hope you may be, and in faith I trust you are, as a people that God has promised his blessings upon, I came not here of myself, but by the influence of the Spirit. For some time past I have received manifestations pointing to the position I am about to assume." (RLDS Ch. Hist. Vol. 3, p. 247)

He was accepted by this conference and was ordained to the Presidency of the High Priesthood by William Marks and others. William Marks was the president of the Nauvoo Stake at the time of the death of the prophet and was also a member of the High Council of the church.

While the tradition of lineage may have played a large part in the minds of the people in the selection of young Joseph, we do wish to emphasize that in his own writings and statements, the first consideration was the will of God and His right of choice. Joseph Smith III served the church until his death in 1914.

On April 14, 1906, a revelation was given to the Reorganized Church by Joseph Smith in which he, as the prophet of the church, designated his successor and we quote from that revelation:

"Inasmuch as misunderstanding has occurred in regard to the meaning of a revelation hitherto given through my servant Joseph Smith in regard to who should be called to preside in case my servant should be taken away or fall by transgression, it is now declared that in case of the removal of my servant now presiding over the church by death or transgression, my servant Frederick M. Smith, if he remain faithful and steadfast, should be chosen, in accordance with the revelations which have been hitherto given to the church concerning the priesthood. Should my servant Frederick M. Smith prove unstable and unfaithful, another may be chosen, according to the law already given." (RLDS D & C 127:8)

35

President Frederick Madison Smith was ordained as president of the church on May 5, 1915 and served in that office until his death on March 20, 1946. Inasmuch as F. M. Smith had no sons, there arose questions in the church as to his successor and how the law of lineage could apply. This was the first indication in the Reorganization where the setting of a precedent or tradition can be an embarrassment. Frederick M. Smith, as prophet of the church, did not leave a document to the church designating his successor. An interesting statement appears in the book *The Story of the Church* by Inez Smith Davis, it reads:

"The choice of a new president in the church follows the definite pattern of all Priesthood choice and ordination as set forth in the law. From the office of deacon up to that of president choice is made by divine call and concurred in by those over whom the one ordained shall minister. However, in the case of president that call to serve *has traditionally come* to one of the descendants of Joseph the Prophet. There is much to commend this procedure, since some orderly method of succession must be followed in order to prevent schism and contention in the body. However, as has been said, ultimate choice rests with the people." (*Story of the Church* by Davis, page 581)

This statement outlines very clearly the position of the Reorganization and its acceptance of the tradition of lineal succession. This, in effect, is another method of advising God as to what His choice should be. This is contrary to the thought in the selections from the Doctrine and Covenants shown earlier in the chapter.

Inasmuch as no revelation was given by President F. M. Smith much discussion ensued. It was stated by some members of the Joint Council (Presidency, Twelve and Presiding Bishopric) that the question of succession had been put to President Smith and he is reported to have designated his brother, Israel A. Smith. When conference assembled to consider the selection of a successor to the deceased F. M. Smith, the Council of Twelve requested the Presiding Patriarch, Elbert A. Smith to seek God's will in the matter. He returned to the conference and confirmed the selection of I. A. Smith. On the strength of the above procedure, Israel Alexander Smith was chosen to preside over the church.

Prior to the death of Israel A. Smith in a tragic automobile accident, a document had been prepared and left in strict confidence with F. Henry Edwards, one of his counselors. This document, now known as section 144 in the Doctrine and Covenants, designated his brother W. Wallace Smith to succeed him as the prophet of the church and was accepted by the conference of April 6, 1958.

A listing of the presidents of the Reorganized Church and their tenure of office is shown in the same manner as shown for the Mormon Church:

PRESIDENT	DATE SUSTAINED	AGE	DATE OF DEATH	YEARS SERVED
Joseph Smith, Jr.	Jan. 25, 1832*	26	June 27, 1844	14+
Joseph Smith III	April 6, 1860	31	Dec. 10, 1914	54+
Frederick M. Smith	May 5, 1915	41	March 20, 1946	30+
Israel A. Smith	April 7, 1946	70	June 14, 1958	12+
W. Wallace Smith	October 6, 1958	57		

To summarize what has been written it is apparent that the Mormon Church has allowed a tradition to develop covering this very important phase of organization as demonstrated by the rights of seniority. It is no longer required that a revelation showing God's choice be received by the church. Acceptance of the choice by the Quorum of Twelve as inspired, is expected of the membership of the church.

The Reorganized Church, while adhering more closely to the instructions of the revelations quoted, have allowed a tradition to grow within the church which again circumscribes God to the choice of a descendent of Joseph Smith. It is in the area of setting precedents in which both churches have erred.

---

* This is the date that Joseph Smith was ordained as president of the High Priesthood. At the organization of the church on April 6, 1830, Joseph Smith was chosen and sustained as the First Elder of the church.

CHAPTER III

SELECTION OF APOSTLES

The second most important group of men in the organization of the Restoration Church are the Twelve Apostles which function as a quorum in the direction of the church and its activities. They are under the supervision of the First Presidency.

Under date of June 1829, a revelation was received by Joseph Smith in which he was told that twelve apostles would be chosen. This was almost a year before the organization of the church in 1830 and it was not until early in 1835 that the first apostles were chosen.

This history of the selection of this first group is of special interest because of the pattern that was set in the choice of the men. After the Saints were driven from Missouri, and efforts had been made to restore them to their lands, the majority of the leaders gathered in Kirtland, Ohio and concentrated on the erection of the temple. It was at this time the prophet was impressed to establish the quorum and requested the three witnesses to the Book of Mormon, David Whitmer, Oliver Cowdery, and Martin Harris, to seek out twelve men for this responsibility. After much prayer and deliberation, twelve men were selected and then ordained to form the first quorum of Twelve Apostles. An interesting feature on the selection of this first group is that none of the men were named specifically by a revelation.

Between the time of the formation of the first quorum of Twelve and the death of the prophet, several changes were made due to the death or disaffection of some members. The replacements were made by the quorum itself with the approval of the prophet. It was in this manner that several new men were added to the quorum right after the death of Joseph Smith to take the place of Lyman Wight and William Smith.

The Mormon Church has continued the same procedure when adding to the quorum as deaths or disaffections occur. The men are nominated by the quorum and then presented to the conference to be sustained. After ordination as an apostle he is then in line under the principle of seniority to become the president of the church. The responsibility is a lifetime task and in the Mormon Church there is no provision for the retirement of an apostle due to age or disability. They can be removed for an act of transgression or can resign if they so desire.

Another development in the Mormon Church relative to the quorum of Twelve is when they are ordained to the office of Apostle, they are also ordained to be prophet, seer, revelator and translator. This grew out of the period when the Twelve assumed the leadership of the church after the death of the prophet. Justification for this procedure is found in the minutes of the dedication of the Kirtland Temple. Reading from church history we quote:

"President Joseph Smith, Jr., then rose, and after a few preliminary remarks presented the several Presidents of the church, then present, to the several quorums respectively, and then to the church as being equal with himself, acknowledging them to be prophets and seers." (RLDS Ch. Hist. Vol. 2, p. 37)

As a result of this teaching there are at least fifteen apostles, prophets, seers and revelators in the Mormon Church. They have just recently ordained an apostle but was not included in the present quorum of Twelve. Later he was assigned to be a counselor to the First Presidency. Also, each member of the Quorum of Twelve has an assistant assigned to aid him in his responsibilities. A question naturally arises, is this the same trend that developed in the early Christian church that ultimately led to the College of Cardinals?

In the beginning of the Reorganization the selection of the Apostles was done by a committee in the same manner as the early church. However, a full quorum was not chosen and for many years they functioned with less than the twelve usually provided for. It was not until March of 1873 that Joseph Smith III received a revelation designating men to be ordained as apostles. This revelation also revealed the names of the men selected to be counselors to Joseph Smith III. From this time forth, all selections to the Quorum of Twelve in the Reorganization have been by revelation.

The writer has no quarrel with the process of selection in the above manner but the question does arise as to the necessity of changing the procedure that was established in the early church. As a result of this method of choosing apostles there have been extensive periods when the quorum was not full in the Reorganization.

Unlike the Mormon Church, when a man is selected to be an apostle in the Reorganization, it is not a lifetime appointment but is subject to being replaced by the selection of another man. Most generally when an apostle is released from the quorum, he is then ordained as a Patriarch and functions in this office for the remainder of his life. Lately there has developed an action that when an apostle has been chosen for a task other than Patriarch, such as a counselor to the presidency, he is said to continue his apostleship in this new task and, in effect, remains an apostle but not in the quorum of Twelve.

On examination of the two churches and the success of each in its method of selection of apostles, the evidence would weigh heavily in favor of the Mormon Church because selection can be made from a basis of experience. Their success not only in business affairs but also in their expansion in membership, can only be attributed to successful administration by expert administrators. This is a field in which the Mormon Church has excelled for many years, especially when they have selected other administrative officers such as stake presidents and ward bishops. They have always sought out men who had proven themselves in an administrative capacity.

CHAPTER IV

OFFICE OF SEVENTIES

In a discussion about the Seventies as an official office in the church, it is necessary to distinguish between the quorum of Seven Presidents of Seventy and the members of the quorum of seventy. This distinction is made in the Doctrine and Covenants as follows:

"And it is according to the vision, showing the order of the seventy, that they should have seven presidents to preside over them, chosen out of the number of the seventy, and the seventh president of these presidents is to preside over the six; and these seven presidents are to choose other seventy besides the first seventy, to whom they belong, and are to preside over them; and also other seventy until seven times seventy, if the labor in the vineyard of necessity requires it. And these seventy are to be traveling ministers. . . ." (RLDS D & C 104:43; Mormon D & C 107:93-97)

The above instructions provide for the selection of seven men to become presidents of seventy to preside over the seventies as a whole. They also become a council Seven Presidents of Seventy which is the third ranking group of men in the church. Should the quorum of the First Presidency and the quorum of Twelve Apostles suddenly be taken, it would be the right and prerogative of the Council of Seven Presidents of Seventy to assume the leadership of the church until such time that God will select another prophet to preside. This position is accepted by both groups of the Restoration.

In their responsibility as the third quorum of the church, it devolves upon them to sit in council with the other two quorums when considering the welfare of the church. The Seventies are always under the direction of the Twelve Apostles in the missionary arm of the church.

In the Mormon church the functioning of the Council of Presidents of Seventy is as shown above. However, pertaining to the members of the quorums of Seventy, there is a different function than that in the original church. A Seventy is the primary missionary of the church under the direction of the Twelve. It was the intent in the early church that all seventies would go on missions for the church as directed. The practice today is not as outlined above. Young men are ordained to the office of Elder and are then called upon to enter a mission for a specific period. When they return from that mission and enter into the activities of local work, they are sometimes called to the office of Seventy and become local or stake missionaries to the wards or stakes to which they belong. Inasmuch as the primary function of a seventy is as a missionary, this cannot be considered too great a departure from the original intent.

In the Reorganized Church the Council of Seven Presidents of Seventy do not sit in council with the First Presidency and the Quorum of Twelve as a joint council. This practice, if it ever existed, was discontinued many years ago. Today, the presiding Bishopric now sits in council with the other two quorums as a joint council considering the welfare of the church and conducting church business during the interim periods between the general conferences.

For many years the Reorganized Church at their general conferences, provided seating for the Council of Seven Presidents of Seventy on the rostrum along with the Twelve and Presidency. This practice has been discontinued and they are no longer honored with this type of consideration.

The function of a Seventy in the Reorganized Church is to be a missionary concentrating strictly on this type of activity. In the early days of the Reorganization this was the major function and many outstanding missionaries were developed. In recent years, more and more of the appointees, the majority of which are seventies, are being assigned to administrative functions throughout the church. A recent revelation to the church admonished them to appoint local Seventies to function within the stakes and local congregations and this is now being done by the church.

CHAPTER V

PRESIDING BISHOP

The first statement pertaining to the office of Bishop in the church appears in section seventeen of the Doctrine and Covenants (RLDS); and in section twenty of the Mormon edition. This particular section outlines the duties and responsibilities of the various officers in the two priesthood groups. The quotation referred to is as follows:

"Every president of the high priesthood (or presiding elder), bishop, high councillor, and high priest, is to be ordained by the direction of a high council, or general conference." (RLDS D & C 17:17; Mormon D & C 20:67)

This revelation was given at the time of the organization of the church on April 6, 1830.

In February of 1831, another revelation was received in which Edward Partridge was designated to be the first bishop of the church. It reads:

"And again, I have called my servant Edward Partridge, and give a commandment, that he should be appointed by the voice of the church, and ordained a bishop unto the church, to leave his merchandise and to spend all his time in the labors of the church; to see to all things as it shall be appointed unto him in my law in the day that I shall give them." (RLDS D & C 41:3; Mormon D & C 41:9, 10)

Following this, a revelation was received in May of 1831 outlining the responsibilities of the Bishop and that made him the financial officer of the church of that time. He was to devote his time to the temporal affairs of the church in purchasing lands and receiving the offerings and consecrations of the members. He was to distribute the lands and consecrations of the people according to the needs and wants of the members and was to establish storehouses as the church prospered. All of this is found in the fifty-first section of both editions of the Doctrine and Covenants.

As a result of the above instructions, bishop Edward Partridge became the first Trustee-in-Trust for the church even though not mentioned as such in the Doctrine and Covenants. In the purchase of lands in both Jackson County and at Kirtland, Ohio, his name appeared on practically all of the transactions for real estate. Based upon this action, the Reorganized Church followed the same practice and made the presiding bishop the trustee-in-trust for the church.

Later another very important position of responsibility was placed upon the presiding bishop and is found in a revelation given to the church in November of 1831. It is found in both editions of the Doctrine and Covenants as section sixty-eight. This responsibility is to preside over the Aaronic Priesthood of the church and to direct them in their duties in cooperation with the president of the Melchisedec priesthood.

In March of 1835 further instructions were received in a revelation on priesthood that are found in both editions of the Doctrine and Covenants. In the Reorganized edition it is known as section one hundred and four and in the Mormon edition it is section one hundred and seven. This revelation reiterates the responsibility of the bishop to preside over the Aaronic priesthood.

Bishop Edward Partridge served in this office until his death, May 27, 1840. In January of 1841, Bishop George Miller was selected by revelation to succeed Bishop Partridge as presiding bishop of the church. He did not succeed him as the trustee-in-trust for the church. At a special conference held in Nauvoo on January 30, 1841, Joseph Smith, president of the church, was made the trustee-in-trust and continued in this office until his death in 1844. On the precedence of this action, the Mormon Church has continued the practice of the First Presidency being the Trustee-in-Trust for the church. This position has now evolved into the Corporation of the First President.

While at Nauvoo, the church began the practice of using bishops as presiding elders of the ward or congregations. The fact that a bishop must first be ordained a high priest permits the use of the bishop in this capacity. This same procedure has been followed by the Mormon church since that time.

The official position of the Mormon church has been stated by Apostle John A. Widtsoe in his book *Priesthood and*

Church Government on page 284. Under the title "Powers and Duties of the Presiding Bishop" is the following statement:

"FIRST DUTY, TO PRESIDE OVER THE LESSER PRIESTHOOD OF THE CHURCH.

The first duty of the Presiding Bishop is to preside over the Lesser Priesthood of the Church, which includes the holding of the keys of this ministry. D & C 68:14, 23.

He possesses "the Priesthood of Aaron, which holds the keys of the ministering of angels, and of the Gospel of repentance, and of baptism by immersion for the remission of sin." D & C 13.

OBLIGED TO CONSULT WITH THE FIRST PRESIDENCY.

The Presiding Bishop, who presides over all Bishops, and over all of the Lesser Priesthood, should consult the First Presidency in all matters of policy pertaining to the Bishopric. IP 39.

ADMINISTRATION OF TEMPORAL AFFAIRS.

In their capacity of exercising jurisdiction over the traveling and local Bishops of the Church, the Presiding Bishopric has charge of all temporal matters under the direction, necessarily, of the First Presidency. The tithing, donations, and offerings of the members of the Church are under their care, both in receipt and in distribution. This includes the care of the poor, and the numerous other purposes for which the funds donated by the people may be used. In other words, the members of the Presiding Bishopric are receiving and distributing agents, under the direction of the Trustee-in-Trust. Thus the financial operations of the Church are localized and centralized in this one body. (As noted in an earlier chapter, the office of Presiding Bishop is incorporated for this purpose.) This jurisdiction over the Bishops of the Church grows out of the fact that the Presiding Bishopric is ex officio the presidency of the Aaronic Priesthood in all the world. (Courses of Study for the Quorums of the Priesthood. 107:15)

JUDICIAL FUNCTION.

It is the duty of the Presiding Bishopric, with twelve High Priests as counselors, to act as a body of judges to try any charges that may be made against one of the First Presidency. This is the only body by which such a person may be tried. (D & C 107:82, 83.) This court has been convened once for this purpose. After the death of the Prophet Joseph Smith, Sidney Rigdon, who had been his counselor, was tried before the Presiding Bishopric, and condemned. This occurred in 1844. It is further stipulated that if charges are brought against the Presiding Bishop himself he can be tried only by the First Presidency. (D & C 68:17-24; 107:82, 83; CSQP 24, 25.)"

The Mormon Church, to more effectively administrate the various temporal affairs of the church, have set up various corporations and these are known as the Corporation of the President, the Corporation of the Presiding Bishopric, the Corporation of the Stake President, the Corporation of the Ward Bishop and several more for the handling of the Welfare Program.

The outstanding success of the Mormon Church and its financial status, attests very strongly for the wisdom of the methods they have adopted.

In presenting the position of the Reorganized Church on the function and responsibility of the Presiding Bishop there is considerable variance when compared to the Mormon Church. The procedures followed by the Reorganized Church have led to a great deal of conflict and division in the church that never should have occurred. To justify the above statement it will be necessary to review much of the history of the Reorganization beginning with the formation in 1860.

"On the seventh of April, 1860, Israel L. Rogers was ordained Bishop of the Church, under the hands of Elders Blair, Gurley, and Powers, as directed by President Joseph Smith." (RLDS Ch. Hist. Vol. 3, p. 252)

From this action, Bishop Rogers became the first presiding bishop of the Reorganization.

During the early years of the Reorganization there was great fear that aspiring men would take advantage of the people through the control and collection of the tithings and offerings. It was felt that this would place undue

46

opportunity for power in the hands of one man and to offset this, the first revelation given to the Reorganized Church on October 7, 1861, recognized the possibility by the following:

"In order to place the church in a position to carry on the promulgation of the gospel, and as a means of fulfilling the law, the Twelve will take measures in connection with the bishop, to execute the law of tithing; and let them before God see to it, that the temporal means so obtained is truly used for the purposes of the church, and not as a weapon of powers in the hands of one man for the oppression of others, or for the purposes of self-aggrandizment by anyone, be he whomsoever he may be." (RLDS D & C 114:1.)

This placement of the Twelve as more or less supervisors over the bishopric resulted in considerable friction as the church began to grow.

It should be inserted here that no revelation as such, appears in the Doctrine and Covenants which specifically states the Presiding Bishop is to be the Trustee-in-Trust for the church. It is implied only in the statements where the bishop is designated to handle the temporal affairs of the church. Had the Prophet, Joseph Smith, Jr., been aware of any such revelation, he would not have permitted the action that was taken at Nauvoo that made him the Trustee-in-Trust.

The fear of one man dominance became a very important factor in the history of the Reorganization and it led to many of the actions taken by the church. It led to the emphasis placed upon democratic action and constantly increased the importance of the general conferences in the church. All this was based upon the principle of "common consent" as stated in the Doctrine and Covenants. In the chapter on General Conferences much more is stated as to the development of democracy in the church.

From the receipt of the revelation quoted above in which the Twelve were advised to work with the bishop in gathering and distributing the tithes and offerings, resentment began to grow, not only by the bishop but by many others in the church and culminated in a resolution passed at the General Conference held in St. Louis, Missouri, on April 6, 1869.

This resolution reads:

> "Resolved that it is not the true policy of the Church of Jesus Christ of Latter Day Saints that the Twelve shall control the funds of the church in the hands of the Bishop, *but that the Bishop shall be amenable to the General Conference alone.*" (RLDS Ch. Hist. Vol. 3, p. 520.)

At the same conference another resolution was passed pertaining to the establishment of a "School of the Prophets" which contains the following statement:

> "Resolved that in the opinion of this conference, the true policy of the church, in this matter, is to be found in the epistle of the Twelve to the church on tithings and offerings, viz.: through the branch presidents as Bishop's agents should all moneys come into the church treasury, and that the spiritual authorities of the church should discountenance the paying of moneys directly to the Bishop, where that policy works to the injury of the poor in districts or branches. . . ." (RLDS Ch. Hist. Vol. 3, p. 521.)

The above quotations are given to show seeds of division had been sown that were to prove disastrous to the church in later years. It appears that the first resolution was not taken seriously because it was not until the fifteenth of April, 1894, that a revelation was received relieving the Twelve from the responsibility put upon them in the previous revelation. Other interesting factors are also mentioned in this revelation and certain portions are being quoted:

> "Thus saith the Spirit unto the elders and the church: (1) My servants have been harsh one with another; and some have not been sufficiently willing to hear those whose duty it is to teach the revelations which my church has already received. Until my people shall hear and heed those who are set in the church to teach the revelations there will be misunderstanding and confusion among the members. (2) The burden of the care of the church is laid on him who is called to preside over the high priesthood of the church, and on those who are called to be his counselors; and they shall teach according to the spirit

48

of wisdom and understanding, and as they shall be directed by revelation, from time to time. . . ." (RLDS D & C 122:1, 2.)

This portion of the revelation acknowledges the existence of division in the eldership on some questions, one of which was the status of the Presiding Bishop and the Quorum of Twelve. Another was the interpretation of the tithing law. Later, in the same revelation, is found the reason given for having placed upon the Twelve the responsibility with the Presiding Bishop as shown in the first revelation given to the Reorganization. The quotation is as follows:

" . . . the one whom I called to preside over the church, had not yet approved himself unto the scattered flock; and I gave this command unto the quorum next in authority in spiritual things that the scattered ones, and those who had been made to suffer might have assurance that I would not suffer that he whom I called should betray the confidence of the faithful, nor squander the moneys of the treasury for the purposes of self. And for the reason that the law of tithing was but little understood, and could not be observed, unless it should be taught, and enforced by the precepts of the chief missionaries of the church. It was not then intended, nor is it now, to burden them with the duty of looking after the disbursements of the moneys in the treasury, or the management of the properties of the church; except as it may be at times necessary to do so in council with the presidency, the high council in case of exigency, the bishopric, bishops, or bishop's agents abroad, or the conferences; and in accordance with the agreement hitherto made. Whatever burden the quorum may have felt rested upon them in this regard, they are now absolved from, the end designed by it having been reached. . . ." (RLDS D & C 122:5.)

Along with the releasing of the Twelve from the direct responsibility of supervising the bishopric, there is another implication contained in the revelation. It indicates that the prophet had now proven himself as president of the church and was now in a position to assume the full direction of the church which included the supervision of the presiding bishopric along with other quorums of the church.

49

At the time the church decided to incorporate as an organization under the laws of the State of Illinois, included in the charter granted by the state and as provided by the church, the Presiding Bishop was designated to be the Trustee-in-Trust for the church and under the law is the only one eligible for this responsibility.

Another protion of the same revelation quoted above has important information bearing on some of the friction that had developed up to this time. It refers to the relative position of the quorums in the church:

> "The quorums in respect to authority are designed to take precedence in office as follows: The Presidency, the twelve, the seventy, in all meetings and gatherings of the member-ship, where no previous organization has been affected. Where organization has been arranged and the officers have been ordained and set in order; the standing ministry in their order; high priests, elders, priests, teachers, and deacons; the parallels are; in the presidency, the president and his counselors; in the second presidency, the twelve; in missionary work, first the twelve; second, the seventy; in the standing ministry, the presidency, second, the high priests; third, the elders, then priests, teachers, and deacons in their order." (RLDS D & C 122:9.)

It should be noted that the presiding bishopric is not mentioned in this presentation of responsibility.

It is very unfortunate that the above revelation did not resolve in the minds of many of the leaders, the friction that had developed. The contention grew and finally climaxed at the general conference of 1925. A recital of some of the events leading up to this conference will shed some light on the things that transpired. It was at this conference that the clash of authority between the first presidency and the presiding bishop was debated and a decision made. One of the outstanding causes that brought the division to a head was the financial position of the church.

Around 1920 a campaign to raise funds for the erection of an auditorium was successful and approximately $500,000 was subscribed. Because the friction and animosity continued to grow among some of the leaders, the financial contri-butions to the church began to drop and the church had difficulty in meeting its operating expenses. The presidency became concerned about the fulfillment of the obligation to the membership relative to the building of the auditorium for which money had been donated. They began pressing the presiding bishopric to start with the construction. Due to the poor financial position of the church, the bishopric could not see their way clear to commence this task. As the financial condition worsened, it was necessary for the presiding bishop to borrow funds to meet operation expenses and rather than borrow the money from outside sources, they decided to borrow from the Auditorium fund. This action added to the friction between the presidency and the bishopric until the bishop called for a joint council session. The council that was called consisted of the Presidency, Twelve and the Order of Bishops and from its session came the ultimate break.

In the June 4, 1924 edition of the *Saints' Herald*, the presiding bishop as president of the Board of Publications, announced they had taken over control of the *Herald* and announced a new group of editors. Since the beginning of the Reorganization the editorship of the *Herald* had always rested upon the First Presidency and generally reflected the official position of the church. The action of the Bishop opened the *Herald* for much controversial material and much was written in an attempt by each group to state their position. This is the first and only time in the history of the church that the power of Trustee-in-Trust has been exercised. It demonstrated very clearly that in the hands of certain types of men, the power and authority can exceed that which is believed to have come from God and resting in him who has been accepted as the prophet of God. So the reader may decide the merits of each position, the statement of each is quoted.

The Presiding Bishop's position is stated in an "open letter" that appeared in the *Herald* and reads:

"TO THE PRESIDENT, MINISTRY, AND MEMBERSHIP OF THE CHURCH: Greeting:
The controversy regarding church government, which began several years ago among the leading quorums, has now spread throughout the membership, and a crisis has been reached which demands serious consideration. There are fundamental issues which must be decided before peace can come to the church. We believe that the

organic law, supplemented by the experience of more than half a century on the part of the Reorganization, has established certain definite and abiding principles which are essential to progress. We issue this open letter so that a frank consideration of them may be had throughout the church. We believe that the coming General Conference, in full possession of the facts, should speak and settle this controversy in a definite, constructive manner. Only in such conference settlement can our people be reunited, confidence reestablished, and the cause of the Master advanced.

We affirm our belief in the following principles and pledge our adherence thereto:

1. General Conference, the enactments of which combine both the inspiration of God and the will of his people, *is the highest authority in the church.*

2. To obtain the common judgment, and to insure the cooperation and support of the people, all general church programs and policies must be submitted to the General Conference for consideration and decision before being initiated.

3. The law recognizes two general divisions in the administrative work of the church—spiritual and temporal, and specifies 'that the temporalities of the church are to be under the charge and care of the Bishopric.' *In temporal affairs the bishop acts as trustee-in-trust for the church and is directly responsible to the General Conference.* (Emphasis by author)

4. All quorums, departments, and institutions within the church shall operate on budgets appropriated by General Conference. The bishop shall limit expenditures to such budgets and General Conference appropriations.

5. We accept the Bible, Book of Mormon, and Doctrine and Covenants, which contain the constitutional law of the church, and recognize the rights and powers of the priesthood as therein defined. We declare for the government in the church by lawful and orderly processes and hold that General Conference enactments are binding without exception upon members, officials, and quorums."

To avoid too much in personalities the names of the signers of the above open letter are not shown. However, it was signed by two members of the Quorum of Twelve, the presiding bishopric and several other outstanding leaders of the church.

In the June 18, 1924 issue of the *Herald*, there is a notice by the First Presidency which reads:

"TO THE CHURCH:

I regret to find it necessary to denounce the action of the Board of Publication as reported by the board in the *Herald* of two weeks ago.

The Board of Publications has assumed unwarranted powers in the matter, and the church must now be informed that the Presidency has not only disapproved the action of the board but has made formal protest. It will be noted that not even the usual courtesies observed in change of editors were extended to us.

For the first time since 1865 the editorial columns of the *Herald* do not represent the Presidency. It will be clear that the "official" character of the *Herald* has thus been changed.

The action of the board is not alone unwarranted but greatly to be deplored at this time. FREDERICK M. SMITH, President of the Church." (*Saints' Herald*, Vol. 71, No. 25, p. 578.)

Following the above notice there appears a lengthy article outlining the actions considered by the council that has been called and also includes the position taken by the First Presidency and a majority of the council. To aid the reader in comprehending the differences between the Bishopric and the Presidency this statement is as follows:

"This church, as defined by the late Joseph Smith, is a theocratic-democracy—not man-made, but of divine appointment and origin. (Matt. 16:18; Doctrine and Covenants 1:5, 17:7; I Nephi 3:221; III Nephi 10:1.) The government of the church is by divine authority through priesthood. (Doctrine and Covenants 68:4; Acts 20:28.) The government in its objective is beneficent, and its purpose is betterment of human conditions. The divine authority becomes operative through the consent of the governed— the common consent indicated in the law (Doctrine and Covenants 25:1; 27:4). It is divine government among the people, for the people, and for the glory of God and the achievement of his purposes towards ideal conditions. God directs the church through clearly indicated channels (Doctrine and Covenants 43:1, 2; 27:2); and his voice is the directing power of the church; but to this the assent of the people must be secured.

In organic expression and functioning there must be recognized grades of official prerogative and responsibility (Doctrine and Covenants 104; 122:9.), with *supreme directional control resting in the Presidency* as the chief and first quorum of the church (Doctrine and Covenants 122:2, 9; 104:42). This control it is presumed is beneficent. Protection against prostitution of this power is amply provided in the law.

To carry into effect the purposes of the church, effective administration is imperative, and organic solidarity is maintained only by effective discipline, which is in consonance with the beneficent purposes of the church, but yet strongly enough administered to prevent the purposes of the organization being frustrated by individual caprice and rebellion. Authority to be effective must be respected. This view of the organization of the church affirms the interdependence of departments and co-ordination of action and holds *General Conference as the instrument of the expression of the will of the people.*" *Saints' Herald*, Vol. 71, No. 25, p. 579. (Italics by author)

The statements shown became the basis for an over-whelming discussion in the columns of the *Herald* which culminated at the General Conference held in Independence, Missouri, in April of 1925. When the final vote was taken on the document presented by the presidency, it resulted in an overwhelming victory in favor. The actual vote was 351 for and 97 against.

Following the adoption of the president's position a revelation was presented to the conference and was accepted. This revelation provided for the acceptance of the resignation of the Presiding Bishop and his counselors. It also provided the selection of a replacement. It also approved of the conference acceptance of the joint council document referred to above as the position of the presidency.

When the conference was called upon to sustain the various officers of the church, several of the signers of the "open letter" were not sustained. Among these were two members of the Twelve. One of these later returned to the church and was accepted but the other withdrew and started an organization of his own. Several others joined the Church of Christ Temple Lot (Hedrickites) and become apostles and officers of that organization. The split that occurred in the church was one of the greatest tragedies in its history. It has not yet fully recovered and will not do so until the seeds of potential division cease to exist.

During the Great Depression of the thirties, the conference of 1932 returned to the presiding bishop some of the controls previously held and it was not until the World Conference of 1968 that the issue seems to have been put to rest by means of a revelation, a portion of which reads as follows:

"3. Instructions given formerly are to be observed, and since the office of bishop is a 'necessary appendage' to the high priesthood and members of the Order of Bishops are charged with the ministry of temporalities, they will act in support of leadership given by the spiritual authorities for the achievement of the purposes of my church. Temporal officers are to be supported in their rightful place, but must be guided by the needs of the field in their work of helping to furnish the means to finance my program." (RLDS D & C 149:3.)

When this document was presented to the conference all of the quorums with the exception of the Order of Bishops, accepted it and it was not until the president gave a clarification that the bishops gave their approval.

Whether or not this highly divisive problem has been permanently resolved remains to be proved by the future.

CHAPTER VI

PRIESTHOOD AND QUORUMS

Possibly one of the most outstanding characteristics of the Restoration Movement will be found in its Priesthood organization and its functioning in the church. Unlike other church organizations which select an individual to become the pastor of their group and place upon him all of the responsibilities of ministering to them, the Restoration divides this responsibility among many different individuals. This is accomplished through the unique priesthood organization given to the church by the prophet Joseph Smith. This organization is believed to be the same as that established by Christ when he organized his church.

In the November 1956 issue of *Reader's Digest* there appeared an article under the title "Why Ministers Are Breaking Down," which was condensed from *Life* magazine of August 20, 1956. The article was written by the Rev. Wesley Shrader, a Baptist clergyman for 19 years who at the time the article appeared was Assistant Professor of Pastoral Theology, Yale Divinity School. Quotations used from his article are to emphasize the wisdom of the organization of the Restoration. On page 56 of the *Reader's Digest* we read:

" . . . Size of salary seems to have nothing to do with it. The principle reason is that the minister's role, as conceived by the members of church congregations, is one no human being, not even one of the Twelve Apostles, could adequately fill. . . ."

"And he is expected to be a specialist in six separate roles: administrator, organizer, pastor, preacher, priest, teacher."

God, realizing that no one individual has all of the qualifications necessary to do a complete task of ministering to the people, established the priesthood organization which consists of two major orders: first, the Melchisedec priesthood and second, the Aaronic priesthood. Each of these priesthood orders has a definite and specific type of service to render in the church. The Melchisedec priesthood is in general, recognized as the presiding body and in direction of the spiritual affairs of the church. The First Presidency, the Quorum of Twelve Apostles, High Priests, Seventies, Patriarchs, Bishops and Elders comprise the membership of this order. The Aaronic Priesthood consists of Priests, Teachers and Deacons whose responsibilities are primarily local in aspect. The Aaronic Priesthood is presided over by a Bishop which indicates also that the Aaronic Priesthood is concerned in the temporal affairs of the local group.

In the above type of organization, it can readily be seen that the problems of over-work on the part of an individual is not necessary and should never be a problem in the mental health of those endeavoring to serve God.

Both churches of the Restoration recognize the above form of priesthood organization but differ in the calling of men and in the use to which they are required to serve. These differences are to be explored. The basic belief of both churches is couched in the following statement by the Prophet Joseph Smith:

> "We believe that a man *must be called of God, by prophecy*, and by the laying on of hands, by those who are in authority, to preach the Gospel and administer in the ordinances thereof." (Epitome of Faith.) (Italics by author.)

Even before the Church was organized in April of 1830, men were called and ordained to the priesthood. Joseph Smith and Oliver Cowdery received their ordination almost a year before the church was formed. However, even though the prophet had been instructed and was authorized to ordain men to the Melchisedec Priesthood, it was necessary to have a formal organization that could approve and accept the men called to minister to them. This procedure continued up to the time of the prophet's death and for some time thereafter.

For many years after their arrival in Salt Lake Valley, the Mormon Church continued the procedure as it was in the early church, calling men to the priesthood on the basis of their capabilities. It was not until around 1877 that a change developed. To confirm the position of the church prior to this time a quotation made by Brigham Young in 1854 at the general conference held in October of that year was referred to:

"When you have got your Bishop, he needs assistance and he ordains counselors, priests, teachers and deacons, and calls them to help him; he wishes men of his own heart and hand to do this. He says 'I dare not even call a man to be a deacon, to assist me in my calling unless he has a family.' It is not the business of an ignorant young man, of no experience in family matters to inquire into the circumstances of families, and know the wants of every person. Some may want medicine and nourishment, and to be looked after, and it is not the business of boys to do this; but select a man who has got a family to be a deacon, whose wife can go with him, and assist him in administering to the needy of the ward." (J of D 2:89)

The above quotation does indicate that some suggestion may have been made to Brigham Young that some younger men be ordained. However, it was not until around 1877 that the change began to take place in the church. In an article published in the *Improvement Era* of June 1957 by Joseph Fielding Smith, an explanation of the beginning of the ordination of boys to the Aaronic Priesthood is made. From this article we quote:

"In July 1877, the First Presidency, who were President Brigham Young, John W. Young, and Daniel H. Wells, issued a circular in which we find the following:

'When priest and teachers visit the Saints, according to the instruction of the Book of Doctrine and Covenants, the experienced priest and teachers should have as a companion a young man, so that the latter may have the opportunity of learning the duties of his calling, and become thoroughly wise and efficient in the discharge thereof.'

It would be excellent training for the young men if they had the opportunity of acting in the offices of the lesser priesthood. They would thereby obtain very valuable experience, and when they obtain the Melchisedek Priesthood they would be likely to place a higher value upon it.' " (*Improvement Era*, Vol. 60, June 1957, p. 383)

Continuing from the same article by Joseph Fielding Smith:

"This same year (1877), there was a general reorganization and setting in order of the wards of the Church, and counsel was given regarding the activities of the quorums of the priesthood." (*Ibid.*, p. 383).

This appears to be the beginning of the practice of calling boys to the Aaronic Priesthood which is now the practice of the Mormon Church. This makes the Aaronic Priesthood the training ground for the Melchisedec priesthood and has made advancement in the priesthood automatic. To substantiate this statement, a quotation from a book by Dr. John A. Widtsoe titled *Priesthood and Church Government:*

"The First Presidency of the Church has authorized the following schedule of ages for ordination to and advancement in the priesthood:

Three years' experience and training for the Deacons—12, 13 and 14 years of age.
Two years' experience and training for the Teachers—15 and 16 years of age.
Two years' experience and training as Priests—17 and 18 years of age. Priests are eligible, if worthy, to be ordained Elders 19 years of age." (P C G, p. 170).

It has since been learned that a change has been made from that shown above to a new schedule in which Deacons serve for two years (12 and 13), they are then ordained as Teachers and serve in this office for two years (14-15 and 15-16). They are then ordained Priests and serve in this office until selected to be Elders which usually occurs when they reach the age of 18.

In the above procedures, no recognition of special aptitudes are involved and no recognition of specific qualifications of the individuals to properly fulfill the responsibilities of these callings. To illustrate, the function of a Teacher as given in the Doctrine and Covenants reads:

"The Teacher's duty is to watch over the Church always and be with and strengthen them; and see that there is no iniquity in the Church, neither hardness with each other, neither lying, backbiting, nor evil speaking; and see that all the members do their duty, and he is to take the lead of meetings in the absence of the elder or priest, and is to be assisted always, in all his duties in the church, by the deacons, if occasion requires; but neither teachers nor deacons have authority to baptize, administer the sacrament, or lay on hands; they are, however, to warn, expound, exhort, and teach, and to invite all to come unto Christ." (Mormon D & C 20:53-59; RLDS D & C 17:11).

From the above quotation it is learned that the teacher is more or less the investigating officer of the church and in some measure, is the policeman of the organization. This immediately raises the question of maturity and wisdom to fulfill these important responsibilities. Can a boy 14 or 15 years of age be mature enough to investigate difficulties between a husband and wife or between members of the church? The same question arises in reference to the other offices of the Aaronic Priesthood namely, deacons and priests.

The early age at which Joseph Smith had his first experience has been utilized to counter the question of maturity. He was not yet fifteen when the event occurred but it was not until seven or eight years later that God felt he had matured enough to assume his work. He was 22 years of age when he received the plates of the Book of Mormon and was 24 when he was ordained to the Aaronic Priesthood.

In the quotation from the Doctrine and Covenants showing the responsibilities and duties of the teacher, we read: ". . . but neither teachers nor deacons have authority to baptize, administer the sacrament . . . " It is very difficult to reconcile the practice in the Mormon Church in allowing the Deacon and Teacher to serve (administer) the sacrament in their services. The problem arises out of the misinterpretation of the word 'administer.' Reading from a dictionary the following is the definition of the word 'administer':

"To take or have the charge of; manage; regulate; to take charge of and settle, as an estate, by will or official appointment."
"2. To supply or provide with (something); apply; inflict; cause to take." (*The Modern Dictionary* - Funk & Wagnalls Co.)

For the church to justify their practice in using the deacons

60

and teachers as servers of the emblems, they give a new interpretation of the word "administer" which is to bless or pray over the sacrament which is usually done by the priests. The above definition of the word does not include this interpretation.

The above practices by the Mormon Church raise many questions relative to the calling and functioning of the priesthood and do need to be answered. What is the purpose of priesthood in the church? Is a man called to the priesthood because of his special qualifications for the office or because he has reached a certain age? There is a quotation in the Doctrine and Covenants that is pertinent to these questions and it reads:

"Therefore, let every man stand in his own office, and *labor in his own calling;* and let not the head say unto the feet it hath no need of the feet, for without the feet how shall the body be able to stand? Also, the body hath need of every member, that all may be edified together, that the system may be kept perfect." (Mormon D & C 84:109-110; RLDS D & C 83:21.)

It is common practice in the Mormon Church that when young members of the Aaronic priesthood are called upon to function in their office, they are accompanied by an older member of the Melchisedec priesthood and therefore, do not "stand in his own office" nor "labor in his own calling."

Events that have occurred in the life of the author to which he was involved, show how both churches have not always followed the right procedure in the use of the priesthood and the offices involved. While serving as Associate Pastor (Counselor) in a congregation, a request was received by either the Stake President or the Presiding Elder (Pastor) from a member wishing to have his name removed from the church records. As this took place during World War II when gasoline was rationed and the author had access to the scarce product, the Presiding Elder requested the author to accompany him and the Stake President in calling on the party to verify the request. On arrival at the home of the party making the request, it was suggested by the Stake President that it would be unwise for all of us to enter the house as it would tend to overwhelm the person called upon. The author was requested to wait in the car while the two officials made their call. The period of waiting gave ample opportunity to weigh the events taking place. First of all, the task that was being performed should have been the responsibility of a member of the priesthood ordained as a Teacher. The fact that the two top officials of the Stake were doing what should have been done by another officer, indicated an extreme lack of confidence in the properly ordained men of the Stake. This experience occurred in the Reorganized Church.

A like misuse of the priesthood function occurred very recently in the Mormon Church and the author was involved. In September 1969, the author was summoned to a Bishop's Court at which time his excommunication was to be considered. Shortly before the date of the trial, two members of the Melchisedec Priesthood delivered a summons on which each had signed as Teachers. At the trial it was requested by the author, inasmuch as both men were in attendance, what true office in the priesthood did each hold. One indicated he was a High Priest and the other that he was an Elder. The question was then raised as to why each had signed as a Teacher. Their response was that they were block teachers but when advised there was no such office provided for they realized the point that was being made. The Bishop corrected his copy of the summons but the author retained his as it was given to him.

It is this misuse of the priesthood in both churches that is to be questioned. This does not question the right of a member of the Melchisedec Priesthood to function in the lower offices when circumstances so require. It is more readily understood when the Mormons resort to this practice because Teachers in that church are ordained as boys when they are fourteen and fifteen years of age and it would not be proper for them to handle such serious cases.

There are some isolated instances where real young men were ordained to the priesthood during the days of the prophet but it was not in the same manner as now being practiced by the Mormon Church. Don Carlos Smith, a brother of the prophet, was ordained and sent out as a missionary when he was fifteen. It is certainly not the intent of the author to limit God in his wisdom, in the calling of those to serve him.

There is no question but what has been related above is an illustration of the attempts by man to improve on that

62

which God has revealed and has happened many times in the history of Christ's church.

The Reorganized Church uses a different approach to the calling of men to the priesthood. They do not place the distinction of grade in the calls, it is rather a recognition of an individual's aptitudes and capabilities to the specific office to which he is called. There is no age limit involved and a man may be ordained as a youth and continue in that office for the rest of his life should his aptitudes so require. When a call is received, it is presumed that God is responsible and that he recognizes within the man the qualifications for the office to which he is called. As men grow and gain wisdom and knowledge, they can be called to other offices in the priesthood, not by way of promotion, but according to the direction of God.

While on the topic of priesthood, it is necessary to give consideration to the organization of the priesthood as given to the church. In the Doctrine and Covenants we find this instruction:

"Of necessity, there are presidents, or presiding offices, growing out of, or appointed of, or from among those who are ordained to the several offices in these two priesthoods." (Mormon D & C 107:21; RLDS D & C 104:11.)

And further on in the same section of the Doctrine and Covenants:

"To the Church of Christ in the land of Zion, in addition to the church laws, respecting church business: Verily, I say unto you, says the Lord of Hosts, there must needs be presiding elders, to preside over those who are of the office of elder; and also priests, to preside over those who are of the office of a priest; and also teachers to preside over those who are of the office of teacher, in like manner; and also the deacons. . . ." (Mormon D & C 107:59-62; RLDS D & C 104:31.)

This same revelation also designates the number of men in each category that comprises a quorum. There are twelve deacons in a quorum of deacons; twenty-four teachers; forty-eight priests; and ninety-six elders. There is no specific number required in the formation of the high priests quorum.

63

It is through this priesthood and its organization that we find the real genius of the Restoration movement. When the priesthood and the quorums are functioning according to the will of God, the success of the organization is assured.

The Mormon Church has continued the organization of the priesthood into quorums and has used them for the instruction and training of the members to the point they have effected one of the finest organizations in the world for the accomplishment of their purpose. Every man or boy, when ordained to the priesthood, is immediately assigned to a quorum and continually meets with them for direction and guidance in efforts to be of service.

The Reorganization, during its early formative years, followed the same pattern and organized the men into quorums and at one time, they had as many as eleven quorums of elders in the church. Over the past fifty years quorum organization in the Reorganization has constantly dwindled and has been deemphasized to the point that only in the Center Stake and one adjoining, are there any organized quorums as such. At the present time there is no specific study material provided by the church for use in quorum activity, nor are there regular priesthood meetings held for the edification and counciling of the priesthood. The author was ordained an elder in 1943 and has never had the privilege of belonging to an elder's quorum.

It is very possible that many of the apparent weaknesses of the Reorganization can be attributed to their failure to organize their priesthood according to the instructions given to the church by God for that purpose. The relationship of quorum organization and the general conferences will be discussed in another chapter.

CHAPTER VII

WORSHIP SERVICES

In making a comparison between the two churches, serious consideration must be given to the type of services conducted, the purpose for which services are held and whether or not the services, as held, accomplish what God has in mind.

In the early days of the church under the prophet Joseph Smith, no definite plan of procedure was outlined by him as to the manner of conducting the services. However, the primary function at a service in his day was the preaching of the Word. One of the peculiar features of the early church was the lack of concern for the erection of church buildings in which to worship. Because of the undeveloped condition of the frontier, this lack of building churches also applied to other organizations. The first building of which there is any record was the erection of a schoolhouse by a group that came to Independence, Missouri. This schoolhouse was located in what is now Kansas City, Missouri. The next building of importance mentioned in the history of the church was the Temple at Kirtland, Ohio. This building was the first and is the only building standing today that was erected under a direct command from God. It is now in the possession of the Reorganized Church.

From the plans and layout of the building, plus the instructions given as the purpose for its erection, we learn what was uppermost in the minds of the men receiving the instructions. The building was arranged primarily for the schooling and teaching of the members of the church. While there is a sanctuary on the main floor that could be used for preaching, etc., it was also provided with curtains that could be lowered and divide the room into separate sections. It has rostrums at each end of the room that were designated for the use of the two orders of priesthood. The Melchisedec at one end and the Aaronic at the other. The seats were movable and could be adjusted to permit those occupying them to face either direction. In the revelation the building was designated to be the home for the School of the Prophets. From this it is apparent that the main concern of the leaders of the church was for the instruction of the people and the priesthood. This appears to have been the major concern all during the lifetime of Joseph Smith. The temple being built in Nauvoo at the time of his death, was for the same purpose plus providing a building in which the conferences of the church could be held.

From that which has been recorded we find very little to guide us in the manner in which services are to be conducted. We do realize that in the early church and for many years after the death of the prophet, there was no such organization as the Sunday School. This developed many years later.

To make a comparison of the two churches today requires a description of their services and endeavor to learn what the purpose is and how well it accomplishes that purpose. In order to do this an attempt will be made to describe them so the reader can make whatever judgment he wishes.

Before attempting the description of services, it should be mentioned that the Mormon Church endeavors to get the greatest utilization of their buildings possible. They do this by having two and sometimes three wards (congregations) meet in the same building. They stagger the times of the services to enable each ward to meet as a unit. The reader should keep this in mind when the hour of service is mentioned.

A typical Sunday in the Mormon Church begins with the meeting of the priesthood at the ward meeting house. Here they meet according to the office held and are instructed from manuals and lesson material provided by the general church. This service usually begins at nine in the morning. At ten-thirty the Sunday School assembles and at this service the Sacrament is served followed by some preliminary exercises. They then separate into class groups and the balance of the morning is devoted to teaching and study. On the first Sunday of each month there is an afternoon service which is known as the Fast Service. For this service the members are expected to fast (refrain from eating) from the morning and noon meals and contribute the money thus saved to the Fast offering fund of the church. This fund is devoted primarily to the welfare of the poor. The Sacrament is served at this service and is followed by prayer and testimonies. There is usually no service held in the evening of the first Sunday of the month. On other Sundays, an evening service is held and is known as the Sacrament Service. At this service, the emblems of the Lord's Supper are served and followed different speakers selected by the bishop of the ward. Sometimes the members are called upon to speak extemporaneously but this is the only service at which preaching would be a part.

It would be well to insert here a description of the serving of the emblems of the sacrament. This is one of the functions within the church that was outlined by revelation and about which there are some specific instructions. In the Doctrine and Covenants there are two prayers that are to be used in the blessing of the emblems. These prayers are in the twentieth section of the Mormon Doctrine and Covenants and in the seventeenth section of the Reorganized edition. The following instructions are also found in this book:

" . . . I say unto you, that it mattereth not what ye shall eat, or what ye shall drink, when ye partake of the sacrament, if it so be that ye do it with an eye single to my glory; remembering unto the Father my body which was laid down for you, and my blood which was shed for the remission of your sins; wherefore a commandment I give unto you, that you shall not purchase wine, neither strong drink of your enemies; wherefore ye shall partake of none, except it is made new among you." (Mormon D & C 27:2-4; RLDS D & C 26:1.)

Later permission was given to use water in place of wine if necessity so required. On the strength of this, the Mormon Church now uses water when the sacrament is served.

In the Mormon Church services when the sacrament is served it is usually done with two priests preparing the emblems and then asking the blessing on each as outlined in the Doctrine and Covenants. It is then taken by the deacons and teachers and served to the presiding officials and then to the congregation. It should be remembered that the deacons and teachers are usually boys. They do not serve each individual but allow the container holding the emblems to pass along the row from person to person until it is received at the far end of the row. There are no restrictions on those partaking and they allow unbaptized children to partake.

With the serving of the sacrament twice in one day, a serious question arises as to the real meaning or efficacy in the minds of the partakers. The real purpose of this ritual in the church is for the renewing of covenants made at baptism. Certainly, it should not be necessary that this be done twice the same day. Will not too frequent participation tend to destroy the real meaning and importance of the act?

From the above description of the Mormon Church services it can be seen that the real emphasis for Sunday services is placed upon education or teaching of the members. Preaching, as it is found in the sectarian churches does not occur.

Realizing the inadequacy of using one day a week for the teaching and developing of their members, the Mormon Church has developed several other forms of service. One of the most outstanding of these is the Relief Society, which is the official women's organization. This organization is much older than the Sunday School as it was first organized at Nauvoo, Illinois by Joseph Smith and was presided over by his wife, Emma Smith. There is also the Mutual Improvement Association which is divided into two organizations known as the Young Men's and Young Women's Mutual Improvement Association. Each of these function as a means of training with study material provided. More will be said of these in a later chapter. Another of the organizations they have provided is the Primary Association which provides for additional training for children and services are held on a weekday in the afternoon following school. They also have the Genealogical Society which also conducts classes pertaining to genealogy.

One of the more unique and outstanding functions developed by the Mormon Church is the Family Home Evening. For many years the church has advocated the reserving of one night during the week for home instruction. It has recently been reemphasized and expanded through the development of lesson material to be used. A manual has been provided by the general church authorities that contains lessons for an entire year. The purpose is to put back into the home, the responsibility of the parents to instruct their children. This is in line with the instructions given to the early church that parents are responsible for the training of their children.

From what has been written above it can readily be seen that the emphasis of the Mormon Church is on teaching and instruction and are following closely the precepts of the early church. They have not relied upon tradition and procedures of other churches as a guide for their methods of worship but have been completely independent and self-reliant and in so doing, have become a very distinctive organization.

To compare the Reorganized Church with the Mormon Church, the same procedure should be used describing the type of services conducted by them. In the early days of the Reorganization, they relied greatly upon the preaching service, preaching in homes and school houses as the opportunity afforded. As the church grew in numbers, they began the erection of houses of worship out of which their present services evolved. They adopted the Sunday School as the main source for the teaching of the members. They later developed another organization for instruction that was known as the Zion's Religio Literary Society which, for many years, specialized in teaching the Book of Mormon. It also functioned as the social outlet for the young people.

To describe a Sunday and its services in the Reorganized Church, we find quite a difference from that conducted by the Mormon Church. The day begins usually at nine-thirty in the morning. This is the start of Sunday School and the first twenty minutes or half-hour is devoted to various types of preliminary exercises after which they separate into classes for study. The general church offers study material of a graded variety for the use of classes from children up to the teen-age group. Other material is offered for the use of adult classes but is generally left up to the classes to select the material to be used. The Sunday School service is over by ten forty-five. At eleven o'clock the major service of the day is held and is devoted to preaching. This preaching is done by a member of the priesthood or visiting general church officers. Most activities are centered around making the preaching service the most important of the day. The exception for this is the service held on the first Sunday of each month, which is the Communion Service and is for the purpose of serving the Lord's Supper. This service is conducted with much more solemnity and ceremony than in the Mormon Church. It is usually announced that they are "close communionists" and do not permit anyone not baptized into the church to partake of the emblems. When serving the emblems, the priests or elders do not allow the container to leave their hands and in so doing, individually serve each member.

On Sunday evening the services held in the Reorganization sometimes vary a great deal and in some instances, no services are held. When they are held it is usually another preaching service. On Wednesday evening of each week they hold a prayer service similar to those held in many of the sectarian churches. This is a prayer and testimony meeting. There are no regularly scheduled priesthood meetings as held in the Mormon Church.

Anyone familiar with the services held in the various protestant churches, will recognize the similarity of the worship services held by the Reorganization. It would appear that the Reorganization has patterned in many ways, their procedures and services from the general format of other churches rather than to have developed a distinctive type of their own as did the Mormon Church.

Several years ago the author, while in conversation with a member of the Mormon Church, pressed him for a criticism of the Reorganization. He was very reluctant to make an observation but after much persuasion, he made the following statement: "Your church has not departed far enough." When pressed for an explanation of what he meant, he replied: "It has not departed far enough from the churches God said were an abomination." This comment was not very impressive at the time it was made; however, the passing of time and the observation of events since that time have brought back the real import of the criticism. The question arises, has the Reorganization been so anxious to avoid the mistakes of the early members of the church when they came to Missouri that they have bent over backward to avoid being different? The author is of the firm conviction that God restored the church because it was necessary to do so. Had he seen the possibility of so reforming the other churches that they could meet with His approval, there never would have been a necessity for a Restoration. Of late there has arisen within the Reorganization the criticism that the church was becoming too "Protestantized" as an organization.

To summarize the comparison of the two churches, it is apparent that the Reorganization does not emphasize the teaching and instruction of their membership and priesthood to the extent it is done in the Mormon Church.

CHAPTER VIII

LOCAL ORGANIZATION

Because mechanical organization plays an important part in the success or failure of a project, we need to compare the mechanics of organization between the two churches.

There is very little information from the early church pertaining to local congregations as such until the church settled at Nauvoo, Illinois. It was at this place that the development of both stake and local groups occurred.

The city of Nauvoo was divided into wards much the same as now done in most cities as political boundaries. However, in Nauvoo these wards became local congregations and were presided over by a Bishop (High Priest) and two counselors and the ward clerk. Under the direction of the Bishop was the priesthood in that ward. There is not much information in reference to the types of services that took place but we can assume they endeavored to meet the needs of the people.

The Mormon Church has continued the same organization as developed at Nauvoo. The people are divided into wards and stakes. The ward is presided over by a Bishop with two counselors. There is also a ward clerk but he has no presiding rights but is to maintain a record of the activities of the ward. Various committees are appointed to assist the Bishop as needed. The local priesthood, specifically the Aaronic, are under his direction. The Bishop is responsible for the collection of all tithes and offerings which he sends directly to the Presiding Bishop of the church. It is of interest to note that a collection plate is never a part of the services of the Mormon Church. The Aaronic priesthood are organized as block teachers and endeavor to visit the home of each member in the block assigned, at least once a month. They are always accompanied by an older member of the Melchisedec priesthood living within the ward and who wish to take part in this service.

The Reorganized Church did not follow the plan as it was in operation at Nauvoo by making a presiding elder of a bishop. Because the church was so scattered at its formation, they had no opportunity to organize a city and develop it in the same manner as did the Mormon Church. As the church grew and new groups were added they began to call them branches. For many years this was the accepted term used when referring to them. In each branch they elected annually a presiding elder and he selected his counselors. They also elected a branch clerk to maintain the records. Among other officers elected they had a presiding priest, presiding teacher and a presiding deacon. Under this organization the presiding elder utilized the several priesthood leaders to direct the activities of those priesthood members within the branch. This form of organization has gradually disappeared and different methods have been experimented with and tried. For many years the church dropped the title of presiding elder and substituted the term pastor. This appears to have been an adaptation from other churches. There is an effort in some areas to do away with the term pastor and return to the use of presiding elder. (The term pastor is not in the Doctrine and Covenants). With the expansion of stake organization within the church, there have been many changes made pertaining to the local group. They are no longer called branches but are known as congregations and they are directly supervised by the Stake President. The local presiding elder is now considered an assistant to the stake president who is considered the pastor of the stake. This is because of a resolution passed by general conference of April 5, 1952 and reads:

"Stakes are the most highly coordinated units of church organization. *Ideally a stake is not an association of branches* but a well integrated organization of related congregations. For this reason it is advisable that all the congregations in the stake shall be under the supervision, direct or indirect, of the stake presidency. The presiding officers of these congregations being assistants to the stake presidency. The selection of these congregational presiding officers should be made at the stake conferences, with the right of nomination resting concurrently with the stake presidency and the people." (*Rules and Resolutions.* Stake organization paragraph 35.)

The above resolution in effect, makes the stake the basic unit in the church and eliminates the congregations or branches from this category, and leaves them nonautonomous as a unit.

To comment on this and to compare it with the organization of the Mormon Church and their form of stake organization, there is a very distinctive difference. The Mormon Church recognizes the ward or congregation as the basic unit of the church and all activities usually center in that group. The Mormon interpretation appears to be much more realistic and feasible in church operation. The real function of the stake in the Mormon Church is the coordination of activities between various wards belonging to the stake. The stake does not assume the control of each ward in the same manner as done within the Reorganized Church. Another weakness of the stake organization in the Reorganized Church is the lack of set guidelines that have endured the test of time. Much of the details of stake organization is left to the individual stake president and as a result, therefore, stake operations are not uniform or standard.

The lack of a tried and tested operation such as stake organization can have a devastating effect upon the membership of the church. The desire of the membership is to have the feeling of permanency in the direction of the affairs of the church, the same as in the doctrines and message of Christ, and they look to the leadership for this. If it is hesitant and unsure, then will the members be unsure. The failure to organize the priesthood into quorums as provided by the law also contributes to the feeling of inadequacy that seems to be present within the stakes. This is a matter that needs the most earnest attention within the Reorganization.

CHAPTER IX

MISSIONARY ACTIVITIES

In a discussion of the missionary functioning and how they compare within the Mormon Church and the Reorganized Church, we find one of the major differences that exists outside of doctrine.

Missionary activities began in the early church immediately following the organizational meeting of April 6, 1830. History records that four men were selected by the prophet to travel to the western frontiers in western Missouri and eastern Kansas, to bring the gospel to the Indians of that territory. This was also the beginning of the migration of the Saints to the West.

It is well to examine the mechanics of the calling of these men. We know that the church was in no financial condition to support these men in their journeys and they would have to rely upon their ingenuity to survive. The church was not in a position to support the families of the men while they were away so it fell upon the membership of the church to care for the families according to their needs and circumstances. In spite of this great handicap, these men were so devoted to the Restoration that they fulfilled the mission to which they were assigned. What should be emphasized here is the fact that the task was a voluntary one and was not done for monetary considerations. This same practice continued in the church during the lifetime of the prophet. Men would be called upon to journey to mission fields in an endeavor to spread the Gospel, then they would return and try to rehabilitate their economic status and that of their families with the view of again being able to fill another mission. These men were devoted and voluntarily consecrated their lives as best they could to the work of the church. They were always dependent upon the area in which they labored for the sustenance needed.

Prior to 1838, the bishop's primary responsibility was to accept the consecrations of the members and to assign inheritances in those areas where the Saints were gathering. We find no record referring to the collection of moneys for the support of the church leaders or the missionaries. These leaders, in order to survive and serve the church, entered into various types of enterprise. There were printing presses, general stores and all of the various professions necessary in any community. These enterprises were owned by the leaders and others qualified to perform the tasks. The majority of the people at that time were farmers and the main source of income was from agriculture.

The same situation prevailed at Nauvoo. All of the leaders of the church had either a business or vocation from which they derived their livelihood. At no time were they dependent upon the church for their sustenance. It should be emphasized that up to the death of the prophet, no record of a professional ministry was found.

The Mormon Church has continued this policy until today, as a church organization, they have no professional ministry involved. It is not to be considered that those employed by the church to handle the details of office management, etc. are professional ministers. The missionaries of the Mormon Church are usually young men though not always so, because anyone can receive a call to go on a mission providing they can sustain themselves while performing the task. When the young men are called, it is necessary that their families support them financially during the period for which they are assigned. The church does assume the responsibility of supplying their return expenses. They now have approximately thirteen thousand young men and women missionaries in the field. This can well account for the phenomenal growth the church has shown.

The same policy is in effect pertaining to the General Church officers. None of these men are remunerated by the church. They are not dependent upon the church for their livelihood and in this sense, cannot be considered professional ministers regardless of the amount of time devoted to the services of the church. There are some instances where the mission presidents and some temple presidents are given a living allowance but it is wholly upon the circumstances of the individual. In the stakes and wards where the real ministry is performed, all of the work is done by men consecrated to the work of the church and their only recompense is in the joy that comes from serving God by serving His people.

The many tourists and visitors to the Temple Square in Salt Lake City are not always aware that the guides are generally prominent business men who take time off from their businesses to serve the church, by welcoming and telling the story of their church to these visitors. Those who have made this trip, know how well that story is told.

The Reorganized Church has followed a somewhat different approach to the missionary work. In the early days of the Reorganization, the principle was the same as in the early church. Men would take the responsibility of missionary activity in the various fields and would rely upon the people in the area to sustain them and in turn they would endeavor to secure sufficient to take care of their families at home. Many had to take time out from their church activities and return home to replenish their financial needs. The church was not financially able to support them and their families. This is shown by what one reads in church history. On several different occasions, it was necessary for the Presiding Bishop to accept a receipt for tithing from the church in lieu of a deficit that existed because sufficient funds were not received.

As the church began to grow and the financial condition improved, it began to assume the responsibility of caring for the families of the missionaries. These funds were taken from the tithes and offerings that were collected. This eliminated the periodic return of the missionaries and led to a more or less permanent assignment as a missionary. As this policy grew and the church became more financially sound, more and more men began entering the mission field as a lifetime vocation. Their dependency upon the church for their material needs became greater as time passed.

The ultimate objective to this type of evolution is a paid ministry and this is what has developed in the Reorganization. This is illustrated by the assignment of men to a certain field and then designating a certain city as the objective. In all of these instances, the appointee became the presiding elder of the congregation which was his objective. Of course, the church looked to the congregation to support the man so assigned, but in many instances, the local groups were unable to do so and the responsibility fell back upon the general church.

During the Great Depression of the thirties, the church's finances became so precarious that it was necessary to eliminate a large number of missionaries from the field because they could no longer give the support and assistance

76

to them and their families. Because of this, greater reliance upon the functioning of the local ministry was essential and the policy of full-time presiding elders was phased out.

Since World War II, the church has regained financial stability and is now continuing the policy of appointing full-time missionaries and stake officers. They have instituted the setting up of reserves to assure the appointee of income when they are retired. While the appropriations made to the missionary or appointee is not considered a salary, it is based upon his family's wants and needs and in the end result, constitutes an annual income on which he is to pay his tithes and the Social Security taxes.

All general church authorities, department heads, stake presidents, stake bishops, and (in some areas) district presidents are staffed by church appointees who are, in fact, professional ministers. It should be emphasized here that what has been said should in no way, be construed as questioning the sincerity, devotion and commitment of these appointees to the Restoration movement. The comparison is to enable those who may have an interest in the work to better understand the differences between the two organizations.

In the opinion of the writer, God's work can best be done by men thoroughly converted and with a love for their fellowmen. This type of devotion can seldom be purchased. One of the most debilitating factors of professional ministers is the effect upon local men called to the priesthood. There is a natural tendency on the part of men to avoid doing those things that are done by someone hired for that purpose. The only way a man can justify a position as a full-time presiding elder, would be by assuming the responsibilities of visiting and ministering to the membership, not only by preaching but also by going into the homes and actually doing the many things that the several officers of the priesthood should be doing. God knew how impossible it is for one man to be all things, he therefore provided the various priesthood functions. When a man is hired to perform these tasks, the local men then become apathetic and lose interest in the work. The Reorganization is today, paying the penalty for some of these policies.

CHAPTER X

GENERAL CONFERENCES

The first instructions given to the Restoration movement in reference to the handling of church business was in a revelation that was given to Joseph Smith before the organization of the church in 1830. The revelation referred to is section seventeen in the Reorganized edition of the Doctrine and Covenants and section twenty in the Mormon edition. It reads the same in both books and quoting from the thirteenth verse of the Reorganized edition:

"The several elders composing this church of Christ are to meet in conference once in three months, or from time to time, as said conferences shall direct or appoint; and said conferences are to do whatever church business is necessary to be done at the time." (RLDS D & C 17:3.)

The above quotation is the first and most significant statement pertaining to the holding of conferences and the reference to the "several elders" of course, refers to the members of the Melchisedec priesthood. To affirm that the above meant the priesthood of the church and not the regular membership, is shown in a number of revelations received at various times. Referring to just one of these revelations:

"Hearken, O ye elders of my church, who have assembled yourselves together, in my name, even Jesus Christ, the Son of the living God, the Savior of the World, inasmuch as they believe on my name and keep my commandments; again I say unto you, hearken and hear and obey the law which I shall give unto you; for verily I say, as ye have *assembled yourselves together according to my command-ment* wherewith I commanded you, and are agreed as touching this one thing . . ." (RLDS D & C 42:1; Mormon D & C 42:1-3.)

It can only be inferred from the above quotations that it was and is the responsibility of the eldership to transact the business of the church and from all data that can be found pertaining to the church during the lifetime of the prophet, indicates that the church business was handled in this manner. There are some instances where the membership as a whole did participate in some conferences but it was primarily to give their consent to actions taken. We do find in the Doctrine and Covenants of both churches, minutes of meetings by the High Council that were accepted by the church for incorporation into the church policy but no resolutions adopted by the membership while in session are available.

The first evidence that the membership participated or attended the conferences took place in Nauvoo. There is evidence that the membership were called upon to sustain the leadership and the program in which they were involved. One example of this was the meeting called by stake president, William Marks at Nauvoo to hear the claim of Sidney Rigdon after the death of the prophet. It was at this meeting that the Twelve assumed control and presented to the people assembled, the opportunity to accept Sidney Rigdon or to accept the leadership of the Twelve. There is also the record of a conference being held in the partially completed temple in Nauvoo in October of 1845.

The Mormon Church has followed the practice that occurred in Nauvoo, such as the conference held in Salt Lake City in 1852, when the doctrine of polygamy was first presented to the church. We find no record of debate or even of a vote being taken to approve that which was presented. Several leaders spoke to the congregation in reference to the subject. However, the action of approval came when the conference was called upon to sustain the leadership. Present day conferences in the Mormon Church are still conducted in this manner.

Due to the large number of members that attend the conference, the Mormon Church has found it necessary to reserve a large portion of the Tabernacle for the seating of stake presidents and ward bishops that attend. Passes are issued to them to assure better representation of the priesthood at conferences.

The principle of "common consent" in the Mormon Church is demonstrated in the right to accept or reject the leadership and their programs. All matters are settled within the various quorums and no discussion as such, occurs on the floor of the conference.

The conferences held by the Reorganized Church are much different and an investigation of its evolution is in order. In the early days of the Reorganization the conference met and it was composed of priesthood and membership. However, it is of interest to note that the minutes of the conferences always show the number of priesthood in attendance. All official actions were taken by the priesthood without the vote of the membership who were attending. The exception to this precedure was when a revelation was presented, after it had been accepted by the various quorums, it was presented to the body as a whole and the membership were then privileged to vote.

It appears that a desire for democracy in the church was stronger than in the group that traveled west for we see a gradual evolution from priesthood action to a delegate system. It should be emphasized that the introduction of the delegate type conference was not instituted by revelation but was traceable to an attorney who drafted the details of a delegate system and it was presented to the church and adopted in the 1880's. This system provided a means whereby members from various parts of the country could select someone to represent them at the conference. It also provided that the Melchisedec Priesthood should have ex officio rights in the conference. This form continued up to the conference of 1964, when a resolution was passed that took the right of ex officio from the Melchisedec Priesthood as a whole and left only church appointees, department heads and certain members of the Melchisedec (High Priests) the right of ex officio.

Joseph Smith III, son of the martyr and president of the Reorganization, described the church as a theocratic Democracy and this was reiterated by his son, F. M. Smith. The interpretation of the theocratic democracy is a "God led Democracy." It is in this type of organization that the principle of common consent is demonstrated by the right of the people to accept or reject what is presented. This appears to be the method Christ used with his disciples. This is the method used by the prophet in his presentation of revelation to the church. The right to debate, revise or alter was not a part of this. The only choice was to accept or reject and this is basically common consent.

With the development of the general conference into a democratic organization giving to conference the appellation "the highest legislative body in the church" the Reorganization has changed the concept of the church from a theocratic democracy to a democratic theocracy, and in place of God-led democracy, they now have a conference-led democracy.

The author cannot visualize that Christ or any prophet chosen by God to function in bringing to the people His will, would be subject to this type of democratic action. By observing the actions that have transpired under the democratic type conference, conclusions can be formed. This has been done by the author for many years. A number of incidents could be narrated that have proven extremely embarrassing to the church due to the privilege extended to members of the conference, to arise and propose any motion he may desire.

At one time the situation become so serious that the president of the church offered his resignation. Another incident that has previously been mentioned was the crisis of the conference of 1925, when the presiding Bishop opposed being responsible to the First Presidency as the directing head of the church. (Refer to chapter V.) Another was the introduction of resolutions to eliminate certain sections from the Doctrine and Covenants. Still another was the action by the conference to eliminate a hymn from the hymnal. All of these actions were on the floor of the conference and publicized in the press. Can the damage from such adverse publicity ever be overcome? Would it not have been far wiser to have had these problems discussed by the various quorums of priesthood, men selected by God to transact the business of the church?

With a general conference that is recognized as the "highest legislative body in the church" cannot that body institute legislation on doctrine? The author, at one general conference arose and asked the presiding officer (the president) whether or not the conference had the right to legislate doctrine and the reply was in the affirmative. These are some of the more serious problems that arise when the church becomes too democratic. An authoritative church cannot exist as a true democratic organization but it can with the doctrine of "common consent" which was practiced in the early church.

The Mormon Church holds a general conference twice each year, one in the Spring and the second in October. The Reorganized Church now holds a general conference once every two years. Neither of the churches lives up to the requirement of "once in three months" as given in the revelation. However, both churches hold quarterly stake conferences which does, in some respect, comply with the instructions. The stakes in the Reorganized Church do not always hold quarterly conferences unless circumstances demand it.

There is another matter in which the two organizations should be compared when considering their general conferences and this pertains to the financial matters. In the Mormon Church a financial statement is never presented for the conference that shows income or expenditures for any given period. A statement showing the worth of the church is never considered as a part of the conference deliberations. For this reason, the membership is never called upon to approve or disapprove any churchwide program. The membership is never aware of the amount of tithing collected or offerings given. An article in *Fortune* magazine of April 1964, estimated the annual income of the church at $110,000,000. The financial position should be of concern to the membership and, in the opinion of the author, it should be presented at one of the general conferences. A budget is never presented to the church for approval and as a result, the membership are not well informed as to some of the major projects of the church.

The Reorganized Church has always made it a practice to submit financial statements showing the income and expenditures for a given period. It was a common practice at one time to print the names of the appointees and the amount they received from the church for the period. This practice has been discontinued in recent years and is no longer a part of the financial statement. The annual budget is also presented to the conference for action and it is thoroughly analyzed before approval is given. In this way, the membership of the Reorganization are much better informed as to what their church is doing and what programs are being emphasized.

There is very good reason for each of the organizations to give some very serious thought to a reevaluation of their conference procedures.

82

CHAPTER XI

JOSEPH SMITH

The preceding chapters have primarily compared the mechanical functions of the two churches. The next task will be to give consideration to other factors such as scripture and doctrine. To begin with, a comparison of the attitudes of each church toward the prophet Joseph Smith is extremely important.

The Mormon Church has great reverence for the prophet, almost to the point of idolizing him. It is because of this attitude that many things were introduced into the church which are in error. Many of the introductions will be discussed in later chapters. It is only through this reverence by the people that the leaders could attribute to Joseph Smith, the responsibility for everything that was introduced. The people failed to remember something which is extremely important in relationship to a man called of God to act as his prophet. It should never be forgotten that any man chosen by God is still human and subject to human error. Joseph Smith, on many occasions, so reminded the people. It is even so indicated in the Doctrine and Covenants in revelations that reprimanded the prophet for his errors. We know Joseph succumbed to the pleadings of Martin Harris and because of this, he lost his power to translate the Book of Mormon. The important thing to be remembered is that a man can only be a prophet and speak for the Lord when God uses him for that purpose. It is when he speaks by the power and gift of God, that he is the prophet of God. It should never be accepted that every time he spoke, he did so by the power of God. It is in this area that the Mormon Church has gravely erred, inasmuch as they have taken statements from funeral sermons, portions of letters written, items written in his journal and from many hearsay sources, and have given them scriptural importance. By using this reverence for Joseph Smith, many things have been added to the church and when an analysis is made, it will be found that most of the doctrines in which the two churches differ, are the result of this misconception of the prophet. More will be said on this later.

The Reorganized Church have a very different attitude on this subject. They do recognize Joseph Smith as the prophet of God but do also remember that he did not always speak as a prophet. They recognize his humanness and his frailties. They do accept the revelations that he gave to the church and that appeared during his lifetime. They also realize that some men gathered around the prophet in Nauvoo, who were aspiring and ambitious for power and endeavored to influence him in many ways. Many have accused the Reorganized Church of teaching that Joseph Smith was a fallen prophet but this is untrue. At no time has God indicated disapproval of the prophet and his work and it certainly is not the prerogative of the church to anticipate that this will happen.

However, there have been some people aligned with the Reorganization that are endeavoring to prove the prophet was confused at the time of his death. This has been of serious concern to the author. The belief that the prophet became confused is not true and such a belief can have a devastating effect on the Restoration movement. Knowing that confusion such as they advocate, is not an overnight happening, a question immediately arises as to when the confusion began. This has then opened the door for the undermining of the entire work of the prophet, and does put in doubt, many of the things he taught. An illustration of just what can arise in a situation may be of interest. The author was sitting in a Sunday School class and a high priest was the instructor. During the discussion, occasion arose to refer to section one hundred seven in the Reorganized Doctrine and Covenants. When the teacher read the reference, he stated that he did not accept that particular revelation. Realizing that the various revelations appear in chronological order in the book, the teacher was asked if he accepted number one hundred six or how far back was it necessary to go for his acceptance. This points out the serious implications that arise when accusations are made that the prophet was confused at the time of his death; When did it begin and how serious was it at the time of his death? It should be remembered that the illustration used above is only the reaction of one individual and should not be construed as the position of the church. The real danger lies in the potential influence of the holder of this particular viewpoint upon those who come into contact with him. It is from men expressing their personal opinions and having high positions in the church, that has been responsible for the thinking of some that the Reorganized Church believed Joseph Smith to be a fallen prophet.

From the above comparisons it is apparent that extreme viewpoints can be very destructive to the Restoration if allowed to flourish. From the over-adulation by the Mormon Church, there has developed within the church, unquestioned obedience and the infallibility of the leadership. The word of the "living oracles" has become of far greater importance than the written word. Complete obedience to the leadership is absolutely essential for man's salvation according to their beliefs. While in conversation recently with a member of the Mormon Church, an individual holding the office of bishop, made the statement that if the president of the church told him to burn down the building in which they were meeting, it would be his duty to do so without question. The philosophy of blind obedience has been one of the greatest tragedies of the human race and especially so when religion is involved. Intelligent obedience should be the objective of all religions and especially so for the Restoration.

A very interesting article appeared recently that represents the Mormon position and should be included in this chapter. It is taken from *Dialogue*, Vol. II, No. 4, Winter 1967, p. 26. It is a footnote of an article written by Armand L. Mauss in which he includes some very important quotes:

"One of the more moot questions, especially on subjects of this kind, is the question of what is 'official doctrine' and what is not. One would think that we should regard as official Church doctrine at least the Standard Works of the Church and those occasional pronouncements given by the First Presidency and/or the Twelve acting in formal and unanimous concert. Beyond that, there are many open questions, and the purport of my remarks in this paper, of course, is to deny the doctrines or opinions offered in books written by individual Church leaders, of however high callings, are binding upon the Latter Day Saints. In a lecture delivered on July 7, 1954, to Seminary and Institute teachers attending a BYU Summer Session, the late President J. Reuben Clark, Jr., dealt with this question and offered what I would regard as helpful counsel. He first referred his listeners to the Doctrine and Covenants 68:2-4, in which we are told that "scripture" is that which is spoken by those leaders who are "moved upon by the Holy Ghost," which implies, according to President Clark, that it is possible for leaders sometimes to speak *without* being so moved. Among the exact words of President Clark which bear particularly upon my contention are the following (all taken directly from this lecture): " . . . only the President of the Church, the Presiding High Priest, is sustained as Prophet, Seer, and Revelator for the church, and he alone has the right to receive revelations for the Church, either new or amendatory, or to give authoritative interpretations of scriptures that shall be binding on the Church. . . . Yet we must not forget that the prophets are mortal men, with men's infirmities. . . . Asked if a prophet was always a prophet, Brother Joseph quickly affirmed that a prophet is a prophet only when he is acting as such (from the Documentary History of the Church, Vol. V, p. 265). . . . Even the President of the Church has not always spoken under the direction of the Holy Ghost, for a prophet is not always a prophet. I noted that the Apostles of the primitive Church had their differences and that in our own Church, leaders have differed in their views from the first. . . . When any man, except the President of the Church, undertakes to proclaim one unsettled doctrine, as among two or more doctrines in dispute, as settled doctrine of the Church, we may know he is not 'moved upon by the Holy Ghost,' unless he is acting under the direction and by the authority of the President. . . ." As for the critical question of how to tell when a doctrine is pronounced by a prophet or leader who is "moved upon by the Holy Ghost," President Clark suggests only a *subjective* test; i.e. in the final analysis, we can tell when our leaders are so moved only when we ourselves are so moved, which has the effect, he points out, of shifting the burden from the speaker to the bearer."

The above is a direct confirmation of the position taken by the author and it is important to keep this statement in mind as further consideration is given to the introduction of doctrine and changes that have taken place in the books of scripture.

CHAPTER XII

BOOKS OF SCRIPTURE

The Bible

The Restoration Movement, because of its belief in the doctrine of continued revelation by God to his people, has an entirely different approach to the Bible as a source of information than most religious organizations professing Christianity. A statement such as the one above, requires more detailed explanation to really understand the position of the two churches and their concepts of the Bible as scripture.

Early in his experience, Joseph Smith learned through his responsibility of translating the Book of Mormon, the real value of scripture and its important status in bringing man to an understanding of God and his will. It is through scripture or the recorded history and experience of man, that future generations can learn and appreciate God's handiwork. Scripture is generally known as sacred writings by those who accept them. It is the attitude toward these "sacred writings" that poses the real problem confronting professed Christians of today.

There are several denominations, especially among the "protestant" groups, that attribute to the scriptures, many things beyond the intent of the original authors. To many, the Bible has become actually words that have been written by God himself. Many others believe that the Bible is the last revealed word of God to mankind. It has become the basis on which church organizations have justified the discontinuance of God speaking to men at the present time as he did in ages past. This has led to such reliance upon the Bible, that those believers have become almost in fact, "Bible Worshipers." Regardless of the historical background and the opinion of many scholars, there are those who believe the Bible is infallible and that every word is the word of God from cover to cover.

The restoration cannot fit into any of the above extremes because of the basic belief in the unchangeability of God in his relations with mankind. It is their belief that God will communicate with men today, as he did in prior ages, and will continue to do so until the end of time. That scripture will continually be coming forth from his people for the benefit of later generations. The Book of Mormon is the evidence of this belief and is accepted by the Restoration as a continuation of scripture.

Shortly after Joseph Smith had completed the translation of the Book of Mormon and had organized the church, he was directed to make some corrections in the Bible under the direction of the Spirit of God. Associated with him in this task was Oliver Cowdery and later Sidney Rigdon. Under date of July 2, 1833, in Joseph's journal there was a statement as follows:

"Having finished the translation of the Bible, a few hours since, and needing some recreation, we know of no way we can spend our time more to divine acceptance, than endeavoring to build up Zion." (*Times and Seasons*, Vol. 6, p. 802)

The prophet used a copy of the King James translation of the Bible for this task and the manuscript and Bible were left in the care of his wife Emma, who later, through her son Joseph Smith III, gave it to the Reorganization. It was published by them and is known as the "Inspired Version" and is accepted by them as scripture. Portions of the inspiration received by Joseph Smith, while translating, were published at different times, but the Bible, as a whole, was not published until done so by the Reorganization.

To clearly present the position of the Restoration relative to the Bible, a statement by Joseph Smith is presented. In 1842, he wrote a letter to John Wentworth of Chicago, Illinois, editor and proprietor of the *Chicago Democrat*. In this letter he outlined a short history of the Restoration that included a concise statement of the beliefs of the church. This statement is generally known as the Epitome of Faith or Articles of Faith. In this statement of beliefs he made the following assertion: "We believe the Bible to be the word of God as far as it is translated correctly." With this statement, the Restoration position is very clear in that it accepts the Bible as containing scripture (sacred writings) but does not accept it as the infallible word of God.

The position of the Mormon Church is based upon the above statement of belief but they do not accept the Inspired Version as published by the Reorganization because they believe it was not completed. They have accepted portions of this version and have incorporated them in the "Pearl of Great Price" which will be discussed later. They use the King James' translation as their authoritative Bible.

A very interesting statement about the Mormons and their relationship to the Bible is found in Hubert Howe Bancroft's *History of Utah* on page 833 and is as follows:

"Mormonism in its religious aspect is simply the acceptation of the bible, the whole of it, literally, and following it to its logical conclusions."

The Reorganized Church accepts at face value practically all translations that have been made of the Bible recognizing the potentials of errors that creep in when the real problems of translation are considered. They do accept the Inspired Version as the most authentic, because they feel the corrections made were done under the direction of the spirit of God.

Realizing that many readers do not have access to the "Inspired Version," it may be of interest to incorporate some of the corrections in this volume for comparison. Because the King James translation is more universally accepted, the comparison will consist of quotations from it and the corresponding quotation from the Inspired Version:

KING JAMES	INSPIRED VERSION
Genesis 3:8; And they heard the voice of the Lord God walking in the garden in the cool of the day.	Genesis 3:13; And they heard the voice of the Lord God, as *they were* walking in the garden, in the cool of the day.
Deuteronomy 14:21; Ye shall not eat of anything that dieth of itself; thou shalt give it unto the stranger that is in thy gates, that he may eat it; or thou	Deuteronomy 14:21; Ye shall not eat of anything that dieth of itself; thou shalt *not* give it unto the stranger that is in thy gates, that he may eat it; or thou

KING JAMES	INSPIRED VERSION
mayest sell it unto an alien; for thou art a holy people unto the Lord thy God. Thou shalt not seethe a kid in his mother's milk.	mayest not sell it unto an alien; for thou art a holy people unto the Lord thy God. Thou shalt not seethe a kid in his mother's milk.
Matthew 6:13; And lead us not into temptation, but deliver us from evil: For thine is the kingdom and the power, and the glory, forever, Amen.	Matthew 6:14; And suffer us not to be led into temptation, but deliver us from evil: For thine is the kingdom, and the power, and the glory, forever and ever, Amen.

The last quotation of the above will be from the Lord's Prayer as quoted from Matthew and should be so recognized. Believing that God does not lead us into temptation, the above wording is much more in harmony with the teaching of a loving Father.

CHAPTER XIII

BOOKS OF SCRIPTURE

Book of Mormon

For the benefit of the reader not familiar with the Book of Mormon, a little of its history will be presented. It will be recalled that Joseph Smith had his first "experience" in the spring of 1820, and after a period of three and a half years, he became concerned about his position with God. The depth of this concern caused him to again seek God in prayer, and as a result of this effort, he was again the recipient of another vision; on this occasion, he was visited by the angel Moroni. In this vision he was told of some hidden metallic plates with engravings and, if he would prove himself worthy, he would be given the privilege, at the end of four years, to receive and translate the plates. On September 22, 1827, he was allowed to get the plates and to begin the translation.

The translating proceeded with various people acting as scribes for the prophet; among these were his wife Emma and Martin Harris. When about 116 pages of manuscript had been translated, Martin Harris pleaded with the prophet to allow him to show them to his wife. After much pleading he was allowed to do so, even though the prophet had been advised not to do so. For some reason that has never been explained, the manuscript of 116 pages was lost and never recovered. Because of his disobedience, the power to translate was taken from the prophet and for a long period nothing was accomplished in translating the plates. Later, in the year of 1828, the power to translate was again given to the prophet and again his wife Emma and others assisted him, but the translation proceeded very slowly and up to April 5, 1829, only some 14 or 15 pages had been written. It was on this date, April 5, 1829, that Oliver Cowdery met Joseph Smith for the first time. Oliver stated that he had been directed to come to him and offer his services as scribe. This has been verified by examination of the original manuscript which shows the first 14 or 15 pages in various handwritings of different individuals. The balance of the manuscript being the handwriting of Oliver Cowdery.

One of the most interesting facts about the translation of the Book of Mormon is the time it took to translate. Joseph Smith received the plates on September 22, 1827, and up to April 5, 1829, only about 14 pages of manuscript had been written. On April 7, 1829, Oliver Cowdery began acting as scribe. In June of 1829, Joseph Smith secured the copyright for the Book of Mormon. Assuming that the translation was completed during the month of June, it appears that the translating of the balance of the book took a period of from sixty to seventy-five days. A printer's copy was then begun, and in August of 1829 the process of printing the Book of Mormon began. The production of a printer's copy accounts for the two original manuscripts that existed. One of these manuscripts was placed in the cornerstone of the Nauvoo House and the other was in the care of Oliver Cowdery. At his death in 1850, this manuscript was given to David Whitmer, one of the three witnesses to the plates. After the death of David Whitmer, one of his heirs presented the manuscript to the Reorganization for a consideration. It is now preserved and in the vault of one of the largest banks in Kansas City, Missouri.

During the remodeling of the Nauvoo House Mr. Bidamon, husband of Emma Smith after the prophet's death, found the manuscript that had been placed in the cornerstone. The condition of the manuscript was bad because of moisture. A portion of this manuscript was given to each of the churches by Mr. Bidamon and the Mormon Church has been able to preserve several sheets of this manuscript. Some reproductions have been made by them. The portions received by the Reorganized Church were so badly deteriorated they were unable to preserve them.

There are practically no differences existing between the two churches relative to the Book of Mormon. They both accept it as scripture and, because of its translation by divine assistance, do accord to it greater authenticity than the Bible. The outstanding difference between the churches is the manner of versification and chaptering of their editions. It is extremely unfortunate that it was not possible for them to standardize all editions in the same manner the Bible is standard in its format.

The first edition of the Book of Mormon was not divided

into chapters and verses as found in modern versions. The first real attempt to versify was in an edition published in England around 1852. After the division of the church at the death of Joseph Smith, the two major factions produced their own versions of the book. This resulted in a real diversity in chapters and verses without any thought of coordination between them. For this reason, a cross reference is necessary in order to make general use of either the LDS (Mormon) or the RLDS (Reorganized) versions. The author, having prepared such a cross reference, felt that it might be of use to the reader and therefore, has included it in this volume. It is as follows:

MORMON EDITION		REORGANIZED EDITION		MORMON EDITION		REORGANIZED EDITION	
I Nephi	1	I Nephi	1	II Nephi	5	II Nephi	4:1
	2		1:24		6		5:1
	3		1:59		7		5:46
	4		1:99		8		5:70
	5		1:146		9		6:1
	6		2:1		10		7:1
	7		2:7		11		8:1
	8		2:40		12		8:17
	9		2:92		13		8:39
	10		3:1		14		8:65
	11		3:37		15		8:71
	12		3:96		16		9:1
	13		3:135		17		9:14
	14		3:201		18		9:39
	15		4:1		19		9:61
	16		5:1		20		9:82
	17		5:55		21		9:116
	18		5:168		22		9:132
	19		5:218		23		10:1
	20		6:8		24		10:23
	21		6:30		25		11:1
	22		7:1		26		11:58
II Nephi	1	II Nephi	1:1		27		11:116
	2		1:59		28		12:1
	3		2:1		29		12:42
	4		3:1		30		12:75

MORMON EDITION	REORGANIZED EDITION	MORMON EDITION	REORGANIZED EDITION
II Nephi 31	II Nephi 13:1	Mosiah 24	Mosiah 11:44
32	14:1	25	11:77
33	15:1	26	11:105
Jacob 1	Jacob 1:1	27	11:150
2	2:1	28	12:1
3	2:48	29	13:3
4	3:1	Alma 1	Alma 1:1
5	3:30	2	1:53
6	4:1	3	1:98
7	5:1	4	2:1
Enos 1	Enos 1:1	5	3:1
Jarom 1	Jarom 1:1	6	4:1
Omni 1	Omni 1:1	7	5:1
Words of Mormon 1	Words of Mormon 1:1	8	6:1
Mosiah 1	Mosiah 1:1	9	7:1
2	1:28	10	8:1
3	1:92	11	8:48
4	2:1	12	9:1
5	3:1	13	9:62
6	4:1	14	10:32
7	5:1	15	10:86
8	5:53	16	11:1
9	6:1	17	12:1
10	6:26	18	12:62
11	7:1	19	12:126
12	7:45	20	12:181
13	7:100	21	13:1
14	8:15	22	13:30
15	8:28	23	14:1
16	8:70	24	14:21
17	9:1	25	14:59
18	9:28	26	14:79
19	9:74	27	15:1
20	9:108	28	15:36
21	9:140	29	15:52
22	10:1	30	16:1
23	11:1	31	16:78

MORMON EDITION	REORGANIZED EDITION	MORMON EDITION	REORGANIZED EDITION
Alma 32	Alma 16:121	6	2:118
33	16:174	7	3:1
34	16:201	8	3:32
35	16:240	9	3:67
36	17:1	10	3:112
37	17:31	11	4:1
38	18:1	12	4:48
39	19:1	13	5:1
40	19:28	14	5:54
41	19:62	15	5:87
42	19:81	16	5:109
43	20:1	III Nephi 1	III Nephi 1:1
44	20:61	2	1:38
45	21:1	3	2:1
46	21:29	4	2:39
47	21:78	5	2:82
48	21:123	6	3:1
49	21:149	7	3:36
50	22:1	8	4:1
51	23:1	9	4:26
52	24:1	10	4:53
53	24:50	11	5:1
54	25:1	12	5:44
55	25:27	13	5:93
56	26:1	14	6:1
57	26:70	15	7:1
58	26:118	16	7:24
59	27:1	17	8:1
60	27:14	18	8:28
61	28:1	19	9:1
62	29:1	20	9:37
63	30:1	21	9:86
Helaman 1	Helaman 1:1	22	10:8
2	1:37	23	10:26
3	2:1	24	11:2
4	2:35	25	11:22
5	2:63	26	11:28

MORMON EDITION		REORGANIZED EDITION		MORMON EDITION		REORGANIZED EDITON	
III Nephi	27	III Nephi	12:14	Ether	6	Ether	3:1
	28		13:12		7		3:37
	29		13:54		8		3:67
	30		14:1		9		4:1
IV Nephi	1	IV Nephi	1:1		10		4:43
Mormon	1	Mormon	1:1		11		4:90
	2		1:21		12		5:1
	3		1:63		13		6:1
	4		2:1		14		6:35
	5		2:26		15		6:72
	6		3:1	Moroni	1	Moroni	1:1
	7		3:24		2		2:1
	8		4:1		3		3:1
	9		4:57		4		4:1
Ether	1	Ether	1:1		5		5:1
	2		1:22		6		6:1
	3		1:60		7		7:1
	4		1:94		8		8:1
	5		2:1		9		9:1
					10		10:1

CHAPTER XIV

BOOKS OF SCRIPTURE

Doctrine and Covenants

The third book of scripture that is of utmost importance to the Restoration is the Doctrine and Covenants. It is also this book that emphasizes the major differences between the two organizations. The Doctrine and Covenants is a selection of the revelations received by the prophet Joseph Smith during his lifetime, both preceding and following the formation of the church on April 6, 1830. Recognizing that scripture is the record of the revealment of God's will to man, makes the selection of these revelations a modern day book of scripture and it is so regarded by both churches.

On November 1, 1831, leaders of the church decided to gather together the various revelations and to have them published. The members of the church had purchased a printing press and sent it to Independence, Missouri, and they were thus in a position to do the printing of the revelations. With this press they also began the printing of the first publication of the church which was known as the EVENING AND MORNING STAR.

While in the process of printing the revelations they had received from Kirtland, Ohio, troubles began to develop between the Saints and the people living in the area. These feelings became so strong they began attempting to drive the Saints from the area. The mob raided the printing plant at Independence and scattered the type and the material that had been printed, into the streets. Part of the material scattered were the revelations that were to appear in the Book of Commandments. From this material the mob scattered, they salvaged some of the pages that had been printed and these were bound into a volume that became known as the Book of Commandments. The Church of Christ (Temple Lot) in Independence, Missouri, have placed great importance on the Book of Commandments and have made several reproductions and they have them for distribution.

Because the Book of Commandments was never completed, it was never accepted officially by the church and it was not until some time later that another edition was authorized.

In the very early years of the church, the prophet did not always have a scribe available to record the many revelations as he received them. When it was decided to publish them, it was necessary for him to recall what he had received and to write for publication. When he received copies of what had been produced in the Book of Commandments, he became aware of the need for some revision in many sections. Some items had been overlooked and others needed some amplification. Punctuation and grammatical construction needed improvement and it was for this reason that when comparing the present Doctrine and Covenants with the Book of Commandments reprint, many differences are noted. It can easily be understood that when he saw the revelations in print, other portions which he had not remembered when writing them, were brought to mind; under these circumstances the revisions were made. Who is to question the right of the prophet to interpret what he received? Some of the early dissidents in the church used the changes made by the prophet as an excuse to justify their position and among these was David Whitmer. The Church of Christ (Temple Lot), also known as "Hedrickites," have taken this position since their beginning and have never accepted later editions of the Doctrine and Covenants.

In 1835, the prophet again accumulated a selection of the revelations and these were published in the first edition of the Doctrine and Covenants that was published at Kirtland, Ohio, and was accepted by the church officially. This edition became the first fully authorized publication of the prophet's revelations.

By comparing the Book of Commandments with the 1835 edition, the proof of the incompleteness of the book is shown. The last revelation appearing in the Book of Commandments is section sixty-five. This appears as section sixty-four in both the Mormon and Reorganized editions of the Doctrine and Covenants, and was section twenty-one in the 1835 edition. On comparison section 65 of the Book of Commandments ends in the middle of verse 36 of section 64 in the Mormon edition and ends in the middle of paragraph seven of the sixty-fourth section in the Reorganized edition. Because the content of the revelations in the current editions is the same as the 1835 edition, the unfinished status of the Book of Commandments is evident.

The author has made a detailed study of the Doctrine and Covenants and has compiled an analysis for the benefit of the reader. This analysis will be included at the end of this chapter. It was started with the Mormon edition of the present time because the sections are listed in chronological order and are listed in the same manner in the Reorganized edition. The same procedure was followed when printing the Book of Commandments, but when the first edition of the Doctrine and Covenants was published in 1835, a different method was used. For this reason, a cross reference will be of real assistance to the reader in understanding the comparisons that are made.

The second edition of the Doctrine and Covenants was issued about September 1844, from Nauvoo, Illinois, by John Taylor, a member of the Quorum of Twelve and editor of *Times and Seasons*. Inasmuch as the second edition was published about two months after the death of the prophet, it can be assumed that he approved the material that appeared in this edition. It included the revelations received by the prophet after those published in 1835. Among these are the revelation on Tithing and the erection of the Temple at Nauvoo, which included some instruction of the doctrine of Baptism for the Dead. The first European edition was published in Liverpool, England under the supervision of Wilford Woodruff.

In 1876, the Mormon Church officials endeavored to replace all of the previous editions of the Doctrine and Covenants because they had made a revision and wanted all of the members of the church to have a copy of this edition. It is this revision that is subject to serious question because of the new doctrines that had been introduced into the church. In this new revision they eliminated one section on marriage which was number 101 in the 1835 edition. They added twenty-five that had never before appeared in any authorized edition by the Prophet Joseph Smith. Inasmuch as the prophet made the selection of those in the 1835 edition and also presumably those in the 1844 edition, it is somewhat presumptuous for someone, thirty-two years after his death, to publish purported revelations which he did not include. If an honest comparison is to be made, there is real need to analyze this change in what is considered modern day scripture.

It was mentioned above that in the 1876 edition a section was deleted. This section was not specifically a revelation but was the action taken by the High Council in Kirtland, Ohio, in which the position of the church on marriage was presented. The important reason for the elimination of this section was due to the following quotation taken therefrom:

"Inasmuch as this Church of Christ has been reproached with the crime of fornication and polygamy; we declare that we believe that one man should have one wife; and one woman but one husband, except in the case of death, when either is at liberty to marry again." (RLDS D & C 111:4)

With the introduction of section 132 of the new Mormon Doctrine and Covenants into the book, it would be very inappropriate for the one on marriage to remain. It was a direct contradiction to the new section. It is unfortunate that the other references to this subject could not also be eliminated. Reference is made to section forty-two:

"Thou shalt love thy wife with all thy heart, and shall cleave unto her and none else." (Mormon D & C 42:22; RLDS D & C 42:7.)

There is also another quotation of interest:

"Wherefore it is lawful that he should have one wife, and they twain shall be one flesh, and all this that the earth might answer the end of its creation." (Mormon D & C 49:16; RLDS D & C 49:3.)

There is very serious and legitimate doubt as to the true authenticity of the section 132 of the Mormon Doctrine and Covenants. This was first presented to the church at a conference in Salt Lake City, Utah, in August of 1852. This is eight years after the death of Joseph Smith. Because the prophet died without ever affirming or denying the existence of the document and that his wife, Emma, consistently denied his connection with it, it is necessary to rely only upon hearsay testimony which would not be acceptable in the courts of the land. Many books have been written giving

100

detailed documentation on this subject and for this reason it is not to be extensively covered in this chapter. It is necessary, however, to go into several phases when making a comparison because factors, other than polygamy, are involved.

Another of the additions made in 1876 in the Mormon edition is as follows:

"Dear and well-beloved brother, Brigham Young, verily thus saith the Lord unto you: My servant Brigham, it is no more required at your hand to leave your family as in times past, for your offering is acceptable to me. I have seen your labor and toil in journeyings for my name. I therefore command you to send my word abroad, and take especial care of your family from this time, henceforth and forever, Amen." (Mormon D & C 126)

This is purported to have been given in July of 1841. By checking church history, we learn that Brigham Young and all other members of the Twelve were continuously making journeys after that date and most all of them were absent from Nauvoo at the time of the prophet's death. It can only be assumed that either the instructions were overlooked or that it was later added to the Doctrine and Covenants for prestige purposes.

Possibly the most astonishing additions made are sections 121, 122, and 123. These "purported revelations" are extracts from a letter written by Joseph Smith, Hyrum Smith, Lyman Wight, Caleb Baldwin, and Alexander McCrae while they were imprisoned in the jail at Liberty, Missouri. This letter was first published in Volume 1, No. 7 of the *Times and Seasons* in Nauvoo, Illinois, in May of 1840. Two months later an addition to the letter was published in Volume No. 9 of the same publication and is found on pages 131-134. The date of publication of the above letter is important when viewed in the light of later publications when portions of the letter were included in the Doctrine and Covenants as revelations or with implications as such.

The second edition of the Doctrine and Covenants was published in Nauvoo in September of 1844, four years after the publication of the letter. This second edition did not include any portion of the letter, and assuming the prophet made or supervised the selection of the material used, it is very apparent that he did not consider the material in the letter as revelation. It was not until the revision of the Doctrine and Covenants in 1876 by the Mormon Church that they appeared and became a part of the book.

While it is apparent that the publication of the letter or any portion thereof, was not approved by the prophet to be scripture, this is not the major objection to be raised. When an analysis is made of the contents of the letter as published in the Doctrine and Covenants and as it appeared in the *Times and Seasons*, do we find the real cause for question. Not all, but most of the verses of section 121 as it appears in the Doctrine and Covenants, are altered by additions, interpolations, omissions, or even completely new material. The first five paragraphs of the letter are not used, and verse one of section 121 starts with the sixth paragraph. The seventh, eighth and ninth paragraphs are then omitted, and in the middle of the tenth paragraph, verse seven of section 121 continues through verse twenty-five. Most of paragraph eleven is omitted, but the last part of this paragraph is used, being verses 26 to 32. From the long twelfth paragraph part of one sentence is used; the second sentence, making verse 33. No use is made of the last paragraph.

Because of its great length, it is not possible to include the entire letter in this volume but to give the reader an opportunity to visualize what has transpired, some excerpts are being shown. To show them in the most convenient manner for comparison, the material from the letter as published in the *Times and Seasons* is shown in the column on the left and the corresponding data as published in the Mormon Doctrine and Covenants is shown immediately adjacent on the right. Beginning with the first verse of section 121 in the Doctrine and Covenants we find the following:

ORIGINAL LETTER	DOCTRINE AND COVENANTS
"O God! where are thou? and where is the pavilion that covereth thy hiding place? how long shall thy hand be stayed, and thy pure eyes behold from the heavens, the wrongs and sufferings of thy people and of	1. "O God! where are thou? And where is the pavilion that covereth thy hiding place? 2. How long shall thy hand be stayed, and thine eye, yea thy pure eye, behold from the eternal heavens, the wrongs of thy

thy servants; thine ears be penetrated with their cries?
How long, O Lord! shall they thus suffer, before thine heart shall be softened towards them, and thy bowels be moved with compassion towards them?

O Lord God Almighty, maker of heaven, earth, and seas, and of all things that in them is, and who controleth (controlleth) and subjecteth the devil and the dark and benighted dominions of Shaole. Stretch forth thy hand, let thine eye pierce, let thy pavilion be taken up, let thy hiding place no longer be uncovered, let thine ear be inclined, let thine heart be softened, and thy bowels moved with compassion towards thy people; and let thine anger be kindled against our enemies, and in thy fury let fall the sword of thine indignation and avenge us of our wrongs."

people, and of thy servants, and thine ear be penetrated with their cries?
3. Yea, O Lord, how long shall they suffer these wrongs and unlawful oppressions, before thine heart shall be softened towards them, and thy bowels be moved with compassion towards them?
4. O Lord God Almighty, Maker of the heaven, earth, and seas, and of all things that in them are and who controlleth and subjecteth the devil, and the dark and benighted dominion of Shayole! Stretch forth thy hand; let thine eye pierce; let thy pavilion be taken up; let thy hiding place no longer be covered; let thine ear be inclined; let thine heart be softened, and thy bowels moved with compassion toward us;
5. Let thine anger be kindled against our enemies; and in the fury of thine heart, with thy sword avenge us our wrongs."

Beginning with the twenty-eighth verse of section 121 of the Mormon Doctrine and Covenants is the following:

"atime when nothing shall be withheld, when all the glories of earth and heaven, time and eternity shall be manifest to all those, who have endured valiantly for the gospel of Jesus Christ.

28. "A time to come in which nothing shall be withheld, whether there be one God or many Gods, this shall be manifest;
29. All thrones and dominions, principalities and powers, shall be revealed and set forth upon all who have endured valiantly for the gospel of Jesus Christ;

If there be bounds set to the heavens, the seas, the dry land they shall be manifest, as well as the various revolutions of the sun, moon, and planets; and a full development of all the glorious laws by which they are governed shall be revealed in the 'dispensation of the fulness of times' according to that which was ordained in the midst of the council of heaven in the presence of the eternal God, before this world was."

30. And also if there be bounds set to the heavens, or to the seas; or to the dry land, or to the sun, moon or stars;
31. All the times of their revolutions; all the appointed days, months, and years, and all the days of their days, months, and years, and all their glories, laws, and set times, shall be revealed, in the days of the dispensation of the fullness of times.
32. According to that which was ordained in the midst of the Council of the Eternal God of all other Gods, before this world was, that should be reserved unto the finishing and the end thereof, when every man shall enter into his eternal presence, and into his immortal rest."

For many years an effort has been made to learn who the writer was or who authorized the changes as they appear in the above, but it has never been successful. It raises a very serious question pertaining to scripture. Does a later prophet have the right to alter, or add to, that which was previously given by another prophet? If true, other questions arise as to the authenticity of the first prophet and to what extent the Spirit of God participated in the first rendition. Should this be accepted as true, then no scripture will ever be inviolate and could result in a complete undermining of what is believed to be the word of God. Will not the acceptance of this philosophy destroy the belief in the unchangeability of God and his teachings? Only through the unquestioning acceptance of the infallibility of the leadership, could the changing of scripture be acceptable.

The above is a clear illustration of the author's contention that the efforts of man to improve upon that which God has given leads to ultimate apostasy as it occurred in the primitive church. The introduction to a belief in the plurality of Gods is contained in the above alterations to a letter written by the prophet, and others, that was never meant to be scripture.

With all of the additions made by the Mormon Church, all except one were attributed to Joseph Smith. The exception referred to is section one hundred thirty-six. This is a revelation Brigham Young received at Winter Quarters in 1847 while they were gathering for the journey West. It contains instructions for the organization of the Saints in making the trip across the plains. This is the last revelation added to the Doctrine and Covenants by the Mormon Church. They have included the Manifesto, which stopped the authorized practice of polygamy in the church. This is not specifically claimed as a revelation.

Actually, to the Mormons, the Doctrine and Covenants has now become a closed book of scripture. This is apparent because no new revelations that may have been received by the succeeding prophets have ever been published in any editions of the book. Does this mean that no revelations have been received? The Restoration Church was founded on the principle of continued revelation as was amply shown by the prophet Joseph Smith. Many times the author has raised this question of some of the leadership, and has received the reply that whenever the prophet speaks, it is the word of God and should so be considered by the membership. However, when queried as to the publishing in the Doctrine and Covenants and why it has not been done, no real intelligent reply has been given. Recognizing that true scripture is the recording of the revealment of God's will to his people and that it is usually given under the direction of the Spirit, the question then arises as to how future generations will be able to study and understand what God's instructions were if they are not compiled into books of scripture. Not having available the written scripture, it becomes necessary that the membership accept the oral teachings that are handed down from the leadership and opens the door for the introduction of tradition. Students of religion are well aware of the influence tradition can have in a church organization and how it can become more important in the minds of people than actual scripture. It should be remembered that the Prophet Joseph Smith never hesitated to make public the will of God as it was revealed to him by the Spirit and this should be a guiding influence to those who succeeded him.

While a great deal of space has been given to the analysis of the Mormon Doctrine and Covenants, it will not require as much to present the position of the Reorganized Church to this book of scripture. This church has accepted the Doctrine and Covenants as it was published during the lifetime of the prophet and has continued all of the revelations he authorized to be published. They have not deleted any that were printed in the 1835 or 1844 editions. They have, however, added many that were received by succeeding prophets during their administration. By following this procedure, the Doctrine and Covenants is always an open book of scripture for the Reorganization.

At the World Conference of 1968, a resolution was presented to the Reorganization that would alter the format of the present editions. The objective of the resolution was to compartmentize the book by placing all revelations into one section, and taking letters, High Council activities and other data, not specifically revelations, into other compartments. In this way, the true scripture will be separated from that which is more historical in content. A comment can be made that any action on this will not be because God wishes it, nor has he ever expressed criticism of what has been considered scripture by the church. It is another possibility that man is again attempting to improve on that which many believe, was God-given. The question is raised primarily for academic purposes.

Starting with the 1835 edition, the book of Doctrine and Covenants included the Lectures on Faith that were prepared in January of 1835, to be delivered to a class of elders at Kirtland, Ohio, and to be included in the publication of the Doctrine and Covenants. Both churches continued publishing these lectures in their editions until shortly before or after the turn of the century, when it was decided that the lectures, not being revelations, should be eliminated from the Doctrine and Covenants to avoid possible scriptural implications.

As stated earlier in this chapter, a detailed analysis of the various editions of the Doctrine and Covenants has been made and to enable the reader to more accurately comprehend the changes that have been made, this analysis is being included in this book. It should be emphasized that the content of the revelations, as they appear in the various editions with the exception of the Book of Commandments, are the same and there is no controversy as to content. The real controversy is based upon the changes made in the Mormon edition of 1876. To understand the analysis, the author utilized the current editions of both churches and has indicated where each section may be found and whether or not it was in the earlier editions. All sections are listed in chronological order and the time of reception is shown:

ANALYSIS OF VARIOUS EDITIONS OF DOCTRINE & COVENANTS
Compiled by Francis W. Holm

DATE RECEIVED	UTAH D & C	RLDS D & C	B OF C 1833	1835 EDIT.	COMMENTS:
April 1830	1	1	1	1	Preface to D & C.
September 1823	2				Added in 1876
July 1828	3	2	2	30	
February 1829	4	4	3	31	
March 1829	5	5	4	32	
April 1829	6	6	5	8	
April 1829	7	7	6	33	
April 1829	8	8	7	34	
April 1829	9	9	8	35	
May 1829	10	3	9	36	
May 1829	11	10	10	37	
May 1829	12	11	11	38	
May 1829	13				Added in 1876
June 1829	14	12	12	39	
June 1829	15	13	13	40	
June 1829	16	14	14	41	
June 1829	17	15		42	Not in Book of Commandments
June 1829	18	16	15	43	
March 1830	19	18	16	44	
April 1830	20	17	24	2	
April 1830	21	19	22	46	
April 1830	22	20	23	47	
April 1830	23	21	17-21	45	Several items combined after B of C.
July 1830	24	23	25	9	
July 1830	25	24	26	48	
July 1830	26	25	27	49	
September 1830	27	26	28	50	
September 1830	28	27	30	51	

DATE RECEIVED	UTAH D & C	RLDS D & C	B OF C 1833	1835 EDIT.	COMMENTS:
September 1830	29	28	29	10	
September 1830	30	29	31-33	52	Combined after B of C.
September 1830	31	30	34	53	
October 1830	32	31		54	Not in B of C.
October 1830	33	32	35	55	
November 1830	34	33	36	56	
December 1830	35	34	37	11	
December 1830	36	35	38	57	
December 1830	37	37	39	58	
January 1831	38	38	40	12	
January 1831	39	39	41	59	
January 1831	40	40	42	60	
February 1831	41	41	43	61	
February 1831	42	42	44 & 47	13	
February 1831	43	43	45	14	
February 1831	44	44	46	42	
March 1831	45	45	48	15	
March 1831	46	46	49	16	
March 1831	47	47	50	63	
March 1831.	48	48	51	64	
March 1831	49	49	52	65	
May 1831	50	50	53	17	
May 1831	51	51		23	Not in B of C.
June 1831	52	52	54	66	
June 1831	53	53	55	66	
June 1831	54	54	56	67	
June 1831	55	55	57	68	
June 1831	56	56	58	69	
July 1831	57	57		27	Not in B of C.
August 1831	58	58	59	18	
August 1831	59	59	60	19	
August 1831	60	60	61	70	
August 1831	61	61	62	71	
August 1831	62	62	63	72	
August 1831	63	63	64	20	
September 1831	64	64	65*	21	End of B of C.
October 1831	65	65		24	
October 1831	66	66		74	
November 1831	67	67		25	
November 1831	68	68		22	
November 1831	69	69		28	

DATE RECEIVED	UTAH D & C	RLDS D & C	B OF C 1833	1835 EDIT.	COMMENTS:
November 1831	70	70		26	
December 1831	71	71		90	
December 1831	72	72		89	
January 1832	73	73		29	
January 1832	74	74		73	
January 1832	75	75		87	
February 1832	76	76		91	
March 1832	77				Added in.
March 1832	78	77		75	
March 1832	79	78		76	
March 1832	80	79		77	
March 1832	81	80		79	
April 1832	82	81		86	
April 1832	83	82		88	
September 1832	84	83		4	
November 1832	85				Added in.
December 1832	86	84		6	
December 1832	87				Added in - Civil War Prophecy.
December 1832	88	85		7	
February 1833	89	86		80	
March 1833	90	87		84	
March 1833	91	88		92	
March 1833	92	89		93	
May 1833	93	90		82	
May 1833	94	91		83	
June 1833	95	92		95	
June 1833	96	93		96	
August 1833	97	94		81	
August 1833	98	95		85	
August 1833	99	96		78	
October 1833	100	97		94	
December 1833	101	98		97	
February 1834	102	99		5	
February 1834	103	100			
April 1834	104	101		98	
June 1834	105	102			
November 1834	106	103		99	
March 1835	107	104		3	
December 1835	108				Added in 1876
March 1836	109				,, ,,

DATE RECEIVED	UTAH D&C	RLDS D&C	B OF C 1833	1835 EDIT.	COMMENTS:
April 1836	110			,,	,,
August 1836	111			,,	,,
July 1837	112	105			
March 1838	113			,,	,,
April 1838	114			,,	,,
April 1838	115			,,	,,
July 1838	117			,,	,,
July 1838	118			,,	,,
July 1838	119	106			
July 1838	120			,,	,,
March 1839	121**			,,	,,
March 1839	122**			,,	,,
March 1839	123			,,	,,
January 1841	124	107			
March 1841	125			,,	,,
July 1841	126			,,	,,
September 1842	127	109			
September 1842	128	110			
February 1843	129			,,	,,
April 1843	130			,,	,,
May 1843	131			,,	,,
July 1843?	132				Section on Polygamy added 1876.
November 1831	133	108		100	Appendix
	134	112		102	
	135	113			Martyrdom of Joseph & Hyrum Smith
January 1847	136				Revelation to Brigham Young.
June 1830	PGP	22			
	PGP	36			
		111		101	Section on Marriage–Removed 1876

Notes: No revelations added to Utah D. & C. since 1876. Later revelations to Reorganized Church start with number 114.

* Book of Commandments ends in middle of verse 36 of section 64 in the

Utah Doctrine & Covenants. It ends in the middle of paragraph seven of the Reorganized Doctrine & Covenants.

** Sections 121, 122, and 123 are taken from the letter written from Liberty Jail by Joseph Smith and others while imprisoned. These should be compared to the letter as it appears in volume one of *Times and Seasons*. Many unauthorized changes have been made.

CHAPTER XV

PEARL OF GREAT PRICE

There is a fourth book of scripture accepted by the Mormon Church but it is not accepted in this form by the Reorganized Church. Parts of the book are included in other books and are accepted by the Reorganization as scripture and these will be shown in the analysis to follow. This book is known as the *Pearl of Great Price* and was first published in England in 1851.

In the April 15, 1967 issue of the *Saints' Herald*, there was an article that appeared in "Question Time" written by the Reorganized Church Historian, Richard P. Howard and permission was given to include it in this volume. It is very complete and a detailed history of this book and its contents. It was written as a reply to the question, "Why doesn't our church accept the 'Pearl of Great Price' as scripture?" Mr. Howard's reply is as follows:

"Part of it we do accept; part of it we don't. Some background data may help to clarify the situation. When first published in England in 1851, by the Mormon apostle, F. D. Richards, the *Pearl of Great Price* was intended to be a 'new member's tract' to inform and encourage the new converts in the British Isles. It contained fifty-six pages of selected, previously published writings of Joseph Smith, Jr. All evidence at hand suggests that in the 1850's there was no intention to canonize this pamphlet. The contents of the 1851 edition were as follows:

1. Enoch narrative (Inspired Version, Genesis 6:45-6:78), pp. 1-7.

2. Writings of Moses (later Section 22, RLDS Doctrine and Covenants), pp. 8-10.

3. Writings of Moses, cont'd. (Inspired Version, Genesis 1-5:25; Genesis 8:1-18), pp. 10-17.

4. The Book of Abraham (*Times and Seasons*, Vol. III, pp. 703-706; 719-722) pp. 19-29

5. Matthew 23:39-24:56 (Inspired Version), pp. 30-32.

6. Section 77, Doctrine and Covenants, (Utah) pp. 33-34.

7. 'Civil War Prophecy' (Section 87, Doctrine and Covenants, Utah), p. 35.

8. Extracts from the 'History of Joseph Smith' (*Times and Seasons*, Vol. III), pp. 36-47.

9. 'Extracts from the Doctrine and Covenants,' Section 17:20, 21; 17:18; 17:22-23; 17:8-11, 19, 24; Section 104:1-10; 104:11c, 12; 104:13; 43-44; Section 17:1-6 (RLDS editions), pp. 48-54.

10. 'Epitome of Faith' (from the Wentworth Letter, *Times and Seasons*, vol. III, pp. 709-710), p. 55.

11. 'Truth' (a poem by John Jaques), p. 56.

Items 1 through 10 were reprinted from selected writings of Joseph Smith, as previously published in the church journals of the 1830's and 1840's.
Items 1, 2, 3, 5, and 9 were published in our own scriptures by the years 1864 (the first RLDS Doctrine and Covenants) and 1867 (the Inspired Version). Therefore these documents needed no further endorsement by our church. The remainder (items 4, 6, 7, 8, 10), clearly not intended by Joseph Smith, Jr., to be given scriptural status, have therefore required no consideration on the part of our church as to their relative canonical merit.
Incidentally, textual comparison of items 1, 2, and 3 with earlier printings, with the Inspired Version (1867) and with the second edition of the *Pearl of Great Price* (1878) show clearly that the second edition of the *Pearl of Great Price* was altered extensively to conform to the wording of the text of the Inspired Version as published eleven years earlier (1867).

One item was added to the second edition of the *Pearl of Great Price* in 1878: The 'revelation' on the plurality of wives (published in 1876 in the Utah Doctrine and Covenants as section 132). This document (as well as sections 77 and 87) was later removed from the *Pearl of Great Price* (1902 edition), since it is already being published in each edition of the Utah Doctrine and Covenants. The poem 'Truth' by John Jaques was printed in every edition until 1902, when it was discontinued. Two years after the release of the second edition of the *Pearl of Great Price* the October 1880 semiannual conference of the Utah Mormon Church accepted it as one of the standard scriptural works of the church."

We are very much indebted to Richard Howard for the above detailed explanation and history of the *Pearl of Great Price* because it enables a sound method of analyzing the contents of the book. Within this book is found a combination of scripture, history and personal writings that have been canonized by the Mormon Church and it is this canonization that is subject to serious question. The same question arose in the previous chapter when additions were made to the Doctrine and Covenants which then became canonized as scripture when the church accepted the book as one of the standard books of the church.

It is remembered that the first edition of the book was published in 1851, which was seven years after the death of Joseph Smith, Jr., and therefore, he was not in a position to approve or disapprove the action that made his writings have scriptural import. When Joseph Smith wrote his letter to John Wentworth of Chicago, in which he outlined some of the history of the origin of the Restoration and some of his personal experiences and also his statement of what the church believed, there was absolutely no intention by him to be writing scripture or that it should ever become so to the church. Another very important consideration is that the book as it appears today, is much different to the first edition.

The major concern in reference to the *Pearl of Great Price* and what may prove the most embarrassing in years to come, is the part known as the Book of Abraham. This is a 'purported translation' of some papyrus manuscripts that were found with some Egyptian mummies purchased by Joseph Smith and others, in 1835 at Kirtland, Ohio. After he had translated the Book of Mormon and then, by inspiration, retranslated or revised the Bible, it is very easy to understand his great curiosity and desire to try to translate other things. He was very interested in the study of ancient languages and especially Hebrew, and pursued the study in the School of the Prophets or Elder's School that began during the

114

construction and after the completion of the Kirtland Temple. With the discovery of the papyrus manuscripts, it is readily understood the impelling desire on the part of Joseph Smith to attempt the translation. The capability to read and decipher Egyptian was unknown at that time and there was no published information that could assist him in making such a translation. Today Egyptian can be read almost as easily as Greek and some of the other ancient languages.

The first publication of the Book of Abraham was in the *Times and Seasons*, Vol. III, pp. 703-706; 719-722. It appeared without any comment from Joseph Smith and was the only time during his lifetime, that it was printed. Had he considered it to become scripture to the church, would he not have included it in the material selected for publication in the Doctrine and Covenants, that was in process at the time of his death? At no time did he ever claim to have had the direction of the Spirit in the purported translation. This silence on the part of the prophet becomes very significant in the light of later developments and the knowledge that has come to light recently pertaining to Egyptian artifacts.

After the death of the prophet, the mummies and the manuscripts were sold by his wife, Emma and other members of the family, to a Mr. Combs. During the great Chicago Fire, some of the mummies were destroyed and it was believed for many years that the manuscripts also were destroyed. Recently it has come to light that some of the artifacts sold by the Smith family, were discovered in the Metropolitan Museum of Art in New York City. In an article in the *Kansas City Times* of November 23, 1967, it was stated that some ancient documents, which appeared to be the papyrus manuscripts, were turned over to the Mormon Church. Some excerpts from this article are of interest. The material was discovered by Dr. Aziz S. Atiya, an expert on Middle East antiquity, and presented to N. Eldon Tanner, a member of the First Presidency of the Mormon Church. After expressing great appreciation at the recovery of the documents he stated that they would be subjected to intensive study. He also made the following statement: "We just aren't sure yet about all of the text." Continuing some of the quotes from the article;

"However, a drawing showing a man on a slab, with a swordsman beside him, has been definitely identified as the original of an illustration copied in a Mormon book of scripture by Joseph Smith, founder of the church. (Facsimiles are in the *Pearl of Great Price*, author.) Dr. Henry G. Fischer, curator of the museum's Egyptian department, said the drawing, from which Smith made his copy, was part of Egyptian material dating back possibly 3,000 years. As to whether the script contains any of the text of the Mormon 'Book of Abraham' with which the drawing is associated, Dr. Fischer said it was doubtful."

With the discovery of the above manuscripts, greater study and investigation can and is being made by qualified experts. The manuscripts were given to the Brigham Young University at Provo, Utah for investigation and study by Doctor Hugh Nibley. A series of photographs of the manuscripts was published in the February 1968 issue of *The Improvement Era* and starting with the January, 1968 issue of the same publication, there is a series of articles by Doctor Hugh Nibley, professor of history and religion at the Brigham Young University. This series was prepared and written before the discovery of the papyrus manuscripts and is in reply to the republication of a small book by Bishop Franklin S. Spalding, D.D. The main purport of Doctor Nibley's articles is to question the reliability of the men quoted in the book by Spalding.

The Spalding book dates back to around 1912 and was the result of efforts made by him to check the authenticity of the translation of the Book of Abraham from the facsimiles as they appear in the current issues of the *Pearl of Great Price*. Being a Protestant minister, he was interested in proving the prophet in error on the translation. He sent copies of the *Pearl of Great Price* containing the Book of Abraham, to eight prominent scientists and Egyptologists and asked them to pass judgment on the translation of the facsimiles. The reactions of these men are contained in a book by Samuel A. B. Mercer, Ph.D. All of these men declared the "Book of Abraham" was not true. The statement of one of these experts is quoted below and it is interesting to note he is associated with the same organization where the manuscripts were found:

"I return herewith under separate cover, the 'Pearl of Great Price.' The 'Book of Abraham'; it is hardly necessary to say, is pure fabrication. Cuts 1 and 3 (facsimiles) are inaccurate copies of well known scenes on funeral papyri, and cut 2 is a copy of one of the magical discs which in the late Egyptian period were placed under the heads of mummies. There were about forty of these latter known in museums and they are all very similar in character. Joseph Smith's interpretation of these cuts is a farrago of nonsense from beginning to end. Egyptian characters can now be read almost as easily as Greek and five minutes study in an Egyptian gallery of any museum should be enough to convince any educated man of the clumsiness of the imposture." (Dr. Arthur C. Mace, Asst. Curator, Metropolitan Museum of Art, New York City, Dept. of Egyptian Art.)

Dr. Mercer's book contains other statements and they are all in accord with the above statement and it is felt that the one shown would be sufficient to make the point in mind.

There has recently appeared a magazine published by a group of Mormon educators from Palo Alto, California, that is completely independent of church control and is known by the title *Dialogue, A Journal of Mormon Thought* and is published on a quarterly basis. They have published many articles that ordinarily would not have been available and have articles by non-Mormons as well as from their own members. In their most recent issues, they have had articles from experts pertaining to the discovery of the papyrus manuscripts and have sought for interpretations of them. Because there have been so many and it is impossible to include much of what has been written, and to give the reader the opportunity of further research into this question, a summary of what has appeared in *Dialogue* is shown as it appeared in Vol. III, No. 3, Autumn 1968, on page 109; this is at the beginning of an article by Klaus Baer in which he gives a translation of that portion of the manuscripts that is the apparent source of the Book of Abraham:

"Klaus Baer is Associate Professor of Egyptology at the University of Chicago's Oriental Institute, and was one of Professor High Nibley's primary tutors in the art of reading Egyptian characters. Professor Baer journeyed to Provo, Utah, last month and personally examined the papyri. Some *Dialogue* readers may appreciate a recapitulation of papyri articles appearing in this journal. The Winter, 1967 issue carried interviews with Professor Aziz (who was

credited with discovering the papyri) and with Dr. Henry
G. Fischer (Curator of the Egyptian Collection of the
Metropolitan Museum).

Dialogue ran a series of articles dealing with the scrolls
in the Summer, 1968 issue. Professor of Egyptology
John A. Wilson (of the University of Chicago's Oriental
Institute) rendered a 'Summary Report' which identified
the Book of the Dead scrolls once belonging to an
Egyptian lady named Ta-shere-Min. These scrolls tell of
'the terrors which she felt for the next world and about the
great dreams she had for eternal life.' An article by Professor of Egyptology Richard A. Parker (of Brown
University) covered the same ground more briefly, and also
gave a translation of the scroll which became Facsimile
No. 1 in the Book of Abraham which, he said, was 'a
well-known scene from the Osiris mysteries, with Anubis,
the jackal-headed god . . . ministering to the dead Osiris on
the bier.' Richard P. Howard, Church Historian of the
Reorganized Church of Jesus Christ of Latter Day Saints,
gave an historical account to the effect that his church
has not accepted the Book of Abraham as scripture.
The next three articles involved the controversial 'sensen'
scrolls, also called 'The Book of Breathings,' or, as Klaus
Baer labels them, 'The Breathing Permit of Hor.' Two
former Mormons, Grant S. Heward and Jerald Tanner,
combined their talents to make out a prima facie case for
the proposition that Joseph Smith believed that the
Breathing Permit was the Book of Abraham. Some
orthodox L. D. S. scholars also share this view. Heward
and Tanner also produced evidence indicating that certain
gaps in Facsimile No. 2 had been filled in with material
from the Breathing Permit and from a scroll labeled 'Photo
3' in the Summer issue. Then followed a brief translation
of the Breathing Permit by Professor Parker.

Finally, Professor Nibley responded (primarily to Heward
and Tanner). He said that he was not sure that the
'Egyptian Alphabet and Grammer' (a notebook containing
Egyptian characters and parts of the Book of Abraham,
which is in the Church Historian's office) had been
authorized by Joseph Smith; moreover, that even if it had
been, he was not sure that the Egyptian characters
(apparently taken consecutively from the Breathing Permit)
on the left side of each page in the E. A. G. had been

118

intended by its author to have anything to do with the Book of Abraham verses found immediately to the right of each character. See p. 94 of the Summer *Dialogue* for a photo of a page from the E. A. G.; also see footnote 116 in the Baer article for Baer's translation of those Egyptian characters in the left-hand margins of the E. A. G. pages. Professor Nibley indicates that even if the left-hand characters do have something to do with the text material to the right of them, these characters may truly represent all the information to the right of them—in a way that scholars have not yet fathomed. Still another possibility suggested by Professor Nibley is that Joseph Smith may have translated none of the Book of Abraham, but may have received all of it by way of direct revelation. A final defense by Professor Nibley is that there is a marked similarity between the message in the Breathing Permit and the text of the Book of Abraham: ' . . . there is cosmological matter here, with the owner of the papyrus longing to shine in the heavens as some sort of physical entity along with the sun, and Orion; also he places great importance on his patriarchal lineage and wants to be pure, nay baptized, so as to enter a higher kingdom . . .' Professor Nibley has an important summary article in the Summer issue of Brigham Young University Studies and tells us he will soon begin to present the affirmative case for the inspired basis of the Book of Abraham (using materials on Abraham from Coptic and other sources in his monthly *Improvement Era* articles). *Dialogue* will continue to publish scholarly developments and personal responses relating to this important subject." (*Dialogue:* Vol. III, No. 3, Autumn 1968, pp. 109-110).

The author is greatly indebted to the editors of *Dialogue* for their permission to use material from their publication and would suggest to any reader, that a subscription would prove invaluable.

Though the above material is not entirely conclusive and is subject to further investigation, it still raises the possibility of doubts as to the scriptural value of the "Book of Abraham." The fact that Joseph Smith is very silent about this is to be appreciated by those who believe in him. It also points out the potential danger inherent on those who would attribute to the prophet, things he would not claim for himself.

The Reorganized Church has never taken an official stand accepting the *Pearl of Great Price* as one of its standard works. In the early days of the Reorganization some of the leaders used the publication and quoted from the Book of Abraham as it was published in the *Times and Seasons* during the lifetime of the prophet. As individuals, many felt that it might be scriptural but as time passed and more information became available, especially the publication of the Inspired Version of the Bible, which contains a portion of the material published in the *Pearl of Great Price*, the use of the book ceased. It was never a publication of the Reorganized Church.

Discussion of some of the contents of the "Book of Abraham" will appear in later chapters when some matters of doctrine will be considered such as the attitude of the Mormon Church to the Negro and the Doctrine of the plurality of Gods.

The Reorganized Church has avoided the potentiality of embarrassment by its non-acceptance of the translation of the Book of Abraham as scripture.

CHAPTER XVI

PRIESTHOOD AUTHORITY

The right of priesthood authority is one of the most divisive questions between the two churches and is one that merits very serious analysis. The position of the Restoration on this question was stated by Joseph Smith, Jr., in his letter to John Wentworth, which included the statement of the beliefs of the church. The statement is as follows:

"We believe that a man must be called of God, by prophecy, and the laying on of hands, by those who are in authority to preach the Gospel and administer in the ordinances thereof."

The above statement is in complete harmony with the scriptural references pertaining to the same subject:

"Ye have not chosen me, but I have chosen you, and ordained you, that ye should go and bring forth fruit, and that your fruit should remain; that whatsoever ye shall ask of the Father in my name, he may give it you." (John 15:16 I. V.)

There is still another quotation that is very significant and used a great deal in presenting the position of the church:

"And no man taketh this honor unto himself, but he that is called of God, as was Aaron." (Heb. 5:4, I. V.)

A quotation from the Book of Mormon is also given to show the harmony of God's word:

"And again; my brethren, I would cite your minds forward to the time which the Lord God gave these commandments unto his children; and I would that ye should remember that the Lord God ordained priests, after this holy order, which was after the order of his Son, to teach these things unto the people." (RLDS B of M, Alma 9:62, 63; Mormon B of M, Alma 13:1.)

121

The main import of the above quotations is that God has reserved to himself, the sole right of calling men to the priesthood and granting to them the authority to represent him. This is basic to the Restoration and is generally accepted by both organizations. If differences did not exist between the churches, there would be no necessity for further examination. However, because there are differences, further consideration is necessary.

The first callings and ordinations to the priesthood in the Restoration, occurred approximately eleven months before the church was officially organized. Reading from the prophet's statement in church history:

> "We still continued the work of translation, when in the ensuing month (May, 1829) we on a certain day went into the woods to pray and inquire of the Lord respecting baptism for the remission of sins, as we found mentioned in the translation of the plates. While we were thus employed, praying, and calling upon the Lord, a messenger from heaven descended in a cloud of light, and having laid his hands upon us, he ordained us, saying unto us, 'Upon you, my fellow servants, in the name of Messiah, I confer the priesthood of Aaron, which holds the keys of the ministering of angels, and of the gospel of repentance, and of baptism by immersion, for the remission of sins; . . .' and he commanded us to go and be baptized, and gave us directions that I should baptize Oliver Cowdery, and afterwards that he should baptize me. Accordingly we went and were baptized, I baptized him first, and afterwards he baptized me, after which I laid my hands upon his head and ordained him to the Aaronic priesthood, and afterwards he laid his hands upon me and ordained me to the same priesthood, for so we were commanded." (RLDS Ch. H., Vol. I, pp. 34-36.)

Other statements by the prophet have indicated that the messenger mentioned in the above quotation was John the Baptist, who had been authorized by Peter, James, and John to confer the Aaronic priesthood. It is of interest to note that even though the messenger had laid his hands upon their heads, after they had been baptized by each other, they proceeded to ordain each other physically. This same type of experience occurred when the prophet received the Melchisedec priesthood from Peter, James, and John as shown in church history. It is important to remember that these

122

events took place before the organization of the church on April 6, 1830.

One of the major requirements when a man is called to the priesthood is that he must be accepted by the church (congregation ward, etc.) before the actual act of ordination can take place. It was for this reason that the actual ordination of Joseph Smith and Oliver Cowdery did not take place until after the official organization of the church on April 6, 1830, at which time, those present accepted Joseph Smith as the first elder, and Oliver Cowdery as second elder and they then proceeded with the actual ordination of one another. Later, other men were called and ordained to the priesthood. What is emphasized here is the fact that the church, as an organization, did not confer the priesthood upon these men. The church accepted those chosen and in so doing, gave them a license or right to serve them as ministers of God. Because the priesthood, as such, was from God through men previously chosen and not the church, it can rightly be assumed that only God can take that priesthood from the man called. The church, as an organization, can bestow the right or license to render service to the organization and can, therefore, rescind that license.

Although it is not always apparent when a man is in transgression, it is something that cannot be hidden from God. A statement from the Doctrine and Covenants makes this clear:

"Therefore, inasmuch as you are found transgressors, ye cannot escape my wrath in your lives: inasmuch as ye are cut off by transgression, ye cannot escape the buffetings of Satan until the day of redemption." (Mormon D & C 104:8, 9; RLDS D & C 101:1).

The authority of the priesthood must come from God and unless it is recognized by God, it is of no value. It is for this reason that priesthood authority can only be taken from a man by God, who gave it and permits its use. When a man holding the priesthood begins to transgress, he knows in his heart his relationship to God and whether or not God can recognize him. It is in this sense that only through transgression does a man lose the authority of the priesthood.

There appears an important safeguard God has made in retaining to himself the choice and selection of men to the priesthood through others that have been chosen; it is the prevention of priestcraft. When the procedure as outlined by God is followed, human frailties would be somewhat eliminated and the calling of men to the priesthood out of friendship or for organizational purposes for self-aggrandizement could better be controlled. However, if the right to call men was given to the human organization such as the church without the controls outlined above, corruption can easily become a factor in the welfare of the church. This has been one of the major problems confronting the church all through the ages of man.

Christ, while on earth, did not leave the selection of those to assist him in his mission, to the followers that were converted to his teachings. It was he who made the choice and designated them in their responsibilities. The history of what followed and its influence upon the church he organized, is well documented and the great apostasy that followed with development of priestcrafts exist to this day. All of this occurred when the church assumed the right to select its leadership and failed to rely on God for direction.

When God granted to the church as an organization, the authority through chosen men, he also gave safeguards whereby the church could deal with men who became involved in transgression. When a man is found in transgression by those with whom he is associated, it is incumbent upon them to present charges against him to be heard by an Elder's Court or a Bishop's Court. It is from the findings of these courts that action can be taken against him and the most drastic of these is excommunication from the church. It is assumed by the church that if the charges of transgression have been proven, the authority to function in the priesthood has been taken from him by God and the action taken by the church is supplementary to this.

Even though the church has been established by divine direction, it is still composed of human beings and in turn is subject to some human frailties in their behavior. The early church in the Restoration was not immune and many events transpired which have been questioned over the years. With the rapid growth that took place in the early church, it is inevitable that some ambitious and scheming men became involved and at every opportunity, took advantage of situations that would lead to their aggrandizement. This led to friction between various of the leaders and in 1838, led to the excommunication of the Three Witnesses to the Book of Mormon.

Prior to the arrival of Joseph Smith in Far West, Missouri,

124

a group of leaders including David Patten and others, formed a council and charged David Whitmer, Oliver Cowdery and others with various accusations. The most serious against David Whitmer was disobedience to the Word of Wisdom because he drank tea and coffee and used tobacco. Oliver Cowdery and David Whitmer refused to appear before this council and denied their right to sit in judgment. In spite of the non-appearance of David and Oliver, the council met and excommunicated them from the church.

While the above action did embitter these men and others who received the same treatment, it did not affect their testimony as to what they had experienced with the coming forth of the Book of Mormon and witnessing the plates by the hand of an angel. Had they ever denied any portion of their experiences, this would have denoted an act of transgression which would have been justification that God had withdrawn his spirit from them. This never occurred and at no time has there ever been presented, evidence that any of these men were transgressors to the extent that the drastic action taken was warranted.

David Whitmer had in his possession a manuscript of the Book of Mormon given to him by Oliver Cowdery, and preserved it until the day of his death and not once did he ever deny his original testimony. It was from his heirs that the Reorganization received the manuscript they now have in their possession. It is extremely difficult to believe that men of the high character demonstrated by these men, and especially so after the wonderful spiritual experiences they had received, could behave in a manner that would justify the action of the council in Far West. This, however, was just a forerunner of what was to occur later.

Church organizations all through the history of mankind, have been faced with the same problem simply because of the humanness that exists in their organization. One of the greatest examples of history along this line was the period of the "Inquisition" in Spain. The leaders of the church took their position so seriously that they felt it was their duty to eliminate heresy from the church. This meant that all who disagreed with the officials were legitimate candidates for elimination. It got so bad that when anyone desired to have someone eliminated, all he had to do was to file charges of heresy with the church officials and action would be taken.

It is interesting to read in church history what transpired for a time at Kirtland, Ohio.

"On October 18, 1837, the High Council of Kirtland resolved to commence a reform by pruning the church of unruly members. On the twenty-second the church in Kirtland disfellowshiped twenty-two members, until satisfaction should be made, for uniting with the world in a dance." (RLDS Ch. Hist. Vol. 2, p. 110).

In other portions of history we read that members were excommunicated simply because they did not attend church as regularly as was desired by some of the leadership. It is not necessary to point out the dangers of developing such policies and the advantage that can be taken of the members by anyone so inclined. This is the real beginning of the demand for complete obedience to the leadership and explains much of what later transpired in Nauvoo.

It should not be construed by what has been written above that the leadership of the church should not be responsible for the conditions within the church and to take all means necessary to see that the will of God is always paramount. If the gifts of the Spirit promised to the leadership, are fully exercised and especially the gift of Discernment of Spirits, the abuse of authority can potentially be avoided. It should again be emphasized that the church as an organization does license those who are to officiate and therefore, does maintain the right to suspend or revoke any license given. Procedures have been provided whereby the rights of the individual can be safeguarded when they are followed by the authorities of the church. These are found in the functioning of the various priesthood offices, in Elder's Courts and Bishop's Courts with the right of appeal to the High Council.

It has been shown that there exists the potentiality that men may be deprived of their position in the church without having transgressed, provided that the leadership is sufficiently entrenched to compel the membership to accept their actions. It is this type of situation that is stressed in the differences between the Mormon Church and the Reorganization.

After the death of Joseph Smith on June 27, 1844, there arose several claimants to the right of presiding over the church and among these was Sidney Rigdon, who was a counselor to the prophet at the time of his death and, being a member of the quorum of First Presidency, he felt that he should carry on until God selected a successor. Under the direction of William Marks, president of Nauvoo Stake and also a member of the High Council, a meeting of the membership of the church was held for the purpose of allowing Sidney Rigdon to present his viewpoint. This meeting was in August of 1844 and, in the meantime, the various members of the Twelve returned to Nauvoo and, under the direction of Brigham Young as president of the quorum, also appeared at this meeting. Sidney Rigdon was allowed to present his views and then was followed by a great deal of oratory on the part of several members of the Twelve and Brigham Young. They called upon those in attendance to recognize the Quorum of Twelve as the leaders of the church. Both churches accept that this is an inherent right of the Twelve, as the second quorum in the church and therefore is not questioned. What is questioned is that which transpired after this action.

After the church had accepted the Twelve, Sidney Rigdon returned to Pittsburgh and was later excommunicated primarily because he refused to follow the Twelve. William Marks, because he sponsored the meeting for Sidney Rigdon, was dropped from the office of Stake President and also as a member of the High Council. He and many others did not approve of the domineering tactics assumed by the Twelve and refused to agree with them in all that took place. As a result, about six months later William Marks was excommunicated for disobedience. It was during this period that the Twelve took many drastic measures to consolidate their position and that the philosophy of complete obedience was projected which has finally led to the present acceptance by the members of the Mormon Church of the infallibility of their leadership.

The reader should keep in mind that many of the members of the church did not go west with the Twelve and many of these men received the priesthood authority under the hands of the prophet and others authorized. The fact that they did not follow the Twelve West, was not an act of transgression except in the eyes of the Twelve. A true act of transgression is one that separates a man from God. Disagreement with a fellowman is not, therefore, an act of transgression. Some of these men, in their search for the truth, joined with others that were claiming the right of leadership. When they learned their search was not fruitful in finding the truth, they ultimately sought guidance from God which resulted in the formation of the Reorganized Church. Certainly the search for truth cannot be construed as an act of transgression on the part of these men, especially so when they never denied the truth of their conversion or the truthfulness of the Restoration. The Reorganized Church always accepted the members of the early church on their original baptism and also accepted the men who had been ordained in the early church. This acceptance was, of course, subject to not having been charged with serious acts of transgression.

In comparison with the actions of the Twelve, it was required of everyone that entered Salt Lake Valley, that they be rebaptized and reordained. In the chapter on First Presidency it was shown from the journal of Wilford Woodruff, the beginning of this practice. Quoting again:

"About this time President Young felt impressed that he and the brethren of the camp should renew their covenants by baptism. August 6th, the Twelve were rebaptized by President Young. Elder Kimball baptized President Young and the latter confirmed his brethren and *resealed* upon them all their former blessings." " . . . The practice of the Saints coming into the Valley to renew their covenants by baptism was followed for many years. . . ." (*Wilford Woodruff* by Matthias F. Cowley, page 319).

The act of re-sealing has been italicized for emphasis because this includes ordination to the priesthood and is very pertinent to the discussion in this chapter. Does the action taken by Brigham Young indicate that enough transgression had occurred to warrant this serious step? Should the answer be in the affirmative, the question of authority then becomes a very serious consideration.

The Mormon Church has taken the position that the men responsible for the forming of the Reorganization could not do so because they lacked authority. This position is based on the fact that they were excommunicated by the Twelve when they refused to follow them in their leadership of the church.

The Reorganized Church accepts the principle that only God can give the authority to a man and therefore, God only can take it from him. If a man has been ordained properly as outlined earlier, only through personal transgression by him, would that authority be removed by God. It is the contention of the Reorganized Church that the men primarily responsible for gathering the scattered church members into an organization after the main body was driven from Nauvoo, were men who had been properly ordained in the early church and had not transgressed to the extent that God would not accept their ministry.

CHAPTER XVII

TEMPLES AND TEMPLE RITES

The building of temples for worship has always been one of the activities of the human race regardless of the type of religion. However, many different usages are ascribed to the term "temple."

The first account of a special structure for the worship of God, was the command of God to Moses to erect the Tabernacle as outlined in the twenty-fifth, twenty-sixth, and twenty-seventh chapters of Exodus in the Old Testament of the Bible. A detailed description of the structure and its usage is given.

The next temple of importance to the Israelites, was the one erected by Solomon, son of David. This temple is referred to many times as Solomon's Temple and is of unusual import in the discussion of temples in this book because it is claimed by Freemasonry that all of the Masonic rituals were first introduced in this temple and that they have continued up to the present time. The origin of Masonry is supposed to have started during the erection and completion of the temple. So far as actual history can learn, this contention on the part of the Masons cannot be proven. The earliest record indicates that Masonry began in the 1600's in England. It is not the purpose of this book to either prove or disprove these contentions. They are given here mainly because of the part Masonry played in the history of the Restoration.

To properly understand the importance of temples to the Restoration, it is necessary to start early in the history of the church. There are references to temples in the Doctrine and Covenants which are somewhat general in aspect, but the first really definite statement was made in July of 1831 and is as follows:

"Hearken, O ye elders of my church saith the Lord your God, who have assembled yourselves together, according to my commandments, in this land which is the land of Missouri, which is the land which I have appointed and consecrated for the gathering of the saints: wherefore this is the land of promise, and the place for the city of Zion. And thus saith the Lord your God, if you will receive wisdom here is wisdom. Behold, the place which is now called Independence, is the center place, and the spot for the temple is lying westward upon a lot which is not far from the courthouse; . . ." (Mormon D & C 57:1-3; RLDS D & C 57:1).

In another section we find the following quotation:

"And let my servant Sidney Rigdon consecrate and dedicate this land, and the spot for the temple, unto the Lord." (Mormon D & C 58:57; RLDS D & C 58:13).

The above quotations have designated the first place at which a temple was to be erected with the instructions to dedicate the land. From the recorded history we know that the spot for the temple was dedicated and the saints began looking forward to the time they would be in a position to enjoy having a building for their use. As an interesting side light, the stones marking the site of the temple that were placed at the time of the dedication, were uncovered several years ago by the Church of Christ Temple Lot, when they were excavating for the erection of a temple they were planning to build. On the strength of some purported revelations by one of their members, the Hedrickites began the excavation for the foundation and basement of a temple but due to the lack of funds and support, were unable to complete or actually start the erection of a building. Later, with assistance from the Reorganization, the excavation was filled in and sodded over. Visitors to Independence can visit the area and see the stones that are on display in the building now occupying a portion of the Temple Lot.

The next revelation pertaining to the Temple in the Doctrine and Covenants is as follows:

"Verily, this is the word of the Lord, that the city New Jerusalem shall be built by the gathering of the saints, beginning at this place, even the place of the temple, which temple shall be reared in this generation; . . . for verily, this generation shall not all pass away until an house shall be built unto the Lord, and a cloud shall rest upon it, which cloud shall be even the glory of the Lord, which shall fill the house." (Mormon D & C 84:4; RLDS D & C 83:2).

The site has been designated and promise has been given that "an house" shall be built. A temple was never erected on the dedicated site in Independence and the saints were driven from the area before they could even begin the accumulation of material for the building.

Many have felt that the prophecy regarding the erection of the temple in Independence was never fulfilled that therefore, the prophet erred. It is of interest to give some thought to other interpretations relative to this prophecy. The erection of the temple at Kirtland, Ohio, in many ways fulfills the statement:

> "this generation shall not all pass away until an house shall be built unto the Lord, and a cloud shall rest upon it, which cloud shall be even the glory of the Lord, which shall fill the house."

History has recorded many wonderful experiences, the prophet and those associated with him, had in the confines of this wonderful building.

There is, however, another point of view and it is based on the following quotation from the Doctrine and Covenants:

> "Verily, verily, I say unto you, that when I give a commandment to any of the sons of men, to do a work unto my name, and these sons of men go with all their might, and with all they have, to perform that work, and cease not their diligence, and their enemies come upon them, and hinder them performing that work; behold, it behooveth me to require that work no more at the hands of those sons of men, but to accept of their offerings; . . . Therefore, for this cause have I accepted the offerings of those whom I commanded to build up a city and a house unto my name, in Jackson County, Missouri. . . ." (Mormon D & C 124:49-51; RLDS D & C 107:15).

This revelation recognizes the inability of the saints to complete the task assigned them because they were driven out and lost their holdings. This revelation was given in January, 1841 and was given to the prophet who received the other instructions; it can be accepted in the light of rescinding the early commands.

In a revelation given in May, 1833 the prophet received the

detailed instructions for the erection of the temple at Kirtland, Ohio. With the completion of this temple that was
dedicated in 1836, the church fulfilled the instruction to
erect a house unto God.

In the instructions received, pertaining to temples, nothing
of the details of the functions that were to take place within
that edifice, have been revealed. The primary purpose we
find in history and the revelations, is for the education of
the priesthood and the School of the Prophets as it is designated. It should also be brought out that a baptismal font
was never provided for in the Kirtland Temple. Another
interesting feature pertains to the embellishments that
appear on the outside of the building. On some of the newer
structures erected by the Mormon Church, various emblems
such as a handclasp, the Sun, Moon and Stars, the All-seeing
Eye and other emblems sometimes identified with the
Masonic organization, are a part of the structure. None of
these appeared on the Kirtland Temple. A description of this
temple was given in a previous chapter.

After the saints were driven out of Independence and then
from Clay County, they began gathering at a place north and
east of Independence known as Far West. Here, without any
revelation, they began the construction of a temple. When the
prophet arrived there from Kirtland, Ohio, he ordered the
work on the temple to stop. It was a very short time after
this that the saints were again driven from their homes.
It is from here they went to Nauvoo, Illinois, and began the
building of a city at that place.

The next instructions regarding a temple were received by
the prophet in January 1841, and this is found in section 107
of the Reorganized Church edition and section 124 in the
Mormon edition of the Doctrine and Covenants. It is in
this revelation that the first instructions were received
pertaining to the ordinance to be performed in the Temple.
The first instruction relative to baptism for the dead is
given as a function that can only be performed in a temple
set up for that purpose. This doctrine is now the basis for
one of the major functions that is conducted in the Mormon
temples. A discussion of the doctrine of baptism for the dead
will be covered in a later chapter.

It is well to note that up to this time, no building had
been started with the exception of the one in Far West,
without specific instructions received by revelation. This may

be due to the instruction contained in the Doctrine and Covenants as follows: ". . . which my people are always commanded to build unto my holy name" (Mormon D & C 124:39; RLDS D & C 107:12). Up to this time God has always chosen the place and site for the temples to be erected along with specific instructions to build. The Reorganized Church interprets this instruction to mean that God will always command his people when he wishes a temple to be erected. The Mormon Church interprets this to mean that the church is commanded always to build, or in more simple language, it is not necessary to wait for specific instruction from God to erect a temple. It is of interest historically to know that the Kirtland Temple is the only building still standing, that was built under the direct command of God. It is now in the possession of the Reorganized Church.

To review the rites and ceremonies for which the temples are erected, it is necessary to learn more of the history, especially of the period in Nauvoo. It is well known that Joseph and Hyrum Smith had joined the Masonic Organization. Hyrum Smith along with Heber C. Kimball, had belonged to the organization back in the state of New York before they ever moved west. Joseph Smith did not join with them until after they settled in Nauvoo, at which time large numbers of the men also joined the lodges established.

Because of the tremendous influence the Masonic organization had upon the church in Nauvoo, an attempt was made to learn more of the details about what took place during this period. T. Edgar Lyon, historian for the Nauvoo Restoration Corporation, was contacted and from him, the following information was received in a letter dated October 22, 1968:

"The following is the information you **requested** concerning the Masonic Lodge at Nauvoo.

October 15, 1841—Grand Master Jonas issued a dispensation authorizing the Nauvoo Lodge at the request of Masons who had settled at Nauvoo. There were about twenty names on the application, and when it was presented to the Grand Lodge, it was opposed by the Quincy Lodge. Jonas, however, issued it without unanimous approval of the Grand Lodge.

March 15, 1842—Grand Master Abraham Jonas visited Nauvoo and officially founded the lodge under the dispensation issued the previous October. Joseph Smith received the first Masonic degree.

March 16, 1842—Joseph Smith "rose to the Sublime Degree."

October 11, 1842—The Grand Lodge suspended the dispensation of the Nauvoo Lodge as the Bodely Lodge at Quincy had demanded an investigation on July 16, alleging irregularities in initiations.

October 1842—During the convocations of the Grand Lodge of Illinois, complaints presented led to the suspension of the Charter Under Dispensation pending investigation.

November 2, 1842—Jonas had been replaced by M. Helm as Grand Master, and he ordered the injunction of suspension removed and granted the Nauvoo Lodge Under Dispensation authority to form two additional lodges, which were named Helm and Nye Lodges.

Spring of 1843—Despite suspension of the Charter Under Dispensation, the Nauvoo Lodge commenced the erection of its hall.

June 24, 1843—Cornerstone of the Masonic Hall was laid. M. Helm, for political reasons, did not attend although the cornerstone had been engraved with his name on it, as he had agreed to perform the laying of it.

October 1843—An investigating committee appointed by the Grand Lodge the previous fall, made a report that the Nauvoo Lodge was guilty of too rapid advancement of its members, did not maintain adequate records, and had not paid dues for all its members. The Grand Lodge then voted to suspend the charter for one year pending reformation of these practices.

April 5, 1844— The completed lodge hall was dedicated. Five hundred fifty plus Masons attended.

October 1844—The report to the convocation of the Grand Lodge indicated there had been no reformation in the Nauvoo Lodge concerning its faulty practices and the charter was permanently suspended. The three lodges were declared clandestine and were forbidden fellowshipping with other lodges.

October 1844—At this same meeting of the Grand Lodge of Illinois, new charters were issued for the Rising Sun Lodge and the Keokuk Lodge, both of which were dominated by Mormons, but which had not been guilty of the three complaints against the Nauvoo Lodges. By October 1843 the total membership of all the Masonic Lodges in the Illinois jurisdiction (this included the Montrose and Keokuk Lodges in Iowa) was 512. Of this number 285 were in the Nauvoo Lodge, leaving only 227 in all of the other state lodges combined, of whom quite a number were Mormons in the Keokuk and Montrose Lodges.

Commencing in 1843 the Quincy Lodge protested at each annual meeting that the Mormon Lodges at Nauvoo were functioning illegally in spite of the order to desist their activities and were therefore known as a clandestine lodge up to the end of the Mormon occupation in Nauvoo." (Letter from T. Edgar Lyon, historian for Nauvoo Restoration Incorporated. October 22, 1968.)

From the above historical data it is very apparent that Masonry began to play a very important part in the church at Nauvoo. So much so that after receiving a revelation to build a temple in Nauvoo and that the time in which to complete the erection was limited, time was taken away from that task to build a structure to house the Masonic Lodge. This building still stands in Nauvoo and is owned by the Mormon Church. The history of both churches has been extremely silent about this phase in church history at Nauvoo, and the reason for this is best known to the historians.

The subject of the relationship of Masonry to the church would not have been dealt with to such length had there not been other information available but not generally known. This information pertains to incidents that led to a culmination in the death of the prophet Joseph Smith.

In the *Universal Free Mason* publication, Volume XIII, No. 22 and dated April 1922, and starting on page 522, is found an article titled "Masonry and Mormonism" from which the following quotation is taken:

"In the issues of the *'Builder'* of February and March, 1921, and February of the present year there appeared articles on 'A Study of Mormonism in its Connection with Masonry,' written by S. R. Goodwin, a P. G. M. of the Grand Lodge of Utah, and present Grand Secretary, formerly an Anti-Mormon preacher and lecturer in Utah. We are, or should be all, in search of *light*, but let it be clear and not as 'through a glass darkly.'

With the first part and that part of the second paper, in so far as the history of the Mormons in Nauvoo and their connection with Masonry there I have little comment to make, further than to remark that they would have been more historically complete, and laid the writer less open to the suspicion of bias had he mentioned the fact that the mob that murdered Joseph and Hiram Smith were members of the Lodge at Warsaw, and that the plans for the carrying out of the assassination were conceived in that Lodge."

The article from which the above is quoted is quite lengthy and for this reason excerpts only are being taken not out of context, but to illustrate the part masonry had during this period of church history. Another quotation on page 530 of the publication reads:

"Heber (Heber C. Kimball, author) was a Freemason in 1823. He received the first three degrees of Masonry in the Lodge at Victor (New York)."

The article then quotes further from the journal of Heber C. Kimball:

"Hyrum Smith received the first three degrees of Masonry in Ontario County, New York. Joseph and Hyrum Smith were Master Masons, yet they were massacred through the instrumentality of some of the leading men of the fraternity, and not one soul of them ever stepped forth to administer help to me or my brethren belonging to the Masonic institution, or to render us assistance, although bound under the strongest obligations to be true and faithful to each other in every case, and under every circumstance, the commission of crime excepted."

A recent article in the Summer Issue of *Dialogue*, written by Keith Huntress and titled "Governor Thomas Ford and the Murderers of Joseph Smith," contains an apparent confirmation of the quotations from the *Universal Freemason Publication*. The quotation used by Mr. Huntress is taken from an account written by William M. Daniels, "A Correct Account of the Murder of Generals Joseph and Hyrum Smith. . . ." (Nauvoo, 1845), p. 4. Quoting from Mr. Huntress' article:

"William Daniels, who wrote an eyewitness account of the Smith murders, began his story: 'I resided in Augusta, Hancock county, Ill., eighteen miles from Carthage. On the 16th of June I left my home with the intention of going to St. Louis. . . . The next morning a company of men were going from . . . (Warsaw) to Carthage, for the purpose, as they said, of assisting the militia to drive the Mormons out of the country. Out of curiosity, as I had no particular way to spend my time. . . .' " (*Dialogue*, Summer Vol. IV, No. 2, page 45.)

There is only one basic reason for the inclusion of this material on the Masonic organization and the author is convinced that this organization had tremendous influence over what occurred later and especially in reference to the rituals used in the Mormon Temples. Many times has the author sought scriptural justification for the importance of many of the actions that are part of this work. It has always been customary for God to reveal his will to mankind and especially so when sacraments are involved and the ordinances to be performed. The prophet, before his death, gave one revelation and two letters, pertaining to one of the practices now being conducted in Mormon temples. These were instructions on the doctrine of Baptism for the Dead. A detailed analysis of this doctrine and practice will be discussed at length in a later chapter. There are no revelations outlining temple rites and ceremonies available for verification, such as are available in scriptures for the instruction of the believers in Christ. It is this lack of scripture that raises the serious question in reference to the origin of temple rites and ceremonies.

It is not possible to secure a verification from either the Mormon Church or the Masonic organization, that the temple rites had their origin from the experiences as Masons in Nauvoo. This statement is based on the premise that a sincere, active member of the Masonic organization, could not honorably reveal that which occurs in the assembly of the lodges; neither would a Mormon, who has integrity and sincere belief in his church, reveal what he experienced in the temple. There have been many exposures by ex-members of both organizations but, none of them have ever been confirmed as authentic by either organization. Many of the exposures have been made by Masons who have become disaffected for various reasons and are therefore, considered renegades and doubt is cast upon veracity of their revealments because of prejudices that have arisen. This same pertains to members of the Mormon Church who have become disenchanted with the church and have actually become apostates. Their veracity is then questioned for the same reasons.

During the Senate hearings in Washington, D.C. on the eligibility of Reed Smoot to sit as a member of the Senate, Professor Walter Wolfe, formerly an instructor at the Brigham Young College at Logan, Utah, was called to testify before the Senate committee. On February 7, 1906, he testified under oath and gave a complete description of the procedures in the temple. His testimony appeared in the Salt Lake Tribune of February 21, 1906 and is also in the Congressional Record of that period. The description is complete and describes the action from entrance into the temple until completion of the purpose for which they came. Most generally it is either for baptism of the dead relatives or for the purpose of temple marriage for time and eternity. There are other reasons for going to the temple such as special endowments.

It is not the purpose of the author to reveal those things which are sacred to members of the Mormon Church and it is for this reason, excerpts from the testimony of Professor Walter Wolfe are not included. However, the author did verify the truthfulness of the testimony from his father, who had spent many years of activity working in the temple and receiving special anointings. To verify the similarity of the temple rites with the rites practiced in the Masonic organization, it was necessary to have a Mason in good standing, read the testimony of Professor Wolfe and get his reactions. The party to whom it was shown was astounded at the similarity and so expressed himself to the author.

During 1967, the Mormon Church published a special edition of the *Improvement Era* called "Temples and the Latter-day Saints." This issue contains some very beautiful illustrations of temples now erected and also illustrations of the several rooms where various ordinances are conducted. If the reader is interested in further extensive investigation, a copy of Professor Wolfe's testimony should be secured and also a copy of the above issue of the *Era*.

When it is realized how important participation in the Masonic organization was at Nauvoo even to the point that, in spite of the urgent instruction contained in the revelation to build a temple in Nauvoo, they allowed efforts to be diverted for the construction of a building to house the lodge, the relationship becomes very apparent.

When the charter under dispensation was revoked, they could no longer continue to function as Masons. By this time the rituals and practices had become extremely important to them and the possibility of making them a part of the temple activities appears to have grown in the minds of the leaders. It should be remembered that the final action of revoking the charter occurred in October of 1844, which is six months after the death of the Prophet. Heber C. Kimball was a member of the quorum of Twelve and later, when Brigham Young became president of the church, he was chosen to be one of his counselors. Heber Kimball had been a Mason since 1823 and had been very active in the organization; it is not difficult to assume, lacking divine instructions, that he played a very important part in setting up the rituals that have become so important to the church today.

The secrecy surrounding the Masonic Rituals and activities was a very convenient method of covering the lack of divine instructions to the church on temples and, by describing them as extremely sacred and not to be exposed to the world, it was possible to convince the membership. This is another evident result of the acceptance of the infallibility of the leadership and blind obedience to their instructions.

Many of the activities in the temples are known as endowments. These, according to the Mormons, are special blessings pronounced upon individuals for various reasons. These are also known as anointings.

Over the years some changes have occurred in the performance and requirements for temple activities. One of these pertains to the special garments that members are required to wear. With the changing of styles, especially with women, it has been necessary to allow revisions or changes to avoid embarrassment. Those who have attended a Masonic funeral, will be aware of the apron worn by the Masons participating in the service. It is interesting to note that participation in temple ceremonies requires the wearing of an

140

apron which represents the fig-leaf worn by Adam and Eve in the Garden of Eden. This, coupled with signs, handclasps, oaths, etc., are the evidences that have convinced the author as to the origin of the temple rituals.

Anything that has been said pertaining to Masonry, should not be considered as a reflection upon that organization, nor that any actions of individuals should be attributed to the organization as a whole. Neither Masonry or the Church should be held accountable for the rash and thoughtless behavior of individual members.

The Reorganized Church has never participated in the institution of temple rituals as described above. It is their feeling that God will not only reveal where and when a temple should be built, but also instructions as to what should be the activities in that temple. There is a difference in interpretation of the term "endowments" between the churches. In the Mormon Church it has come to mean a special blessing to individuals. In the Reorganization the belief is that endowments will be like those received in the Kirtland Temple which were outpourings of the Spirit of God upon those assembled. It can be for individuals such as received by the Prophet Joseph Smith in the Kirtland Temple and then later as he was associated with other individuals. It is well to note that the rituals now practiced by the Mormon Church, did not originate in the Kirtland Temple. No provision had been made for them in the divine instructions received for the construction of the building. Many wonderful experiences took place in the Kirtland Temple and have been fully revealed in the histories of both churches.

Since the above was written there have been some important changes in the position of the Reorganized Church and its relationship to temples. At the World Conference in April of 1968, there was a revelation to the church through its prophet, W. Wallace Smith (grandson of Joseph Smith) which was accepted by the church. There were several matters of interest to the church contained in this revelation but the portion of interest in this chapter is the following quotation:

"The time has come for a start to be made toward building my temple in the Center Place. It shall stand on a portion of the plot of ground set apart for this purpose many years ago by my servant Joseph Smith, Jr. The shape and character of the building is to conform to ministries which will be carried out within its walls. These functions I will reveal through my servant the prophet and his counselors

141

from time to time, as need for more specific direction arises. (b) Money for this purpose should come from the consecration of surplus by my people inasmuch as the building of houses of worship is one of the purposes of the Storehouse. (c) As you are diligent in moving to effect this project I will pour out the blessings of my Spirit and you will know that I am God." (RLDS D & C 149:6).

After the above document had been presented to the conference, some questions arose and as a result, a clarification was given to the church that was then accepted as section 149A. Contained in this clarification is the following pertaining to the temple:

"It is also to be noted that the full and complete use of the temple is yet to be revealed but that there is no provision for secret ordinances now or ever, although there will be provision for instructional opportunities which will of necessity be restricted to the particular category concerned, *viz*, high priests, patriarchs, bishops, seventies, elders, Aaronic priesthood, and so forth." (RLDS D & C 149A:6).

With the introduction of the above revelation to the Reorganized Church there has been a revival of a hope that has been cherished by Latter Day Saints since the beginning of the church in 1830. The building of a temple has always confronted the church but in the past few years, very little has been said and in the minds of many, it was becoming a forgotten dream. Effects of this silence are indicated in the response many have made: "For what purpose a temple?"

CHAPTER XVIII

MARRIAGE

With the subject of marriage, one of the ordinances practiced in the Mormon temples, we enter into possibly the most controversial subject between the two churches. A detailed and comprehensive discussion of this subject can be found in publications prepared by both churches and can be obtained without much difficulty and for this reason, the observations made here will be more general. To justify the doctrine of polygamy or plural marriage, it is absolutely essential to have hearsay testimony. Due to the unreliability of this type of testimony, the author has confined his quotations to those of record.

To establish the position of the early church during the days of the prophet we should quote the revelations received pertaining to the subject of marriage. From section forty-nine in both editions of the Doctrine and Covenants we find the following:

"And again, I say unto you, that whoso forbiddeth to marry, is not ordained of God, for marriage is ordained of God unto man; wherefore it is lawful that he should have *one* wife, and they *twain* shall be one flesh, and all this that the earth might answer the end of its creation; and that it might be filled with the measure of man, according to his creation before the world was made." (Mormon D & C 49:15-17; RLDS 49:3.)

Also in section forty-two of both editions we find this statement:

"Thou shalt love thy *wife* with all thy heart, and shall cleave unto her and none else: . . . " (Mormon D & C 42:22; RLDS D & C 42:7.)

In 1835, the High Council in Kirtland, Ohio, approved the Doctrine and Covenants which contained the following:

"Inasmuch as this Church of Christ has been reproached

with the crime of fornication, and polygamy; we declare that we believe that one man should have one wife; and one woman but one husband, except in the case of death, when either is at liberty to marry again." (RLDS D & C 111:4).

This section was eliminated from the Mormon Doctrine and Covenants in 1876, and to take its place, they inserted the "purported revelation" on marriage now known as section 132.

In none of the above quotations has marriage been made a doctrine of salvation but they have emphasized the principle of monogamy in marriage. It is also well to note that nowhere in the Bible or the Book of Mormon, has marriage ever been considered as a doctrine of salvation. It is the attempt to take marriage from the area of social custom or practice and placing it among the principles of the Gospel, as a means of salvation, and to make it mandatory for a man to have at least one wife in order to reach Celestial Glory, to which exception is taken. All through the history of mankind marriage has been primarily a social custom. That is why some nations permit the practice of polygamy and in others, the practice of polyandry (the practice of one woman with several husbands).

To continue the examination of attitude of the early church, we find articles in the official church paper, *Times and Seasons* in the February and March issues of 1844, in which men were excommunicated from the church for either practicing or teaching the doctrine of polygamy. This was just shortly before the death of the prophet in June of 1844. Also in *Times and Seasons* we find the following statement as the position of the church:

"As to the charge of polygamy, I will quote from the Book of Doctrine and Covenants which is the subscribed faith of the church and is strictly enforced. Article Marriage, sec. 91, par. 4, says, 'Inasmuch as this church of Christ has been reproached with the crime of fornication and polygamy, we declare that we believe that one man should have but one wife, and one woman but one husband except in the case of death when either is at liberty to marry again.' " (*Times and Seasons*, Vol. 6, p. 894; dated May of 1845.)

It should be noted that this article appeared nearly a year after the death of the prophet so we can safely assume that up to the time of his death, the church recognized the word of God as it had been given to the church by him.

If the statements by the Mormon Church are to be accepted, Joseph Smith has been accused of being in polygamy as early as 1838, and some have claimed he received the "purported" revelation as early as 1832, without supporting data. However, the purported "revelation" they introduced on marriage, they claim was received on July 12, 1843. This purported "revelation" was first made public in Salt Lake Valley in August of 1852, eight years after the prophet's death and at a time when he could not defend himself from the charges. If the charges of the Mormon Church are accepted as true, it must then be admitted that Joseph Smith was a very inconsistent leader, to publicly teach one doctrine and an entirely different one in private. It is very hard to believe that such duplicity would not have destroyed his leadership.

On many occasions a challenge has been issued to Mormon elders to produce one bit of evidence, acceptable in a court of the land as evidence, wherein Joseph Smith had expressed his approval of what they attribute to him, but none has ever been presented. The only evidence that has been presented is hearsay testimony and which is mostly self-serving. An interesting comment on this question by T. Edgar Lyon, historian for the Nauvoo Restoration Incorporation:

"As you are more than likely aware, the issue of polygamy is one of the most vital and most difficult and illusive subjects which separate the two churches. I am willing to grant that no specific documentation can be provided in the form of an official document signed by Joseph Smith concerning this institution. On the other hand there are published statements in which he denied its practice in the Church." (Letter from T. Edgar Lyon, dated October 22, 1968.)

The author is aware of the fact that many questionable actions were taking place in Nauvoo during this latter part of the prophet's life. Whether or not the prophet was responsible or if it was the result of activities of men surrounding him, the introduction of false doctrine can never be acceptable to those who have a sincere love of God. It can only be attributed to the human weaknesses of man. This again points out the danger of blind acceptance of those things that may be uttered by a man, even though he is recognized as the prophet of God when so used. Remember that he is only human and not infallible.

There are a number of affidavits sworn to by women claiming to have been wives of Joseph Smith. Knowing that the practice of sealing women to husbands, is a part of the Celestial Marriage theory, it can easily be explained why some women were willing and sincere in providing the affidavits. Several of these women, even though married to other men, requested the privilege of being sealed to the prophet. Eliza R. Snow claimed to have been sealed to the prophet and later became one of Brigham Young's wives. Believing as strongly as they did in what was being taught by the leaders, they were permitted to be sealed to the prophet for eternity, as this would make them wives of the prophet in eternity. Thus, after this action had been taken, they did consider themselves as wives of Joseph Smith and this is what was attested to.

To really understand why these women felt as they did, we need to know some of the beliefs that are involved. According to Mormon doctrine, a wife must be called forth from the grave by her husband, using the name given her in the temple marriage ceremony when the sealing took place, at the time of the resurrection if she is to spend eternity with him in Celestial Glory. With this understanding, it is not difficult to evaluate the claims as they were presented. It is very remarkable however, to note that while Joseph and Emma, his wife, were prolific in giving birth to children, not one of the women claiming to have been the wife of the prophet, ever gave birth to any children as a result of that marriage. Several of the women married other men and had children by them. One of these women was Zina D. Huntington. Reading from the *Historical Record*, Vol. 6, page 233, we find the following:

"Zina D. Huntington, afterwards the wife of Pres. Brigham Young, sealed to the Prophet October 27, 1841, Dimick B. Huntington officiating."

The dates shown should be very carefully noted on the quotations given. From the *Times and Seasons*, Vol. 2, p. 374, is the following:

"Married, in this city, March 7, (1841), by Elder John C. Bennett, Mr. Henry Jacobs and Zina D. Huntington."

146

According to the record, the marriage to Mr. Jacobs occurred approximately five months prior to the purported marriage to Joseph Smith. It is also a matter of record that two sons were born to this marriage. Reading from her testimony as published in *Women of Mormondom*, by Tulledge, pp. 327-330:

"So on the ninth of February, 1846, on a clear cold day, we left our home at Nauvoo. . . . I will pass over the tedius journey to the Chariton River. . . . On the bank of the Chariton an incident occurred, ever eventful in the life of woman. . . . We had traveled one morning about five miles, when I called for a halt in our march. There was but one person with me, Mother Lyman, the aunt of George A. Smith; and there on the bank of the Chariton I was delivered of a fine son. On the morning of the 23rd, Mother Lyman gave me a cup of coffee and a biscuit. . . . These days of trial and grief were succeeded by my journey to Winter Quarters, where in due time I arrived, and was welcomed by President Young into his family."

The son born in the above narrative was the second son of Henry Jacobs as the father. With the death of Joseph Smith in June of 1844, it is physically impossible for him to have been the father. It has never been claimed by anyone that Joseph Smith was the father.

From the statements made above, it becomes quite obvious that many contradictions have occurred and these do justify serious questioning of the teachings of those who introduced this doctrine in Utah.

Another point of interest to the author was the attempt to learn when the first plural children were recorded. Wilford Woodruff, one of the Twelve at the time of the death of the Prophet, did not take a plural wife until April, 1846, and his first plural child was born March 25, 1847. Brigham Young's first plural child was born June 19, 1845. It is difficult to document or secure information of this type due to the manner in which records were maintained. However, it is an interesting approach to an intriguing question.

One thing is certain and that is, a doctrine such as polygamy does not develop overnight but must go through a process of evolution. Any doctrine, to be acceptable to those to whom it is presented, must have an appeal. For this reason it is necessary to go back into history a little to trace the beginning of the doctrine in Nauvoo. It has been reported that a man by the name of John C. Bennett, came to Nauvoo in its early days as a city. He ingratiated himself with a number of the leaders, including the Prophet. However, we find the Prophet was skeptical of the man's morals which ultimately led to his excommunication from the church. Bennett is generally conceded as the one suggesting the idea of spiritual marriage. An idea that anyone, properly married by the leaders of the church, should be married for time and eternity. It is apparent that the idea appealed to the Prophet because, in his testimony before the city council at Nauvoo in June of 1844, testified, when questioned about the purported revelation that was referred to in the *Nauvoo Expositor*, that what he taught was that a man should marry in view of eternity. That it was a means whereby marriage became a very important part of the church's belief and, by making the marriage covenant an eternal covenant, the incidence of divorce would become much less. By persuading men that a covenant of marriage to a woman, when performed by a man with the priesthood, would become an eternal covenant in the same manner that baptism is an eternal covenant. There is a tremendous social value in this type of doctrine. The Roman Catholic Church, by making divorce almost impossible, has to a large extent, practiced this theory for centuries. There is a very real possibility that the prophet realized this and permitted the introduction of the eternity of the marriage covenant.

An article in the *Kansas City Times* for Wednesday, November 15, 1939, entitled "Exploring Your Mind," by Albert Edward Wiggam, makes the following statement:

"Should engaged and young married couples be strongly warned about the dangers of divorce? No! It should be assumed from the beginning that marriage is for life and that divorce is never to be thought of. Today a good many young couples marry with the notion that if it does not prove satisfactory they can end it by divorce. But they should be taught not that divorce is dangerous—but that it is practically unthinkable and that they are entering a partnership for *time and eternity*."

A statement such as this gives credence to what previously has been said.

148

However, it is but a short step from something that appears extremely rational to something very different from the original intent. To continue a rationalization of marriage for time and eternity, we realize that during this particular period it was not uncommon for a wife to die during childbirth or for other reasons. This, of course, left the husband eligible to marry another woman. When the question of the eternity of this second marriage was considered, the same principles applied. The covenant being made was just as important as the first. When later they introduce the doctrine that the next life was to be somewhat a continuation of this life and that families would be together on the other side, we can begin to see a natural evolution. If a man was permitted to marry more than one woman while on earth and that these women would be his wives in heaven, it is only natural that they concluded that if having more than one wife was permissible in heaven, it would be just as much so on earth. Had they remained with the moral aspect of the eternity of the covenant, no harm could have arisen.

While there is not much factual evidence proving the above theory, it does give a concept that could have taken place. It is because we cannot produce any real factual evidence other than hearsay, and that hearsay evidence is given quite some time after the death of Joseph Smith, that we assume the foregoing theory. During the Prophet's lifetime the only official statements recorded to him, prove his stand against any such doctrine of polygamy or of making marriage a principle of salvation.

There is one other bit of evidence to show where the Prophet's interest was at the time of his death. While in Carthage Jail on the morning of June 27, 1844, the day he was killed, he wrote the last letter of his life to his wife Emma and his family. This letter is in the possession of the Reorganized Church in Independence, Missouri, and can be seen there. The contents of this letter are shown below:

"Carthage Jail, June 27, 1844, 30 past 8 a.m.
Dear Emma:—The Governor continues his courtesies and permits us to see our friends. We hear this morning that the Governor will not go down with his troops to-day (to Nauvoo) as was anticipated last evening; but if he does come down with his troops you will be protected; and I want you to tell Bro. Dunham to instruct the people to stay at home and attend their own business, and let there

be no groups or gathering together, unless by permission of the Governor they are called together to receive communications from the Governor, which would please our people. But let the Governor direct. Bro. Dunham, of course, will obey the orders of the government officers and render them assistance they require. There is no danger of any "exterminating order." Should there be a mutiny among the troops, (which we do not anticipate—excitement is abating,) a part will remain loyal and stand for the defense of the State and our rights. There is one principle which is eternal—it is the duty of all men to protect their lives and the lives of their households whenever necessity requires, and no power has a right to forbid it, should the last extreme arrive;— but I anticipate no such extreme. But caution is the parent of safety.

Joseph Smith.

P.S. Dear Emma:—I am very much resigned to my lot, knowing I am justified and have done the best that could be done. Give my love to the children and all my friends, Mr. Brower and all who inquire after me; and as for treason, I know that I have not committed any, and they cannot prove one appearance of anything of the kind, so you need not have any fears that any harm can happen to us on that score. May God bless you all. Amen.

Joseph Smith.

P.S.—Twenty minutes to ten.—I just learn that the Governor is about to disband his troops.—All but a guard to protect us and the peace,—and come himself to Nauvoo and deliver a speech to the people. This is right, as I suppose."

(Historian's comment: This letter we have. The signature and first postscript in Joseph's handwriting.) (RLDS Ch. Hist. Vol. 2, page 771.)

Had the prophet been involved with other women as his wives, would he not have been as much concerned with them as with his wife Emma? Would he not have sent letters to them and especially so if there were children? This information is of much more importance because Joseph Smith went to Carthage with the foreknowledge of his death. He had stated and it is so recorded in the history of both churches that "I am going like a lamb to the slaughter." It is important to remember that Emma Smith denied any

150

knowledge of the purported revelation on polygamy all during her life, and also denied the stories of her husband having more wives. She was the person most vitally concerned and her testimony should receive the utmost credence.

In order that the reader may be in a better position to understand what has been referred to above, it is necessary that some quotations be given to be compared. When section 132 is referred to, it is that purported revelation that was made public for the first time at Salt Lake City in August of 1852. Quotations from this "revelation" will be compared with what was previously given through the Prophet.

One of the first quotations is taken from the Book of Mormon:

"Behold, David and Solomon truly had many wives and concubines, *which thing was abominable* before me, saith the Lord." (Mormon B of M Jacob 2:24; RLDS B of M Jacob 2:33).

Compare this quotation with this from the first verse of section 132:

"Verily, thus saith the Lord unto you, my servant Joseph, that inasmuch as you have inquired of my hand, to know and understand wherein I, the Lord, justified my servants Abraham, Isaac and Jacob; as also Moses, David and Solomon, my servants, as touching the principle and doctrine of their having many wives and concubines." (Mormon D & C 132:1).

It is difficult to believe that God would so emphatically condemn something as abominable and then later reverse himself by justifying it.

There is a difference in the understanding about the Unpardonable Sin which can be seen by the following quotations:

"For behold, if ye deny the Holy Ghost when it once has had place in you, and ye know that ye deny it, behold, this is a sin which is unpardonable." (Mormon B of M Alma 39:6; RLDS B of M Alma 19:8).

151

Now a quotation from modern day revelations in the Doctrine and Covenants.

> "Concerning whom I have said there is no forgiveness in this world nor in the world to come; having denied the Holy Spirit, after having received it, and having denied the only begotten Son of the Father." (Mormon D & C 76:34; RLDS D & C 76:4).

Compare the above quotations with this one from section 132:

> "The blasphemy against the Holy Ghost, which shall not be forgiven in the world, nor out of the world, is in that ye commit murder, wherein ye shed innocent blood." (Mormon D & C 132:27).

We have here two different causes for the Unpardonable Sin. The Book of Mormon and the Doctrine and Covenants published by both churches, contain the above quotations and they are in harmony. The introduction of murder by shedding innocent blood is introduced in section 132 and is not in harmony with any scripture previously given.

There is another quotation from section 132 that has an unusual meaning:

> "Verily, verily I say unto you, if a man marry a wife according to my word, and they are sealed by the Holy Spirit of promise, according to mine appointment, and he or she shall commit any sin or transgression of the new and everlasting covenant whatever, and all manner of blasphemies, and if they commit no murder, wherein they shed innocent blood—yet they shall come forth in the first resurrection, and enter into their exaltation." (Mormon D & C 132:26).

The author has been unable to harmonize the philosophy contained in the above quotation with any scripture previously given in either the Bible, Book of Mormon or the Doctrine and Covenants.

Again quoting from section 132:

> "And again, as pertaining to the law of the Priesthood, if a

man espouse a virgin, and desire to expouse another, and the first shall give her consent, and if he espouse a second, and they are virgins and having vowed to no other man, then is he justified, he cannot commit adultery, for they are given unto him, for he cannot commit adultery with that which belongeth unto him and no one else." (Mormon D & C 132:61).

Without much comment we should compare the above with what had previously been given to the church. The first quotation is from the Book of Mormon:

"Behold, the Lamanites your brethren, whom ye hate because of their filthiness and the cursing which hath come upon their skins, are more righteous than you; for they have not forgotten the commandment of the Lord which was given unto our fathers—that they should have save it were one wife, and concubines they should have none, and there should not be whoredoms committed among them." (Mormon B of M Jacob 3:5; RLDS B of M Jacob 2:54).

And to quote again from the Doctrine and Covenants:

"Thou shalt love thy wife with all thy heart and shall cleave unto her and none else." (Mormon D & C 42:22; RLDS D & C 42:7).
"And again I say unto you, that whoso forbiddeth to marry is not ordained of God, for marriage is ordained of God unto man; wherefore it is lawful that he should have one wife, and they twain shall be one flesh, and all this that the earth might answer the end of its creation." (Mormon D & C 49:15,16; RLDS D & C 49:3).

On the basis of the above quotations and the historical data, we find it very difficult to justify such contradictions as containing the will of God. It does, however, prove that the major differences between the Reorganized Church and the Mormon Church are based upon teachings attributed to Joseph Smith after his death which he could neither affirm or deny. It is the view of the author that God does not do his work in this manner. He has continually advised men to avoid doing things in secret and that his word should be sent to all nations.

Because of its importance there is one other quotation that should be given so that the reader will know just how important this purported "revelation" is to those who accept it:

"For behold! I reveal unto you a new and an everlasting covenant; and if ye abide not by that covenant, then are ye damned; for no one can reject this covenant, and be permitted to enter into my glory." (Mormon D & C 132:4).

It is very apparent that the above quotation requires everyone to accept and practice those things contained in the "revelation" including marriage, either plural or singular, in order to reach Celestial Glory. It is in this quotation that we find marriage being made a doctrine of salvation, which has never been done before. The author can find no justification for this in scripture.

The Reorganized Church has never been a party to the introduction of doctrines as those being discussed, nor have they introduced any "revelations" and attributed them to the Prophet after his death. They have always accepted those things given to the church by the prophet during his life, and they also recognized a very fundamental consideration that a prophet of God can only be a prophet when God so uses and speaks through him. They do not believe that every time he speaks, it is the word of God. This position is somewhat the opposite to that of the Mormon Church. This was discussed in a previous chapter.

There is no better way to close a chapter such as this than by using the statement of Christ, when the question was put to him about what the situation would be in the hereafter relative to marriage. The story is found in the Bible, in both Matthew, Mark, and Luke in the New Testament. The quotation used here is from the story by Luke in the Inspired Version as given to the church by Joseph Smith:

"There were therefore seven brethren; the first took a wife, and died without children. And the second took her to wife, and he died childless. And the third took her in like manner; and the seven also; and they left no children, and died. And last of all the woman died also. Therefore in the resurrection, whose wife of them is she; for seven had her to wife? And Jesus answering, said unto them, the

154

children of *this world* marry and are given in marriage; but they who shall be accounted worthy to obtain that world, through resurrection from the dead, *neither marry nor are given in marriage.* " (Luke 20:29-35)

CHAPTER XIX

BAPTISM FOR THE DEAD

In approaching the analysis of the doctrine of Baptism for the Dead and the position of the two churches pertaining to it, we enter into one of the more emotional doctrines. It appeals greatly to our emotions and love for our relatives and friends and our concern for them in the hereafter. The previous chapter on marriage was also one of great emotional appeal and has greatly aided the Mormon Church in gaining converts.

To examine the history of this doctrine so far as the church is concerned, it is claimed by the Mormon Church that the doctrine was introduced to the Prophet Joseph Smith in the Kirtland Temple at the time of the appearance of Elijah. In the Mormon Doctrine and Covenants we find the following quotation which is used by them to support this conclusion:

"After this vision had closed, another great and glorious vision burst upon us, for Elijah the prophet, who was taken to heaven without tasting death, stood before us and said—Behold, the time has fully come, which was spoken of by the mouth of Malachi, testifying that he (Elijah) should be sent before the great and dreadful day of the Lord come. To turn the hearts of the fathers to the children, and the children to the fathers, lest the whole earth be smitten with a curse." (Mormon D & C 110:13)

This section is one that was added to the Doctrine and Covenants in 1876. It also appears, not as a revelation, but as an item of history in the Reorganization history. There is no specific reference to Baptism for the Dead in this experience but the statement, "the hearts of the children to the fathers" is accepted by the Mormon Church to have that implication.

The first real reference to the doctrine did not take place until the saints were in Nauvoo and about 1840 and 1841, there was talk about it but no revelation was given pertaining to how the rites were to be performed. In January of 1841, the Prophet received a revelation giving specific instructions for the building of a temple in Nauvoo. It is this revelation in which the first statements appear on baptism for the dead. These statements pertain primarily to where these baptisms can be performed. It is in this particular revelation that in "Zion and in her Stakes," and only in a house of the Lord erected for that purpose, can the rite be performed. Reading from the Doctrine and Covenants:

"For a baptismal font there is not upon the earth, that they, my saints, may be baptized for those who are dead; For this ordinance belongeth to my house, and cannot be acceptable to me only in your poverty, wherein ye are not able to build a house unto me." (Mormon D & C 124:29, 30; RLDS D & C 107:10).

For a time they did practice baptizing for the dead in the Mississippi River until the Prophet received the revelation on the temple and he ordered that the practice be stopped until it could be done in the temple. Again it should be borne in mind that no revelation specifically instructing the church to proceed had been received but the practice had started without one.

The Prophet later wrote some letters to the church containing some instructions on the doctrine but, according to his statement in these letters, they were never complete. These letters are incorporated in sections 109 and 110 in the Reorganized edition of the Doctrine and Covenants, and sections 127 and 128 in the Mormon edition. The first letter was written September 1, 1842, and the second on September 6, 1842. While these letters were never given to the church as revelations by the Prophet, he did reveal some of the inspiration he had received on the matter and therefore the letters were published in the editions of the Doctrine and Covenants after his death and both churches have allowed them to remain.

As the church progressed with the erection of the temple in Nauvoo, they erected a temporary baptismal font in the basement and then resumed the practice of baptizing for the dead. This brought on some further instructions from the prophet and we find an article in the *Millennial Star* of May 12, 1844, (a month before his death):

"We may be baptized (for our relatives or) for those whom we have much friendship for; *but it must first be revealed to the man of God, lest we should run too far.*" (*Millennial Star*, Vol. 23, 1861, p. 487)

This quotation will be given further consideration.

The practice of baptizing for the dead was stopped when the saints were driven out of Nauvoo and for the period between 1846 and the erection of the Endowment House in Salt Lake City, Utah in October of 1856, and later the erection of the temple at St. George, Utah. Since that time it has become one of the major responsibilities of the members of the church to seek out their genealogy and that of friends who have passed to the beyond. Because of this endeavor, the Mormon Church today has possibly, the most complete files and records on genealogy that can be found. Great efforts of research have been made by devout members searching old church records and cemeteries in all parts of the world, endeavoring to learn all they can of possible ancestry. All this for the purpose of finding names for whom they can be baptized. They conduct classes in genealogy in all their stakes and wards or congregations. It can certainly become very time consuming and does keep their membership active and interested, especially so if one is inclined to a knowledge of their ancestry.

It is this all-encompassing search to which the Reorganized Church does not agree. They have taken the position that the ordinance of baptism for the dead is a permissive rite and should be done only on the direction of God and in a temple which has been erected at his command.

Following is one of the experiences the Prophet Joseph Smith had in the Kirtland Temple on January 21, 1836, when he and several others met in one of the school rooms of the temple. Some marvelous visions occurred and the Prophet recorded the following quotation which is part of the narrative:

"I saw fathers Adam and Abraham, and my father and mother, my brother Alvin, who has long since slept, and wondered how it was that he had obtained an inheritance in that kingdom, seeing that he had departed this life before the Lord had set his hand to gather Israel the second time, and *had not been baptized* for the remission of sins.

Thus came the voice of the Lord unto me, saying: All who have died without a knowledge of this gospel, who would have received it if they had been permitted to tarry, shall be heirs of the celestial kingdom of our God; also all that shall die henceforth without a knowledge of it, who would have received it with all their hearts, shall be heirs of that kingdom, for I, the Lord, will judge all men according to their works, according to the desires of their hearts." (*Life of Joseph Smith* by G. Q. Cannon, page 189).

In this quotation we have one of the first used to show the fallacy of extreme genealogical research and that it may result in doing "dead works" from which the church has been warned.

One of the basic scriptures used to project the thought that baptism for the dead is essential, is the quotation from the Bible:

"Jesus answered and said unto him (Nicodemus), verily, verily, I say unto thee, except a man be born again, he cannot see the kingdom of God. Nicodemus said unto him, how can a man be born when he is old? Can he enter the second time into his mother's womb and be born? Jesus answered, verily, verily, I say unto thee, except a man be born of the water, and the spirit, he cannot enter into the kingdom of God. That which is born of the flesh, is flesh; and that which is born of the Spirit, is spirit." (John 3:3-6 I V).

This quotation does establish the necessity of baptism for those who accept Christ and is accepted by both churches.

The concern for the people who have died is not new with the Restoration movement because of the practice in the Roman Catholic Church in which masses are said for the spirits in purgatory and the many efforts on the part of loved ones left behind, giving offerings and prayers for those who have died. The text used by the Catholic Church justifying this procedure is taken from the Apocrypha and is found in II Maccabees, the twelfth chapter and starting at the forty-second verse:

"Betook themselves unto prayer, and besought him that the sin committed might wholly be put out of remembrance. Besides, that noble Judas exhorted the people

159

to keep themselves from sin, forsomuch as they saw before their eyes the things that came to pass for the sins of those that were slain. And when he had made a gathering throughout the company to the sum of two thousand drachms of silver, he sent it to Jerusalem to offer a sin-offering, doing therein very well and honestly, in that he was mindful of the resurrection for if he had not hoped that they that were slain should have risen again, it had been superfluous and vain to pray for the dead. And also in that he perceived that there was great favor laid up for those that died Godly. (It was a holy and good thought.) Whereupon he made a reconciliation for the dead, that they might be delivered from sin."

From this quotation it is shown that concern for the sins of those who have died has been in existence for a long time.

Up to this point there has been no discussion as to the eligibility of those for whom the rites of baptism for the dead are performed. To do this we should refer to the vision the Prophet had in the Kirtland Temple which was narrated above. In this vision, the Prophet saw his brother Alvin in the Celestial Glory without having been baptized and when he inquired about this, he was told;

"All who have died without a knowledge of the gospel, who would have received it if they had been permitted to tarry, shall be heirs of the Celestial kingdom of our God."

We have here an indication that baptism was not essential to Joseph's brother Alvin. A statement of this character, of course, needs additional verification and it will be our aim to give this in the following material.

The first scripture to be referred to is in the Doctrine and Covenants and the sections are the same in both editions:

"And then shall the heathen nations be redeemed, and they that knew no law shall have part in the first resurrection." (Mormon D & C 45:54; RLDS D & C 45:10).

In the Book of Mormon there are many references to this subject and for complete clarity of the position taken, it is necessary that they be quoted:

"And these are those who have part in the first resurrection; and these are they that have died before Christ came, in their ignorance, not having salvation declared unto them. And thus the Lord bringeth about the restoration of these, and they have part in the first resurrection, or have eternal life, being redeemed by the Lord." (Mormon B of M Mosiah 15:24; RLDS B of M Mosiah 8:58.)

Another quotation from the Book of Mormon:

"Wherefore, he has given a law; and where there is no law given there is no punishment; and where there is no punishment there is no condemnation; and where there is no condemnation the mercies of the Holy One of Israel have claim upon them, because of the atonement; for they are delivered by the power of him. For the atonement satisfieth the demands of his justice upon all those who have not the law given to them." (Mormon B of M II Nephi 9:25; RLDS B of M II Nephi 6:51.)

In Moroni of the Book of Mormon is the strongest statement made concerning baptism and especially so on the matter of baptizing little children and in the opinion of the author, we find the strongest evidence opposing promiscuous baptism for everyone. To quote:

"For I know that God is not a partial God, neither a changeable being; but he is unchangeable from all eternity to all eternity. Little children cannot repent; wherefore it is awful wickedness to deny the pure mercies of God unto them, for they are all alive in him because of his mercy. And he that saith that little children need baptism, denieth the mercies of Christ, and setteth at naught the atonement of him and the power of his redemption. Wo unto such, for they are in danger of death, hell and an endless torment. I speak it boldly, God hath commanded me. Listen and give heed, or they stand against you at the judgment seat of Christ. For behold that all little children are alive in Christ and also *all they that are without the law.* For the power of the redemption cometh on all they that have no law; wherefore, he that is not condemned, or he that is under no condemnation, can not repent; and unto such *baptism availeth nothing.* But it is mockery before God, denying the mercies of Christ, and the power of his Holy

161

Spirit, and putting trust in *dead works.*" (Mormon B of M Moroni 8:19; RLDS B of M Moroni 8:18.)

It is the position of both churches that when the "law" is referred to in the scriptures, it is the gospel of Christ taught with the authority of Christ. It is also the position of both churches that the authority to teach the Gospel was taken from the earth when the church, established by Christ, apostatized and departed from the true teachings, and made the Restoration a necessity. Both believe that this restoration of authority occurred when the priesthood was conferred on Joseph Smith and Oliver Cowdery in 1830. If this position is correct, then anyone dying prior to that date, certainly died without the law and are "under no condemnation" and "can not repent" and unto such "baptism availeth nothing" and would then come under the category of "dead works."

We could possibly stop here and feel that the doctrine of baptism for the dead had been proven as unnecessary, but this is not so. There are other factors to be considered in which the doctrine can have a legitimate bearing. These are to be considered.

It is and always has been the position of both churches that the Gospel of Christ was also the same as that which was taught to Adam. The prophets that succeeded him, such as Abraham, Enoch and others, including Noah, taught the same doctrine. On the basis of this belief, we realize that the earth has not been without the law for several periods of time. We are going to specifically refer to the period of Noah. It is believed he taught the Gospel and warned the people, if they did not accept, they would be punished and perish in the flood. The reason for referring to this period is contained in the quotation from the Bible:

"For which cause also, he went and preached unto the spirits in prison; Some of whom were disobedient in the days of Noah, while the long-suffering of God wained, while the ark was preparing, wherein few, that is, eight souls were saved by water." (I Peter 3:19,20 IV).

According to the belief of the churches, those who had the opportunity to learn of the gospel but did not accept it, will go to the prison house and again be given an opportunity to hear again the message which is so vital. It is the belief of many that men, who were valiant in this life, bringing souls

162

to an understanding of the gospel, will continue to preach to the spirits in prison and carry the message of Christ to them. It is because of this, there is a place for the doctrine of salvation for the dead. Being a permissive rite and one only practiced in a temple provided under the direction of God, there must, of necessity, be limitations and we find these expressed by the Prophet in an earlier quotation taken from the *Millennial Star*:

"We may be baptized (for our relatives or) for those whom we have much friendship for; but *it must first be revealed to the man of God*, lest we run too far." (*Millennial Star*, Vol. 23, 1861, p. 487).

It is the belief of the author that baptism for the dead can be practiced by the church providing it fulfills all of the above requirements. (1) It must be in Zion or one of her stakes. (2) It must be in the house of the Lord, built according to his direction and command. (3) It must be done by way of revelation to the church so that the work that is done, will be directed by God.

To summarize this chapter we find one of the major differences between the two churches. The Reorganized Church believes but does not practice the doctrine and is waiting for further revelations before they can proceed. The Mormon Church has gone to the other extreme and have not waited upon the Lord to direct the building of a temple and do not wait for the revelation from God instructing them for whom the rite should be performed. Inasmuch as the gospel authority was not restored to earth until 1830, those who died prior to that time, died without the law. The Mormon Church is baptizing for everyone of the ancestors that can be traced, regardless of the time of death and as a result, are doing that which the Book of Mormon says:

"Unto such baptism availeth nothing. But it is a mockery before God ... and putting trust in dead works." (Mormon B of M Moroni 8:19; RLDS B of M Moroni 8:27).

If the reader desires further information on this subject, particularly in reference to either church's position, it can be secured. There is a pamphlet titled "Baptism for the Dead" prepared by Charles F. Hield and Russell F. Ralston of the

Reorganized Church, which presents their view in detail. A pamphlet by Joseph Fielding Smith of the Mormon Church and titled "The Reorganization *vs.* Salvation for the Dead" outlines their position.

CHAPTER XX

TITHING

A study of tithing as a principle of the church enters into one of the more sensitive areas because it affects the individual in a closer physical contact than most principles. It touches a man's pocket-book and his temporal needs and wants and in many ways, affects his way of life. It is also one of the most rewarding acts a man can perform when done in the spirit of working and giving to God and to those of his creation that are in need.

During the first years of the church, the only concern was the gathering of the Saints to the places designated, namely; Independence, Missouri and Kirtland, Ohio. The temporal law in effect in those days was known as the law of Consecration and we find reference to this in the Doctrine and Covenants of both churches. This law of consecration called upon those who had joined the church, and desired to settle in one of the above locations, to consecrate all of their property into the hands of the bishop of the church. The bishop had been instructed to purchase land in the areas to be settled and from this land, inheritances were to be given to those who had consecrated to the bishop. Reading from the Doctrine and Covenants:

"And it shall come to pass that after they are laid before the bishop of my church, and after that he has received these testimonies concerning the consecration of the properties of my church, that they can not be taken from the church, agreeable to my commandments; every man shall be made accountable unto me, a steward over his own property, or that which he has received by consecration, inasmuch as is sufficient for himself and family. And again, if there shall be properties in the hands of the church, or any individuals of it, more than is necessary for their support, after this first consecration, which is a residue, to be consecrated unto the bishop, it shall be kept to administer unto those who have not, from time to time, that every man who has need may be amply supplied, and receive according to his wants. Therefore, the residue shall be kept in my storehouse, to administer to the poor and the needy, as shall be appointed by the high council of the church, and the bishop and his council, and for the purpose of purchasing lands for the public benefit of the church, and building houses of worship, and building up of the New Jerusalem which is hereafter to be revealed, that my covenant people may be gathered in one, in that day when I shall come to my temple. And this I do for the salvation of my people." (Mormon D & C 42:32-36; RLDS D & C 42:9, 10).

Another quotation from the same source:

"And if thou obtainest more than that which would be for thy support, thou shalt give it unto my storehouse, that all things may be done according to that which I have said." (Mormon D & C 42:35; RLDS D & C 42:14).

A very significant statement is made in section forty-nine of the Doctrine and Covenants:

". . . and that he might have in abundance, but it is not given that one man should possess that which is above another; wherefore the world lieth in sin." (Mormon D & C 49:19, 20; RLDS D & C 49:3).

To be fully aware of the teachings of the early church it is necessary that a considerable number of quotations be made and while many may be familiar, it is necessary, for the clarity of what is being written, that these be made. In section fifty-one, given in May of 1831, appears this statement:

"Hearken unto me, saith the Lord your God, and I will speak unto my servant Edward Partridge, (bishop) and give unto him directions; for it must needs be that he receive directions how to organize this people, for it must needs be that they are organized according to my laws, if otherwise, they will be cut off; wherefore let my servant Edward Partridge, and those whom he has chosen, in whom I am well pleased, appoint unto this people their portion, every man equal according to their families, according to their circumstances, and their wants and needs; and let my servant Edward Partridge, when he shall appoint a man his portion, give him a writing that shall secure unto him his portion, that he shall hold it, even this inheritance in the church, until he transgresses and is not accounted worthy by the voice of the church, according to the laws and covenants of the church, to belong to the church; and if he transgresses, and is not accounted worthy to belong in the church, he shall not have power to claim that portion which he has consecrated unto the bishop for the poor and the needy of my church; therefore he shall not retain the gift, but shall only have claim on that portion that is deeded unto him. And thus all things shall be made sure according to the laws of the land." (Mormon D & C 51:1-6; RLDS D & C 51:1).

Again in April of 1832, another revelation was given to the church which adds much to the understanding of the early teachings. It reads:

". . . for Zion must increase in beauty, and in holiness; her borders must be enlarged; her stakes must be strengthened; yes, verily I say unto you, Zion must arise and put on her beautiful garments; therefore, I give unto you this commandment, that ye bind yourselves by this covenant, and it shall be done according to the laws of the Lord. Behold, here is wisdom, also, in me, for your good. And you are to be equal, or in other words, you are to have equal claims on the properties, for the benefit of managing the concerns of your stewardships, every man according to his wants and his needs, inasmuch as his wants are just: and all this for the benefit of the church of the living God, that every man may improve upon his talent, that every man may gain other talents, yea, even an hundredfold, to be cast into the Lord's storehouse, to become the common property of the whole church, every man seeking the interest of his neighbor, and doing all things with an eye single to the glory of God." (RLDS D & C 81:4; Mormon D & C 82:14-19).

From the above quotation we learn that the early church was somewhat communal in its purpose and if proposed in this day of the twentieth century would be labeled communistic in its intent. Its major purpose was to be concerned about the welfare of the members and to see that no one had more than they needed while others were in need. This

167

philosophy conforms with the statement of Christ:"Thou shalt love thy neighbor as thyself."

It should also be remembered that the above instructions were given to a primarily agrarian people and pertained to the establishment of an agrarian society. It was much more possible for them to accomplish this, at the time in which they lived, than it would be today in our highly industrialized society. This is another of the Utopian ideals that man is always philosophizing about, but will not strive to obtain.

It was due to the cohesiveness this type of society developes that brought upon the early members, the antagonism of their neighbors and finally led to their expulsion from Jackson County, and later from Far West and again from Nauvoo. This is not to imply that the communal type of organization was in effect at Nauvoo. However, as a political group, they were very cohesive.

After the saints were driven from Independence and were no longer in a position to carry out the instructions they had received as shown above, new problems began to arise relative to raising the necessary funds for operating as a church. On the 29th of November, 1834, Joseph Smith and Oliver Cowdery made a covenant which introduced for the first time, the tithing to be paid. This covenant is well worth quoting:

"On the evening of the 29th of November, I united in prayer with Brother Oliver, for the continuance of blessings. After giving thanks for the relief which the Lord had lately sent us by opening the hearts of the brethren from the east, to loan us four hundred and thirty dollars; after commencing and rejoicing before the Lord on this occasion, we agreed to enter into the following covenant with the Lord: *viz:*—"That if the Lord will prosper us in our business, and open the way before us, that we may obtain means to pay our debts, that we be not troubled nor brought into disrepute before the world, nor his people; after that, *of all that he shall give us, we will give a tenth*, to be bestowed upon the poor in his church, or as he shall command; and that we will be faithful over that which he has intrusted to our care, that we may obtain much; and that our children after us, shall remember to observe this sacred and holy covenant; and that our children, and our children's children, may know of the same, we have subscribed our names with our own hands.' " (RLDS Ch. Hist. Vol. 1, p. 529).

Due to the confusion that arose after the expulsion and the settling in the new areas, the saints were not aware of what was required of them in giving support to the church and its needs. This confusion led the Prophet to seek from God, some clarification on the matter and as a result, the revelation on tithing was given to the church. To be completely fair in making an analysis, the entire revelation should be quoted, to give the reader an opportunity to draw a conclusion. This revelation is as follows:

"In answer to the question, O Lord, show unto thy servants how much thou requirest of the properties of thy people for a tithing? Verily, thus saith the Lord, I require all their surplus property to be put into the hands of the bishop of my church of Zion, for the building of mine house, and for the laying the foundation of Zion, and for the priesthood, and for the debts of the presidency of my church; and this shall be the beginning of the tithing of my people; and after that, those who have thus been tithed, *shall pay one tenth of all their interest annually*; and this shall be a standing law unto them forever, for my holy priesthood, saith the Lord. Verily I say unto you, it shall come to pass that all those who gather unto the land of Zion shall be tithed of their surplus properties, and shall observe this law, or they shall not be found worthy to abide among you. And I say unto you, if my people observe not this law, to keep it holy, and by this law sanctify the land of Zion unto me, that my statutes and my judgments may be kept thereon, that it may be most holy, behold, verily I say unto you, it shall not be a land of Zion unto you; and this shall be an ensample unto all the stakes of Zion. Even so, Amen." (RLDS D & C 106; Mormon D & C 119).

This revelation was given to the church on July 8, 1838. It is apparent in this revelation that there is a departure from the full consecration of property to the church and in turn receiving of an inheritance. Because of this, it has sometimes been thought that the above revelation is a substitute law for that which was previously given. It has been felt that there is a similarity in the events surrounding Moses when he went to

169

the mountain and received the Law on tablets of stone. When he returned to the children of Israel, he found them worshiping the golden calf and became so enraged that he tossed them to the ground and they were broken. He then returned to the mountain and received the Ten Commandments, which became the law unto the Israelites. They were a substitute law for what was originally given. This same applies to the law of tithing as given above, it is a substitute for the original law of consecration.

Nevertheless, this revelation became the basis on which all interpretations of the tithing law are made. It is from this revelation that we shall compare the two churches and their interpretations. The most controversial part is in the definition of the word "interest" as it is used in the revelation.

To understand the Prophet's use of the term "interest," we refer back to the quotation from church history and the covenant made by him and Oliver Cowdery: ". . . of all that he shall give us, we will give a tenth. . . ." This statement can easily be accepted as all "income." There are many definitions that can be given to the word "interest" such as concern, or attention to, or a return on money invested, and also an increase on net worth. In the opinion of the author, the term "interest" as used in the revelation pertains to the entire interest of the individual, whether it is income from a position, or the profits from a business enterprise. In fact, anything pertaining to the welfare of the individual is his interest. From these definitions, we feel that the best definition of the term used by the Prophet would be "income" rather than the word increase. To substantiate this opinion we quote from church history as follows:

"Therefore, as soon as the Twelve have proceeded to a full and complete organization of the branches abroad, let every member proceed immediately to tithe himself or herself, a tenth of all their property and money, and pay it into the hands of the Twelve, or into the hands of such bishops as have been or shall be appointed by them to receive the same, for the building of the temple or the support of the priesthood, according to the scriptures and the revelations of God; and then let them continue to pay a tenth of their *income* from that time forth; for this is a law unto this church as much binding on their conscience as any other law or ordinance." (RLDS Ch. Hist. Vol. 3, p. 15).

170

This quotation is from an epistle of the Twelve to the church dated August 15, 1844 at Nauvoo, Illinois. This is just two months after the death of the Prophet and followed the acceptance of the Twelve as the leaders of the church in Nauvoo. It is the opinion of the author that the time was too short between the death of the Prophet and the issuance of this epistle to enact a different interpretation of the law other than that held by the Prophet.

In the *Times and Seasons* of July 14, 1845, is another quotation;

"While upon this subject we would remind the brethren of their duty in tithing according to the laws, and commandments given through Joseph the prophet, it is the duty of all saints to tithe themselves one tenth of all they possess when they enter into the new and everlasting covenant; and then one tenth of their interest, or income, yearly afterwards." (T & S Vol. 6, p. 780).

In this quotation and the one preceding we have something introduced that is not exactly as stated in the revelation. We refer to the statement of tithing "themselves one tenth of all they possess." Refer back to the revelation and read the first statement:

"Verily, thus saith the Lord, require *all* their surplus property." Not one tenth as shown above. In this interpretation, both churches appear to be in error. Both churches accept the statement above of tithing one tenth of their surplus when entering the church but differ on the interpretation of the word "interest."

The Mormon Church now teaches the temporal law in line with what has been quoted above. Their method is to tithe the membership one tenth of their income annually. Very little is done pertaining to the surplus. This is left optional with the member. To more clearly state the position of the Mormon Church, a quotation from a book by Dr. James E. Talmadge is given:

"The law of tithing, as accepted and professedly observed by the church today, is after all but a lesser law, given by the Lord in consequence of the human weaknesses, selfishness, covetousness, and greed, which prevented the Saints from accepting the high principles, according to which the Father would have his children live. Specific requirements regarding the payment of tithes were made through revelation in 1838; but seven years prior to that time, the voice of the Lord had been heard on the subject of consecration, or the dedication of all one's property, together with his time, talents, and natural endowments, to the service of God, to be used as occasion may require." (Articles of Faith, page 449).

This statement is in harmony with the author's previous statement. It has not been mentioned, however, that in return for the consecration of his property, the individual then became a steward in the church and was to receive his "just wants and needs" as a responsibility of the church.

With the interpretation as done in the Mormon Church, tithing as a principle, has been simplified and each member, without the need of keeping accounts, is well aware of his obligation to the church.

The system adopted by the Mormon Church has led to a very satisfactory condition for the church financially. By wisely using the funds received, they have been able to establish some very successful business enterprises which add greatly to the annual income of the church. The author has been advised by authorities of the church that when a local congregation or ward, is in need of a meeting house or place of worship, the general church contributes sixty or more percent of the necessary funds and the remaining is raised by the local group. They do not, however, wait for the local fund to be raised before the church makes its contribution. In fact, construction of the building is commenced as soon as possible and in so doing, provides facilities for the congregation to grow and function. This puts them in a much better position to raise funds for their obligation.

It is also a practice of the Mormon Church for the bishop of the ward to forward all tithes collected, to the Presiding Bishop of the church and that approximately sixty-five percent of the ward's budget expenses, are returned to the ward by the presiding bishop. There is no distinction between local funds and the general church funds as such. They do, however, have special offerings, oblation or fast offerings that are separate from tithing; these are all made voluntarily.

A very distinctive feature in the Mormon Church is the practice of not passing a collection plate during a service. One can attend services at any of their wards and will never be asked to make a contribution while there. Every member is expected to visit with the bishop of his ward or the ward clerk and pay his tithing at that time. When he does this, the only question that is asked is whether or not the amount being paid is complete or partial and the bishop so records. The matter is left entirely to the individual and his responsibility to God.

The Reorganized Church has had a much more serious problem due to the interpretation of the tithing law other than that of the Mormon Church. Early in the beginning the Reorganization followed the pattern of the early church and more or less accepted the principle of ten percent of income. To properly place the position of the Reorganization in this respect, we shall quote from volume three of the church history:

"While we regard a tenth as what the Lord requires, we also recognize the right and duty of all who tithe themselves to exercise a prayerful watchcare over its uses, that all may be done agreeably to the will of the Lord. Those who possess nothing beyond the needs of their families, can have no surplus; and as this is the beginning of the tithing required by that law, such cannot strictly be regarded as subjects of the law of tithing. And such as have over and above, or a surplus, of them the Lord requires this surplus, which the Lord calls a tithing, or tenth." (RLDS Ch. Hist. Vol. 3, p. 472).
"Yet the present necessities of the work do require a portion of tithing and consecrations, and we believe that the tithing now required is one tenth of the properties of all who possess a surplus; afterward, one tenth of their annual interest annually." (*Ibid.* p. 474.)

The first quotation is from an epistle of the Twelve dated April 8, 1867. The second is also from the Twelve and is signed by Jason W. Briggs, president and is of the same date.

At a council of the authorities of the church at Plano, Illinois, on May 6, 1872, the following items were adopted among other statements. We will not quote all of the items but those we feel pertinent to the discussion:

"That it is imperative and important that the law of tithing be taught as *tithing*, by the local and traveling ministry including the bishopric. That the principle of consecration, donation, and freewill offering, should be taught as distinc-

173

tive and separate from the law of tithing, by the local and traveling ministry. That any member of the church can tithe himself in accordance with the law whatever may be their temporal condition. That tithing means a tenth, and applies to all persons who have made a consecration of whatever they may have deemed a surplus;—surplus being construed to signify, in this case, that portion of property and money which a member of the church may feel that he can and will spare as a first consecration out of his or her possessions; this tenth required being but the one tenth of the yearly *increase* after such surplus has been given." (RLDS Ch. Hist. Vol. 3, pp 699, 670).

In this quotation we have one of the first uses of the word "increase" in the place of interest.

As the Reorganization developed and grew larger, the controversy on the interpretation of the word "interest" also grew and, because of the animosity toward the Mormon Church and its practices, a desire to do things differently to avoid being associated with the Mormon Church in the minds of the people, the interpretation of "interest" to "increase" became more and more general. However, much controversy continued in the church until it was necessary that instruction from God be given to the church, and this came in a revelation dated April 18, 1909, and is in the Doctrine and Covenants and from which is quoted:

"The attention of the church is called to the consideration of the revelation, (Sec. 106) given in answer to earnest supplication, with regard to temporal things. The word has been already given in agreement with revelation long since delivered to the church, that the temporalities of the church were to be under the charge and care of the bishopric, men holding the office of bishop under a presiding head acting for the church in the gathering, caring for, and disbursing the contributions gathered from the saints of moneys and properties under the terms of tithing, surplus, freewill offerings, and consecrations. The word which has been given at a late period should not have been so soon forgotten and disregarded by the church or any of its members. 'I am God; I change not;' has been known to the church. . . . The church has been directed to accede to the rendition of the bishopric with respect to the temporal law; and until such heed is paid to the word which has

174

been given, and is in accordance with other revelations given to the church, which had been before given, the church can not receive and enjoy the blessings which have been looked for when Zion should be fully redeemed." (RLDS D & C 129:8).

As a result of the above revelation, the Reorganized Church officially adopted the interpretation of the word "interest" in the revelation of 1838, to mean the annual increase of the member. To properly discern what a member's increase would be, it becomes necessary to keep records of income and expenditures. With the interpretation of increase, the allowance of just wants and needs was taken into consideration and it was felt in the Reorganization that the necessities of life were not subject to tithe. Only that which remained after living expenses were taken out, was to be tithed. This then became the tithe of the increase or one tenth of what was left.

The evolvement of this interpretation required the member to present a statement of his net worth each year to the bishop, in order to verify how much his net worth increased or decreased. As a result, regular forms have been prepared and have been made as simple as possible to enable each member to render an accounting of what is now termed, "his stewardship." For many years the filing of tithing statements was more or less optional with the member and is still so. However, in recent years a policy has been adopted by the leaders of the church in council, that future ordinations of men to the priesthood would be subject to the acceptance and compliance with this portion of the financial law. There is also beginning, an effort to teach prospective members the principle of tithing that will enable them to understand and fulfill the requirements from the time of baptism into the church. Many of the new converts are thus rendering their financial statements at the time of their baptism. This is not to be considered as a compulsory requirement.

There is another development in the Reorganization that the writer feels is not according to the law of tithing. This is the separation of the contributions to the local congregations from those to the general church. Only those funds sent to the general church are now considered tithing and that which is contributed locally for the upkeep of the local congregation is now designated as offering. There is no revelation or

175

law that authorizes this distinction. It is the opinion of the author that all funds contributed for the advancement of the church, either locally or on a world-wide basis, come under the law as tithing and should so be considered. Special offerings or donations for specific purposes are different and are not to be used for any purpose other than that so designated.

The above interpretation raises some very serious problems within the church. When a member files a statement and learns from that statement that a large sum of money is due as tithing, the natural inclination is to pay that sum, because it is considered the most important obligation. In the desire to pay off this obligation there will be a tendency to neglect the contributions locally made because these are considered as offerings and are not recognized as important as the tithing. Another factor is also involved due to the fact that when filing a statement, only just wants and needs are deducted and this does not include offerings. Therefore, offerings made to a local congregation, not being a just want or need, are subject to being tithed inasmuch as they are part of the increase.

Previously outlined was the use of tithing as practiced in the Mormon Church and it is different from the policy as followed by the Reorganization. Where approximately 65% of the local congregation's budget is returned to them by the general church, within the Reorganization, none of that which is paid as tithing is returned to the local group. When the need for buildings arise, it is necessary for the group to secure a location and then raise sufficient funds equal to 50% of the cost of the building. The general church will then loan the congregation, an equal amount which is to be paid back over a period of years. By following the procedure, the building of houses of worship proceeds much slower in the Reorganization than in the Mormon Church.

The Reorganized Church, in following their interpretation of the tithing law, have never been an affluent organization and for many years, suffered greatly for the lack of funds. It has only been since World War II, that the church has reached a position where it can be free of debt and has been able to complete the magnificent auditorium building in Independence, Missouri. The extent to which the membership of the church participate in the filing of statements, is of interest and should show the true acceptance of this interpretation of the tithing law. To secure the percentage of the membership

176

filing statements, the conference reports for the 1966 World Conference were used. From the statistician's report, we learn that 20.79% of the membership of the church were filers. This figure would indicate that many of the contributors to the church, do so without filing statements.

Because there are no published statements as to the number or percentage of the members of the Mormon Church that pay tithing, there is no basis on which a comparison in this matter can be made.

CHAPTER XXI

WORD OF WISDOM

On February 27, 1833, there was given to the church one of the most interesting and meaningful revelations received by the Prophet Joseph Smith. This revelation is known as the "Word of Wisdom." To start this chapter and to be in a position to compare the attitudes of the two churches, it is necessary that the revelation in its entirety should be given. The author is fortunate in having available a copy of an excellent book written by Doctor John A. Widtsoe and his wife Leah Widtsoe on the subject of the Word of Wisdom, and from this book we are copying the revelation. It is identical with the revelation as it appears in the Doctrine and Covenants. It is known as section 89 in the Mormon edition and section 86 in the Reorganized edition and the wording is identical. It is being quoted as it appears in the book written by Dr. Widtsoe:

"INTRODUCTION
1. A Word of Wisdom, for the benefit of the council of high priests, assembled in Kirtland, and the church, and also the saints in Zion—
2. To be sent greeting; not by commandment or constraint, but by revelation and the word of wisdom, showing forth the order and will of God in the temporal salvation of all saints in the last days—
3. Given for a principle with promise, adapted to the capacity of the weak and the weakest of all saints, who are or can be called saints.
4. Behold, verily, thus saith the Lord unto you: In consequence of evils and designs which do and will exist in the hearts of conspiring men in the last days, I have warned you, and forewarn you, by giving unto you this word of wisdom by revelation—

NEGATIVE HEALTH FACTORS
5. That inasmuch as any man drinketh wine or strong drink among you, behold it is not good, neither meet in

the sight of your Father, only in assembling yourselves together to offer up your sacraments before him.

6. And, behold, this should be wine, yea, pure wine of the grape of the vine, of your own make.

7. And, again, strong drinks are not for the belly, but for the washing of your bodies.

8. And again, tobacco is not for the body, neither for the belly, and is not good for man, but is an herb for bruises and all sick cattle, to be used with judgment and skill.

9. And again, hot drinks are not for the body or belly.

POSITIVE HEALTH FACTORS

10. And again, verily I say unto you, all wholesome herbs God hath ordained for the constitution, nature, and use of man—

11. Every herb in the season thereof; and every fruit in the season thereof; all these to be used with prudence and thanksgiving.

12. Yea, flesh also of beasts and of the fowls of the air, I, the Lord, have ordained for the use of man with thanksgiving; nevertheless they are to be used sparingly;

13. And it is pleasing unto me that they should not be used, only in time of winter, or of cold, or famine.

14. All grain is ordained for the use of man and of beasts, to be the staff of life, not only for man but for the beasts of the field, and the fowls of heaven, and all wild animals that run or creep on the earth;

15. And these hath God made for the use of man only in times of famine and excess of hunger.

16. All grain is good for the food of man; as also the fruit of the vine; that which yieldeth fruit, whether in the ground or above the ground—

17. Nevertheless, wheat for man, and corn for the ox, and oats for the horse, and rye for the fowls and for swine, and for all beasts of the field, and barley for all useful animals, and for mild drinks, as also other grain.

REWARDS

18. And all saints who remember to keep and do these sayings, walking in obedience to the commandments, shall receive health in their navel and marrow to their bones;

19. And shall find wisdom and great treasures of knowledge, even hidden treasures;

20. And shall run and not be weary, and shall walk and not faint.

21. And I, the Lord, give unto them a promise, that the destroying angel shall pass by them, as the children of Israel, and not slay them. Amen."

In the light of modern day knowledge pertaining to food and diets and also of the effects of indulgence of the use of tobacco and strong drinks, or alcoholic beverages, a very deep appreciation of the above revelation should be in the hearts of all Latter Day Saints, regardless of which faction they belong to. However, in spite of the clarity of this revelation, we find differences between the two churches pertaining to its acceptance.

The Mormon Church, even though the revelation states, ". . . not by commandment or constraint," have made obedience to the revelation one of their requirements for a member to be in good standing. They believe that inasmuch as God felt the need to warn the church, it is incumbent upon the church to heed these instructions with as much concern as any other instructions that have been received. In this attitude they are supported by actions taken in the early church. In Doctor Widtsoe's book he shows a photo copy of minutes of a High Council meeting in Kirtland, Ohio, on February 20, 1834, and it reads:

"The council then proceeded to try the question, whether disobedience to the *word* of wisdom was a transgression sufficient to deprive an official member from holding an office in the church, after having it sufficiently taught him? Counsellors Samuel H. Smith, Luke Johnson, John S. Carter, Sylvester Smith, John Johnson, and Orson Hyde, were called to speak upon the case then before the council. After the counsellors had spoken, the president proceeded to give a decision:—That no official member in this church is worthy to hold an office, after having the words of wisdom properly taught him, and he, the official member neglecting to comply with or obey them: which decision, the council confirmed by vote." (*Word of Wisdom* by Widtsoe, page 27.)

The above quotation very clearly shows the attitude of the early leaders about the importance of the revelation. It upholds the position of the Mormon Church in making it a basic requirement of a member to be in good standing. The major difference between the churches on this subject is the question of whether or not the statement: "not by commandment or constraint" should be considered a commandment.

The one portion of the revelation that seems to have created the most controversy among the members of both churches is found in verse 9 and is as follows: "And again, hot drinks are not for the body or the belly." There has been some reluctance in accepting the fact this statement referred to tea and coffee. Inasmuch that the only hot drinks that are consumed by man are tea, coffee, cocoa, hot toddies and hot soups, there should be no question as to the intent of the revelation. Therefore, to properly conform to the Lord's advice, these hot drinks should not be consumed. Many will take exception to the mention of soups and justifiably so, because the injurious contents in tea and coffee are not present in soups and the only real danger from the consumption of them would be the heat factor. Therefore, the real intent of this verse pertains primarily to those beverages that contain deleterious factors.

The Reorganized Church accepts the word of wisdom as it was given and does interpret its contents the same as in the Mormon Church. They, however, have not stressed the need for fully complying because the initial statement, "not by commandment or constraint," made it primarily a personal matter between the individual and God. They have made an official statement against the use of tobacco and strong (intoxicating) drinks and will not ordain men to the priesthood if they are users of either.

The author has, at various times, been confronted with the query from members of the Mormon Church relative to the Reorganized Church's attitude to the word of wisdom and if we considered it the word of God. The answer always being in the affirmative, the next question is:

"Why then do we see your church officials drinking coffee or tea at public functions, when they know they are violating God's wishes?"

This is something that can only be answered by the individual committing the act and it is not the prerogative of the author to pass judgment. However, it is something that deserves some very serious consideration by all believers in the revealed word of God.

CHAPTER XXII

WELFARE PROGRAMS

Of all the instructions given to the church, particularly during its early period, nothing has been more constantly emphasized than the concern for the poor and needy within the church. This was also one of the primary concerns of Christ while he was upon the earth. A comparison of the two churches and their response to this ever growing problem should be of the utmost interest to anyone interested in either church or, this major social problem. There is much that could be written about this, but it is also a problem as to how much and to whom this information should be given. No church desires to have people become interested in its organization based upon a desire to secure financial stability. It is very possible that this condition existed in the early church, because of its early teaching about a Zionic Community.

We have previously discussed the early program of the church in the chapter on tithing and learned of the plans to share equally in the consecrations made to the church. This philosophy being taught could have been responsible for some joining the church, not because of their desire to serve God, but for a haven of economic security. This could then account for the lack of depth in the convictions of some early members of the church.

It is possible for the above reason that whenever attempts are made to secure literature from either of the churches, they are reluctant to release it publicly. The matter has been discussed with many different people both in and out of the two churches. Close acquaintance has existed between the author and one of the men directing one phase of the Deseret Industries in Salt Lake City, which is a part of the Welfare Program of the Mormon Church. There has also been available a course of study of the Welfare Plan written by Albert T. Bowen, which is very enlightening of the church program as it exists throughout the church.

In section forty-two (both church editions) of the Doctrine and Covenants are the basic instructions pertaining to the church and its temporal concerns and also in this section are the instructions that are to be the foundation of any welfare program. This quotation was used in the chapter on tithing but should again be used when considering the welfare program of the church:

> "And again, if there shall be properties in the hands of the church, or any individuals of it, more than is necessary for their support, after this first consecration, which is a residue, to be consecrated unto the bishop, it shall be kept to administer unto those who have not, from time to time, that every man who has need may be amply supplied, and received according to his wants. Therefore, the residue shall be kept in my storehouse, to administer to the poor and needy, as shall be appointed by the high council of the church. . . ." (Mormon D & C 42:33-36; RLDS D & C 42:10.)

This quotation points out the responsibility of caring for the poor and needy and the purpose for a storehouse. Instructions to the church were given many times following this pertaining to both factors. The storehouse is to become a very important part of the church and its philosophy.

There is another quotation to be used when discussing this program and it is also from section forty-two.

> "Thou shalt not be idle; for he that is idle shall not eat the bread nor wear the garments of the laborer." (Mormon D & C 42:42; RLDS D & C 42:12.)

This quotation should constantly be kept in mind because it is the underlying foundation of any successful welfare program. This is especially true pertaining to the Welfare Program of the Mormon Church. A condensed history of the beginning of this program is of interest and is presented for the benefit of the reader.

In the early years of the Great Depression that followed the market crash of 1929, the church began to be concerned about the welfare of their membership and conducted an extensive survey and investigation. Quoting from *The Church Welfare Plan* by Albert E. Bowen, on page 27, appears the following statement:

> "Of particular concern was the revelation that either through their own reticence to make their conditions

known to the bishops, or through lack of aggressiveness on the part of local church authorities in ferreting out instances of distress or through a preference for help from public agencies, or perhaps from a combination of all these, many church members were receiving relief through public funds."

This disturbed the authorities and at the April Conference of 1935, the stake presidents and ward bishops were requested to bring their 1933 survey and report up-to-date before the Fall Conference. As a result of these reports, at the April Conference of 1936, the church presidency issued a message formally launching the Church-wide and centrally directed welfare plan. Church officials then visited and canvassed the various stakes and missions to instill in them an awareness of the problem confronting the church and its needs. Again quoting from Albert Bowen on page thirty:

"So prompt and generous was the response of the people that at the opening of the October Conference of 1936, the president of the church was able to announce that 98 stakes out of a total of 117 had completed their surveys and filed their reports. These showed that 83% of the reporting stakes were able to provide for all their needy members during the coming winter. The deficiencies in other stakes were readily supplied from surpluses in the more favored ones."

The implementation of the above among the membership resulted in a great deal of very favorable publicity throughout the nation during a period when so many were seeking aid from the government. In the April 1964 issue of *Fortune*, there is an article on Mormonism and from this article by Seymour Freedgood we quote:

"The church through its welfare program has for years been doing something about poverty, and takes care of its own in a way no federal-government bureau can possibly duplicate."

The Welfare Program is operated under the direction of the First Presidency through a general committee that oversees all of the activities throughout the world. Under the General Welfare Committee there are sub-committees for Finance,

Correlation, Building, Agriculture, Industries and Projects, Processing, Clothing, Cooperatives, Storage, Storehouses, and perhaps some others. All service on these committees is voluntary and unpaid except for a few key men whose whole time is required for the work. Some of the compensated workers are recruited from among those who, through age or accident or infirmity, cannot get employment in regular commercial channels, and who, but for the Welfare Program, would be subjects of charitable support, though possessed often of rare ability and fine skills.

Each of the sub-committees mentioned above have been responsible in the area assigned for the development of that phase of the Welfare Plan. For example, the sub-committee on processing was responsible for the development of canneries and other processing facilities as needed. Storehouses were developed by the sub-committee on this project and there are now many of these throughout the nation. There are storage places where the exchange of commodities from one area to another are provided for and can be a place of distribution. The country has been divided into regions and regional executive councils have been set up which are comprised of the stake presidents within the region.

In the stake organization there is a welfare committee which is usually supervised by a member of the stake presidency. There is also a stake work director, the chairman of the bishop's executive council, the Relief Society president, the Stake Relief Society Work Director, the adult Aaronic priesthood representative and the chairman of the stake agricultural committee. This committee coordinates all of the welfare activities of all the wards within the stake.

Within the ward or local congregation, there is also a committee responsible for the development of the welfare program on the local level. This committee is comprised of the ward bishopric, ward work director, a representative of the High Priests, Seventies, Elders, Adult supervisor of the Aaronic Priesthood, the Relief Society president and the Relief Society Work Director. It is in this local organization that much of the program begins, such as collecting furniture, clothing and foods for processing, etc.

The implementation of the welfare program began shortly after the declaration made by the president of the church during the depression. At a time when the nation as a whole, under the direction of the federal government, were plowing under corn and other crops, killing off hogs in order to create an artificial shortage to increase food prices, the various stakes and wards began getting the permission from land owners to cultivate all the vacant ground available. This was done through the various priesthood quorums and also men of the wards that did not belong to the priesthood. Men made idle by the closing of industries, were given an opportunity to assist in the production of their needs and in turn, were permitted to share in the production as needed. Inasmuch as what was produced did not enter into the public market, it did not add to the dilemma facing the federal government but did begin to relieve the government of the cost of sustaining those who were participating. As the members began to realize the importance of what they were doing, the program grew by leaps and bounds. As the raw products were produced, it became necessary to set up the processing facilities for preserving and distribution in usable form. As the program grew, they began the purchase of unused land wherever possible to set up stake farms, sites for storehouses, manufacturing units, etc. It is of interest to note that the church now owns farms in the vicinity of Washington, D.C., Detroit, Michigan, a 320,000 acre ranch near Orlando, Florida on which large herds of cattle are raised. They own several large orange groves both in Florida and California, sugar beet fields in many western states. In fact, the Welfare Organization now has well over $50,000,000 in assets represented by the above holdings. It is easy to see they are well equipped to care for their own.

With all that has been stated above, it may sound to some that here is a haven of plenty and they may be tempted to desire a share. This brings us back to the quotation mentioned earlier in the chapter from the Doctrine and Covenants:

"Thou shalt not be idle; for he that is idle shall not eat the bread nor wear the garments of the laborer." (Mormon D & C 42:42; RLDS D & C 42:12.)

This is very strictly adhered to by the church. An illustration is given in Albert E. Bowen's book and it is as follows:

"A forty-year-old veteran of World War I bought a small farm upon which he was owing $3,000, and was about to lose. At his priesthood quorum meeting he had revealed himself a valuable member. When his condition became

186

known, five High Priests volunteered the monthy payments to save the farm. They helped him get a team and wagon and set him to hauling fertilizer on the Welfare farm, the program furnishing him food and a little money. He fertilized his own land, too. In the spring he was given charge of a ward beet project which he tended with his own land. In the fall when he got his pay he rented some more land and within a year was entirely on his own, with cows and equipment and self-confidence" (page 113).

Not much need be said of this type of assistance and its value to the recipient.

There are regular procedures that must be adhered to for a person to derive benefits from this program. They must be members in good standing in the church and have participated whenever possible in the program needed. Should a need arise, he must then go to his bishop and make known his problem. The bishop is then the individual that authorizes his participation in receiving his needs from the storehouse. It is not publicized and the feeling is that it is one of the rewards of his participation and not one of charity. The Relief Society performs a very important function in the Welfare program and this will be discussed when women's work of the two organizations is compared in another chapter.

It is not to be implied that the church confines its care of the needy to church members only. Where there is a real need in the community, the church will give assistance.

As the program developed and became more successful, surpluses in various commodities were used to secure, by exchange or sale, the commodities not produced by the program that were needed. In this the complete welfare of the participant was assured.

To compare the above program with the welfare program of the Reorganized Church we find that this church has not developed on such a large scale. Over the years the Reorganized Church has carried on many programs for the welfare of its members. They have conducted homes for the aged, children's homes, and also a sanitarium and hospital that has, over the years, been a boon to many of the church. They now operate, through the oblation fund, a home for senior citizens known as Resthaven in Independence, Missouri. At this home, the residents have medical and nursing attention as needed and a great deal is accomplished for the welfare of those that are in need. The church, through the stakes and districts, does a great deal in assisting needy members without public knowledge of these activities. The bishops and bishop's agents are constantly on the alert to learn of the needs of members and endeavor to, in every way possible, relieve and reestablish these members to a better condition. The church also conducts a Social Service Center where furniture, clothes, and various articles are rehabilitated for the benefit of the needy.

Above we mentioned the Oblation Fund and it should be explained that this is a special fund that is an offering given by the members, usually at the sacrament service or the serving of the Lord's Supper. This fund is reserved and used for only one purpose, that is the welfare of the needy of the church.

CHAPTER XXIII

WOMEN'S WORK

It is well to follow the chapter on the Welfare Program with a comparison of the function of the women in both churches. The responsibility of the women in the Mormon Church is very great, especially in relation to the welfare program.

The origin of women's work in the church began in Nauvoo and came about because of a great need within the church at the time. During the early years of settling at Nauvoo and especially in the lowlands of the area, a great deal of sickness was incurred due to dampness, exposure while in flight from Missouri and for many other reasons. This sickness was not confined to any one group, but it was especially serious when many of the mothers and children became ill. Much time and effort was needed from those fortunate enough to remain healthy, in ministering to those who were ill, especially so to the mothers that were incapable of caring for their families because of illness. Emma Smith, wife of the prophet, spent much time rendering this type of service to the sick and needy. Many of these people were new arrivals from overseas and did not always have the necessary funds for their welfare. The responsibility for their care then fell upon the membership of the church.

It was out of conditions such as these that an organization was formed to better enable the women to render assistance. A statement made by the Prophet Joseph Smith as editor of *Times and Seasons* is very interesting and we shall quote from church history, the statement as it appears:

"LADIES RELIEF SOCIETY.

A society has lately been formed by the ladies of Nauvoo for the relief of the poor, the destitute, the widow, and the orphan; and for the exercise of all benevolent purposes. The society is known by the name of the 'LADIES RELIEF SOCIETY of the City of Nauvoo:' and was organized on Thursday, the 24th of March, A.D. 1842. The society is

189

duly organized with a presidentess or chairwoman, and two counsellors, chosen by herself, a treasurer and secretary. Mrs. Emma Smith takes the chair, Mrs. Elizabeth Ann Whitney and Sarah M. Cleveland are her counselors; Miss Elvira Cole is treasuress, and our well-known and talented poetess, Miss Eliza R. Snow, secretary. There was a very numerous attendance at the organization of the society, and also at their subsequent meetings, of some of our most intelligent, humane, philanthropic, and respectable ladies; and we are well assured from knowledge of those pure principles of benevolence that flow spontaneously from their humane and philanthropic bosoms, that with the resources they will have at command they will fly to the relief of the stranger, they will pour oil and wine to the wounded heart of the distressed, they will dry up the tear of the orphan, and make the widow's heart rejoice. Our ladies have always been signalized for their acts of benevolence and kindness; but the cruel usage that they have received from the barbarians of Missouri has hitherto prevented their extending the hand of charity in a conspicuous manner; yet in the midst of persecutions, when bread has been torn from their helpless offspring by their cruel oppressors, they have always been ready to open their doors to the weary traveler, to divide their scanty pittance with the hungry, and from their robbed and impoverished wardrobes to divide with the more needy and destitute; and now that they are living on a more genial soil, and among less barbarous people, and possess facilities that they have not heretofore enjoyed, we feel convinced that with their concentrated efforts the condition of the suffering poor, of the stranger, and the fatherless, will be ameliorated." (RLDS Ch. Hist. Vol. 2, p. 571.)

The above statement contains the basic foundation of all women's work in the Restoration movement and is the heart of the women's organizations in both churches.

The Mormon Church has continued the organization from its beginning in 1842 and is still organized as it was in the days of Emma Smith. For the general church there is a president of the Ladies Relief Society with two counselors and an organization that coordinates the activities of the women for the whole church. This is done by working through the various stake organizations down to the ward level. It is the responsibility of these leaders to develop the general program of women's activities, prepare study material that is used uniformly throughout the church. It is of interest to note here, the lesson material appears in the Relief Society magazine that is published monthly. Because the magazine is published with some seasonal atmosphere, they have made provision that the people in the Northern Hemisphere will study the material that is seasonal at the time. Because of the seasonal difference between the Northern and Southern Hemispheres, the lesson material is designated for a different period in each. An example is given from the August 1966 issue. The material for this issue will be studied the first meeting in November in the Northern Hemisphere and in April, 1967 in the Southern Hemisphere. With the lesson material contained in the monthly magazine of the organization, they can be assured of continuity of material and the uniformity in study.

The general church officers work through the stake organization which is also organized in the same pattern as the general authorities, with a stake president and two counselors and a secretary-treasurer. The stake officers coordinate the activities of the various wards in the stake. At the ward level is found the real work of the Relief Society. It is here that the program is actually executed by the women. An effort is made by the teachers assigned to visit every member in the ward at least once a month. It is while visiting that the women learn of the needy or of the sick in the ward and just what help is needed. Should special assistance be required such as food or clothing, the women report this to the bishop of the ward. In this program of visiting there is close coordination with the priesthood of the ward and those responsible.

The Relief Society women meet every week at the church and the first week is devoted to the study of the doctrines of the church. At the present time they are taking their lessons from the Doctrine and Covenants. The second meeting is devoted to home-making instructions; the third meeting is on social relations and the fourth on cultural refinement. Each of these subjects is covered by material in the Relief Society magazine. To aid young mothers and those mothers with children still too young for school, they provide a nursery for the children with lesson material for those able to benefit. These meetings are generally very well attended by the women.

191

The work of the Relief Society is not always confined to their membership and this can be attested to by the author. On the occasion of the death of his father, who had left the church some twenty years prior and was considered an apostate, it was but a short time after his death that two women of the Relief Society called upon his wife and assisted her in many ways during the period of bereavement, bringing in food and sharing in the household tasks. Their concern for those in distress and the way they give aid and comfort to those in need, speaks well for their devotion to the Savior.

In the Reorganized Church we do not find the continuity of organization as in the Mormon Church. The first official recognition was in April of 1893, at which time an organization was formed and was called the "Daughters of Zion." In 1911 the name was changed to "Women's Auxiliary" for Social Service, and in 1920 it was established as the "Department of Women." The purpose and objectives of the organization are shown below:

PURPOSE: To discover and magnify the divine purpose of each woman through study, worship, fellowship, and service.

OBJECTIVES: (1) Fulfill personal stewardship through spiritual, mental, and physical improvement. (2) Establish Zionic homes with stability, character, and culture. (3) Develop church unity through communication and understanding. (4) Cultivate evangelistic spirit by witnessing and supporting all good works. (5) Encourage worldwide sisterhood.

The above list of purpose and objectives are from the official literature issued by the Department of Women of the church.

The Women's Department of the Reorganized Church is presided over by a director appointed by the First Presidency and sustained at the general conference in the same manner as other appointees. There is a general council of women comprised of nine women from Independence and vicinity, and six associate members from elsewhere in the domestic field. The director acts as chairman of this council. This council then has the responsibility of:

1. Formulating and advising on methods of procedure and policies for the Department of Women in all its phases.
2. Channeling and interpreting the general goals of the church in terms of women's interests, capabilities, responsibilities, needs and purposes.

3. Formulating immediate and long-term goals with special attention to a yearly emphasis.
4. Planning and supervising the preparation of study courses for use of local departments.
5. Planning and preparing reunion courses for women.
6. Planning World Conference activities for women.
7. Planning and supervising General Department of Women's institutes.
8. Providing articles concerning women's work for the *Saints' Herald* and the *Distaff.*
9. Revising *Handbook for the Department of Women* when necessary.

The above gives a comprehensive outline of the many activities programmed for the women. The organization is carried on through the stakes and in the same manner, to the local congregations. It is in the local congregation that the real accomplishment of the women will be observed. One of their major objectives is to visit in the homes of the members and endeavor to meet their need both physically and mentally and spiritually. When these aims are carried through, their function becomes very similar to that of the Relief Society of the Mormon Church. In the Reorganized Church the women do not meet as often but usually meet once a month for study and review of their activities. The women's department in the local congregations is usually of great assistance in raising funds, putting on socials and dinners, adding much to the social environment of the group.

Questions arise when making the comparison of the two organizations and one is, Why did the Reorganization feel the necessity to change their women's organization from that which was established in the early church by the Prophet? Why was the name, adopted by the Prophet, not suitable for their use? The functioning today of the women's department is very similar to that of the various protestant churches and it appears that much of the policies and procedures could have been adopted from them.

A very interesting sidelight on the Relief Society of the Mormon Church was recently made known to the author. The Relief Society is the only auxiliary organization in the church that has the right to maintain its own funds, and from these funds has been able to erect a very fine headquarters building for its use in Salt Lake City, Utah. A visit to this building, when visiting in the west, could be of real value.

CHAPTER XXIV

YOUTH ORGANIZATIONS

Discussing the youth activities of the two churches, we enter into the field of activities which is, in the opinion of the author, one of the most important to either church. Because the future welfare and progress and even the life of the church, rests upon the shoulders of the youth, it is extremely important that the youth should recognize their coming responsibilities. Still more important is the necessity of developing a loyalty and appreciation within the youth that will keep them within the church and actively engaged in church functions. A church that cannot keep its youth, is doomed to extinction. It is, therefore, extremely important that any program developed, must meet the needs of the youth, but must also build within the youth, a testimony of the truthfulness of the Restoration. As we endeavor to compare the program of the two churches, it must be kept in mind what the objectives are and how well they are being accomplished.

In the early church, during the life time of the Prophet Joseph Smith, there is very little written relative to youth activities. There is very good reason for this because of the youthfulness of the leadership at that time. Joseph Smith was only 39 years of age at the time of his death in 1844. Most of the men around him were approximately of the same age. This is considered a youthful age and they had not yet reached the time when the need for the developing of younger leadership had been impressed upon them.

Circumstances and conditions surrounding the church in that early period were such that practically all social activities were centered in the church. There were no distractions for the entertainment of the youth that would cause them to leave the influence of the home and church, such as exists today. This condition probably accounts for not developing youth organizations such as the Sunday School or other means for training the youth.

The major source of entertainment was conducted by the church in socials, dances, etc. We read that the dance around the campfire on the trek west, was the greatest morale builder devised. It was these socials and dances where the young people had the opportunity to intermingle, become acquainted and naturally, which led to greater inter-marriage in the church. It was very early recognized by the Prophet and those associated with him that marriage outside of the church was an indication of weakness:

> "We believe that it is not right to prohibit members of this church from marrying out of the church, if it be their determination so to do, but such persons will be considered weak in the faith of our Lord and Savor, Jesus Christ." (RLDS D & C 111:1. Eliminated from the Mormon D & C in 1876.)

Modern day experience is proving the truthfulness of this quotation. Marriage counselors and social psychologists emphasize the great need of religious compatibility in making a successful marriage. Marriage outside of one's faith has proven one of the severest blocks in marriage. To avoid conditions conducive to the young people seeking mates outside of the church, it is necessary that the church build a program of activities that will keep the interest of their young people centered in the church.

In our comparison of the youth organizations of the two churches, the success of their programs will be measured largely upon how successful they have been in keeping their young people tied closely to the church and its program.

The first organization in the Mormon Church specifically organized for the training and schooling of their young people, occurred on December 9, 1849, at the home of Richard Ballantyne, located at First West and Third South in Salt Lake City, the first Sunday School was held and in 1850, it was adopted officially by the 14th Ward as a regular part of their services. This is the origin of the Sunday Schools so far as the Mormon Church was involved.

On August 25, 1878, in Farmington, Utah, they organized what is known as the Primary Association. This organization provides for the training of young children during the week. Usually all children under the age of twelve attend these sessions which are held after school on a week day.

On November 28, 1869, Brigham Young as president of the church, organized the young women. The following quotation by him outlines the purposes he had in mind:

"I have long had it in mind to organize the young ladies of Zion into an association so that they might assist the older members of the church, their fathers and mothers, in propagating, teaching and practicing the principles I have been so long teaching. There is need for the young daughters of Israel to get a living testimony of the truth." (*MIA Executive Handbook*, page 11.)

Some five years later, June 19, 1875, the young men were similarly organized and the following statement was made by President Young:

"We want you to organize yourselves into associations for mutual improvement. Let the keynote of your work be the establishment in the youth of an individual testimony of the truth and magnitude of the great Latter-day work; the development of the gifts within them that have been bestowed upon them by the laying on of hands of the servants of God; cultivating knowledge and an application of the eternal principles of the great science of life." (*MIA Executive Handbook*, page 11.)

These two organizations were the beginning of the youth organizations known as the Mutual Improvement Associations. They are separate and distinct organizations and the women's group is known as the Young Women's Mutual Improvement Association, and the young men as the Young Men's Mutual Improvement Association. They are generally referred to by their initials, YMMIA and YWMIA. In these two groups most of the social activities of the young people take place. In the chapter on services it was mentioned but not in detail, the method of conducting the services of these two groups. It should be remembered that they are two distinctive organizations and, as a rule, function separately. However, their functions are coordinated by the general church board of each group. They also function in close coordination with the priesthood quorums.

A young person must have reached the age of twelve before he is eligible for membership in either group. From that point on, there is no limitation of eligibility. Their services are usually held on a week night and they are advised never to schedule them for Sunday. An exception is made for the class of Young Marrieds or the Fireside groups; these can meet on Sunday for study. The study period for each group begins usually when school starts in the fall and is conducted for approximately the same periods of time or until June of each year. During the summer months, no class work is conducted but outdoor activities, such as camping, etc. are the rule.

In order to better understand the organization and its potential, a more detailed description should be given. As previously stated, the men's group starts with the boy at the age of twelve. It incorporates the Boy Scout organization and follows that program in all of its phases. In the United States, boys are now admitted to the scout organization at the age of eleven. In the Mormon Church, boys of that age will have their first scouting experience in the Guide Patrol of the Primary Association. At the age of twelve, the boy is then eligible for ordination to the priesthood and also as a member of the Mutual Improvement Association in which he continues his scouting activities. As the boy grows older, he can either remain in the scout troop as a leader, or he can join the Ensign or Explorer group. They usually remain in one of these groups until they graduate from high school. After this they then become "M" men which is comprised of young unmarried men usually of the same age group. As the young people marry, they then join the Young Married group and continue their MIA activities. The above is a general outline of the organization of the Young Men's Mutual Improvement Association.

The Young Women's Mutual Improvement Association (YWMIA) is a paralleling organization and functions as an independent group as such, but their overall activities are coordinated through the general church officials. The age limit for membership in this organization is the same as in the Young Men's group. Girls at the age of twelve are eligible for membership and are known as the Beehive Organization. They continue in this group until they reach the age of fourteen. After two years in this group, they are eligible to become "MIA" Maids and after two years with this classification, they become a part of the Laurel Organization. This group of young women parallels the "M" Man and can stay with the organization until they are married, at which time they join and become a part of the Young Married group. The Laurel group covers a period of two years after which they become Gleaners. These are the girls who have graduated from high school and they remain as Gleaners until they marry.

The motto of the two organizations above is: "The Glory of God is Intelligence."

The official publication by the church is known as the *Era* and can be subscribed to by anyone interested. Study manuals are prepared and provided by the various age-groups and are uniformly used throughout the church.

Above is shown the mechanical organization very briefly and which alone, would be of no great value, but to be really effective, it must have activities that will arouse and hold the interest of the young people. The Mutual Improvement Association has been designated officially by the church, to supply the recreational activities for the people of the church along with the educational portions. This has been done by the use of the following means; Dances, Gold and Green balls, ward and stake. Miscellaneous dances, Drama, Music, Male Choruses, Female Choruses and Mixed choruses. Speech; Talks, Readings, Story Telling, Debating, Ward Speech contests and ward speech festivals.

There is also an athletic program conducted by the MIA throughout the world and where possible, inter-stake and inter-ward contests are held. They have also arranged for final competitions to be held in Salt Lake City. An interesting statement appears in the *MIA Athletic Handbook* which is worthy to quote:

"The MIA interprets the gospel of Jesus Christ as pertaining to the whole individual—physical, mental, social and spiritual. It recognizes the great appeal of competitive athletics as possible means of bringing people into the realms of influence of our church. It sponsors the athletic program, with the understanding that it will be used as a missionary to make converts and build testimonies in the lives of those with whom it deals."

At this point the author wishes to call attention especially to the role dancing has in the youth program of the Mormon Church. At a time when most other religious organizations were taking a stand against dancing as dangerous and potentially immoral, the Mormon Church began using supervised dancing as a recreational activity for their young people and other members of the church.

Having once been a member of the church and having participated in these dances, does provide some justification of the author to pass some judgment pertaining to this phase of the program. Some of the happiest moments were spent with the young people of the church, attending ward and stake dances, etc. At no time was there ever an occasion when trouble arose, but the author at one time, desired to demonstrate a new step and while doing so, was tapped on the shoulder and advised that such behavior would not be tolerated. It was done kindly and with understanding. Participation in these activities did not produce any proclivities to delinquency but did tend to keep up an interest in the church and its associations, and was largely responsible for the hesitancy in leaving the church.

In spite of the position taken by other churches, the Mormon Church utilized dancing to keep their youth tied closely to the church, especially during the period when youth begins the search for lifetime partners.

The program is well organized and as they erected new meeting houses or church buildings, they always provided a building usually called an "Amusement Hall" next to or adjoining the regular meeting house. To appreciate what is being done on a program such as this, a visit to one of their centers to see what has been provided, would be of real value.

In the opinion of the author, the youth program of the Mormon Church is the finest that has ever been developed, and it is attested to by the success they have in holding their youth to the church.

This can best be illustrated by their success they have had in calling their youth to be missionaries. One need only to remember the young men who may have called at your door and presented themselves as missionaries. The fact that they now have over thirteen thousand of these young men and young women throughtout the world, traveling at their own expense or the expense of their family, attests to the devotion and the testimonies they have gained in their early youth activities. When it is remembered that these young men and women are not permitted to date during the period of their mission, it indicates the sincerity and depth of their convictions. We may disagree with some of their philosophy, but we cannot disagree about the tremendous success of their youth program.

In an examination of the youth program of the Reorganized Church, we do not find the continuity of organization as found in the Mormon Church, but we do find similarity of programs and objectives. During the formative years of the Reorganization, very little was done in the way of organizing the youth other than through the Sunday School, which was officially adopted by the church in an action taken by a joint council dated May 5, 1865. The following statement gives the action taken by the council:

"That the First Presidency and the Quorum of the Twelve recommend, that in all branches of the church where it is practicable there be Sunday Schools established." (*True Latter Day Saints' Herald*, Vol. 7, pp. 163, 164.)

It was not until the General Conference of 1892, that any action pertaining to youth organization appeared. In a resolution adopted on April 13, 1892, we find the following:

"No. 365. A report was presented from the Young People's Mutual Improvement Society, of St. Joseph, Missouri, asking that action be taken toward completing an organization of the young people's societies. The matter was 'left with the society for further action as they deem best.' " (General Conference Resolution No. 365.)

An article appeared in *Zion's Ensign* outlining some of the details from which we quote:

"The first formal step toward a general organization was at the General Conference at Independence, Missouri in 1892. A petition from the Young People's Mutual Improvement Society of St. Joseph, Missouri was presented by Elder M. H. Forscutt on April 13th, and on the 16th a temporary organization was effected with F. M. Sheehy, president and J. F. Mintun, secretary. A committee on by-laws was appointed, consisting of J. A. Gunsolly, G. J. Whitehead, C. F. Duncan and J. C. Hitchcock. The work of this committee was reported to a meeting called at the Lamoni Conference of 1893 which met on April 14th. A Constitution was adopted and permanent organization provided for the name the society still bears, and which was suggested by Brother Sheehy and adopted. The department in the *Autumn Leaves* was continued and resulted in the publishing of monthly programs designed to lead and help the societies in their study and work, including the literary part. In time the monthly program gave way to a special publication giving lessons for study and known as the 'Religio Quarterly'. Sister Louis Palfrey Sheldon was for some years, editor." (*Zion's Ensign*, Vol. 25, May 21, 1914, p. 1 of No. 2.)

The name that was adopted at the conference in 1893 was Zion's Religio Literary Society and continued under this title until some time after 1923, when a change was made to "The Department of Recreation and Expression."

From its beginning, the Religio functioned very much upon the same lines as the Mutual Improvement Association of the Mormon Church. A policy was adapted that the primary subject matter for study in the Religio would be the Book of Mormon. They did develop the recreational and literary activities of the young people with readings, debates, recitations, etc. The author recalls one outstanding experience of a program conducted by the Religio of the Stone Church in Independence, Missouri. In an attempt to demonstrate parliamentary procedure, it was decided to hold a mock conference of the church. It was completely organized by having all the quorums of the church represented by various members of the Religio. Motions were introduced and debated, then presented for action. It was an extremely interesting program and did much to demonstrate proper procedure in a deliberative body. There were debates by authorities on the geography of the Book of Mormon and many other activities.

The Religio, from its inception, set up an age limit for membership and this began at the age of fourteen. There was no upper limit and anyone with a desire to attend was permitted to do so. In 'the early twenties, there developed a movement to place a top age limit upon those participating in youth affairs. This began with a series of sermons sponsored by the young people in which it was requested that those over thirty-one years of age refrain from attending in order to reserve the seating for the younger people. This separation of the age groups was the beginning of many problems that possibly had great influence on the demise of the Religio.

This particular period was a time when the author was very closely connected with events that took place in Independence, Missouri. From 1925 through 1927, he was the stake superintendent of the Department of Recreation and Expression, and was president of the Stone Church Religio. He was closely associated with Dr. F. M. McDowell, member of the First Presidency, who had been assigned to oversee the youth activities of the church.

One thing developed during this period, along with the regular study classes, was a special recreation night each week, and the young people of the church under the age of thirty met in the old Stone Church Annex, or "Dining Hall." At these sessions, there were organized games and contests under the supervision of adults. It was at these events that many of the young people met other members of the church and were given an opportunity to become better acquainted and at the same time drawn closer to the church. This did not continue for a long period and was ultimately dropped when the Religio was phased out. It was not until sometime in the thirties that a new organization was formed to replace the Religio. This was the beginning of Zion's League.

One very interesting fact, according to the author's knowledge, pertains to the Boy Scout organization. From what information can be verified, the Reorganized Church was the first church to adopt the Boy Scout program as an official part of the church's youth activities. The first Boy Scout troop west of the Mississippi River was organized by W. O. Hands in 1910, the year that Scouting was first started. The author had the privilege of belonging to a Boy Scout troop in the thirty-second Ward of the Mormon Church in 1910, but at that time the troops were not registered at the national headquarters of the Scout organization. The Mormon Church did not adopt Scouting officially until around 1913.

The Boy Scout program is now the official boys program in the Reorganized Church and the author has participated in this phase of the youth work, having organized one of the troops still functioning in Independence, Missouri, namely Troop 223 organized in 1927.

After the phasing out of the Religio and then later the Department of Recreation and Expression, a number of different groups were formed in an attempt to meet the needs of the young people. These were started in various sections of the country and had various names. Some were called O. B. K's. (Our Brothers Keeper); another was O. T. Z's. (Onward to Zion). The largest that was organized on a regional basis was the Zion's Christian Legion. This was organized in the Michigan District and a portion of the Canadian area adjoin-

202

ing, and was brought about largely through the efforts of Apostle D. T. Williams. In 1937 this organization's name was changed to Zion's League and became the official youth organization of the church.

At the present time the Zion's League now functions in the branch or congregation under the leadership of an adult youth leader. This leader is usually appointed or nominated by the presiding elder of the congregation. Under this direction, a president for the Zion's League group is elected and with the assistance of a "cabinet," leads the activities of the group. The ages involved in the Zion's League range from fifteen through eighteen. Most generally it is comprised of high school age groups.

The Boy Scout program is not under the direction specifically of the youth leader, but functions primarily independent of any other youth organization. The same is true of the Zioneers and the Oriole girls activities. These are separate phases of the youth work and function under programs prepared for them.

The Zioneer program is of very recent origin and is designed to serve the need of the Junior High age group, but because of its newness as a program, it has not been fully tested.

The Oriole girls is an organization of much longer duration. The first "Book of the Orioles" was published in 1915, and the program at that time was conducted under the Young Women's Department of the Women's Auxiliary for Social Service. It is a program that is somewhat similar to the Camp Fire Girls and Girl Scouts, but it is oriented more to the church and endeavors to guide and hold the interest of the girls to the church. In this way it is very similar to the organization of the Beehive girls of the Mormon Church.

The most outstanding weakness of the youth program of the Reorganized church is its lack of permanent continuity. The constant changing of policies and procedures over the years has left the church with an insecure feeling relative to its youth and this in turn has left the youth with a feeling of insecurity. The programs and purposes and materials produced are excellent but have not had the test of time and successful operation over the years.

CHAPTER XXV

EPITOME OF FAITH

One of the outstanding features of the Restoration movement as compared to other religious bodies, is the fact that it never adopted or established a creed. However, there came a time when the Prophet found it necessary to outline the basic beliefs of the church. This is found in his reply to John Wentworth, editor of the *Chicago Democrat*. In this letter the Prophet outlined a brief history of the Church and then completed the letter with thirteen statements of the beliefs of the Restoration and these will be quoted because they are known in the Mormon Church as the Articles of Faith, and in the Reorganization as the Epitome of Faith. The letter to Mr. Wentworth was first printed in the *Times and Seasons* of March 1, 1842. The quotation is taken from a photo-copy of the *Times and Seasons* and is as follows:

"We believe in God the Eternal Father, and in his son Jesus Christ, and in the Holy Ghost.

We believe that men will be punished for their own sins and not for Adam's transgression.

We believe that through the atonement of Christ all mankind may be saved by obedience to the laws and ordinances of the Gospel.

We believe that these ordinances are 1st, Faith in the Lord Jesus Christ; 2d, Repentance; 3d, Baptism by immersion for the remission of sins; 4th, Laying on of hands for the gift of the Holy Ghost.

We believe that a man must be called of God by 'prophecy, and by laying on of hands' by those who are in authority to preach the gospel and administer in the ordinances thereof.

We believe in the same organization that existed in the primitive church, vis: apostles, prophets, pastors, teachers, evangelists, etc.

We believe in the gift of tongues, prophecy, revelation, visions, healing, interpretation of tongues, etc.

We believe the bible to be the word of God as far as it is

translated correctly; we also believe the Book of Mormon to be the word of God.

We believe all that God has revealed, all that he does now reveal, and we believe that he will yet reveal many great and important things pertaining to the kingdom of God.

We believe in the literal gathering of Israel and in the restoration of the Ten Tribes. That Zion will be built upon this continent. That Christ will reign personally upon the earth, and that the earth will be renewed and receive its paradisaic glory.

We claim the privilege of worshiping Almighty God according to the dictates of our conscience, and allow all men the same privilege let them worship how, where, or what they may.

We believe in being subject to kings, presidents, rulers, and magistrates, in obeying, honoring and sustaining the law.

We believe in being honest, true, chaste, benevolent, virtuous, and in doing good to all men; indeed we may say that we follow the admonition of Paul, 'we believe all things, we hope all things,' we have endured many things and hope to be able to endure all things. If there is anything virtuous, lovely, or of good report or praiseworthy we seek after these things. Respectfully, etc. Joseph Smith."

In the above statement we have one of the clearest presentations of what the Restoration movement believes and it is very difficult to understand, how two organizations can agree to the above statement and yet differ so greatly as do the Mormon Church and the Reorganized Church.

It is thought by some that the statement of belief was first written by Orson Pratt but was somewhat condensed by Joseph Smith when he wrote his letter to Mr. Wentworth.

The first publication of the articles of faith by the Mormon Church appeared in the *Pearl of Great Price*, published in England in 1851, primarily for the benefit of new members. In this book, it was published as it appears in the *Times and Seasons*. In later editions of the *Pearl of Great Price*, several changes were made in the context and among the changes, was the one made in the Articles of Faith. This is found in the fourth paragraph as it appeared in the *Times and Seasons* and reads as follows:

"We believe that these ordinances are 1st, Faith in the Lord Jesus Christ; 2d, Repentance; 3d, Baptism by immersion for the remission of sins; 4th, Laying on of hands for the gift of the Holy Ghost."

This same article was changed to read:

"We believe that the first principles and ordinances of the Gospel are: first, Faith in the Lord Jesus Christ; second, Repentance; third, Baptism by immersion for the remission of sins; fourth, Laying on of hands for the gift of the Holy Ghost."

At a quick first glance, the change will not be noted, but the change 'these ordinances' to 'the first principles and ordinances' makes a complete change in context and now permits the introduction of other principles and doctrines that did not appear in the original. It should be remembered that this change occurred many years after the death of the Prophet and is another of the deliberate actions taken by someone to alter what the Prophet had said and making it read differently and yet attribute the statement to the prophet. The author feels this is inexcusable and is again, one of the many teachings introduced after the death of Joseph Smith and attributed to him, something he was unable to either affirm or deny.

At the semi-annual conference of the Mormon Church in October of 1880, the *Pearl of Great Price* was accepted as one of the standard books of scripture, and the Articles of Faith, being included as revised, also became scripture to the church. This was never the intention of the Prophet when he wrote the letter to Mr. Wentworth. It is this deliberate tampering with the writings of the Prophet to which exception is taken. If this practice is condoned and accepted, no writings of any previous prophet is inviolate and the written word then will cease to have much import. This is in line with the teachings in the Mormon Church that the 'Living Oracles' (leaders of the church) are more important than the written word. The incorporation of the Articles of Faith into scripture, in effect established a creed.

The Reorganized Church has never utilized the statement in the Wentworth letter to the extent done by the Mormon Church. It has been printed and distributed by the membership but has never been the subject of any official action by the church. They have accepted the historical portions of the letter and they are found in the history of the church. They have always maintained that they have no creed other than "All Truth."

During the 1930's, the *Saints' Herald* published a series of articles written by some of the leading men of the church in which they endeavored to state the basic beliefs of the church. These articles were never compiled in a book and no official action was taken on them. However, when compiling a church member's manual, there was included a "Brief Statement of Belief" which is shown below:

"WE BELIEVE

In god the Eternal Father, creator of the heavens and the earth.

In the divine Sonship of Jesus Christ the Savior of all men who obey his Gospel;

In the Holy Ghost whose function it is to guide all men unto the truth.

In the Gospel of Jesus Christ which is the power of God unto salvation.

In the six fundamental doctrinal principles of the gospel: Faith; Repentance; Baptism by immersion in water; The Baptism of the Holy Ghost; The Laying on of hands for the healing of the sick, for conferring the Holy Ghost, Ordination, and blessing of children; Resurrection of the dead; and the Eternal judgment.

In the justice of God who will reward or punish all men according to their works, and not solely according to their profession. In the same kind of organization that existed in the primitive church: Apostles, prophets, evangelists, pastors, teachers, elders, bishops, seventies, etc.

In the Word of God contained in the Bible, so far as it is correctly translated.

In the Word of God contained in the Book of Mormon, being a record of divine dealings with men in the new world as in the old.

In the Word of God revealed today and recorded in the Doctrine and Covenants of the church.

In the willingness and ability of God to continue his revelation of his will to men to the end of time.

In the powers and gifts of the gospel: Faith, discerning of

spirits, prophecy, revelation, healing, visions, tongues, and their interpretation, wisdom, charity, temperance, brotherly love, etc.

In marriage as instituted and ordained of God whose law provides for but one companion in wedlock, for either man or woman, excepting in case of death. When the marriage contract is broken by transgression, the innocent party is free to remarry.

In the Book of Mormon declaration: "There shall not any man among you have save it be one wife; and concubines he shall have none."

In the doctrine of Stewardships; that is, that every man is accountable to God for the conduct of his life and the use of his material blessings.

In the Divine Commission to the church to establish a Christian Community called Zion built upon the basis of stewardship and the principle of equal opportunity, and where each member shall give according to his capacity and receive according to his needs." (*Church Member's Manual*, page 109).

A series of radio sermons were prepared by Elder Evan Fry while he was radio minister for the Reorganization which outlined the basic beliefs of the church. They were never published in book form and for this reason are not available for examination. At the present time, a committee appointed as a result of a resolution passed at general conference, are endeavoring to compile a statement of the basic beliefs of the church. The first result of their efforts appeared in the *Saints' Herald* of January 1, 1968, and succeeding statements have appeared monthly since that time:

"We believe in God the eternal Father, source and center of all love and life and truth, who is almighty, infinite, and unchanging, in whom and through whom all things exist and have their being."

The second to appear reads:

"We believe in Jesus Christ, the Only Begotten Son of God, who is from everlasting to everlasting; through whom all things were made; who is God in the flesh, being incarnate by the Holy Spirit for man's salvation; who was crucified, died, and rose again; who is mediator between God and man, and the judge of both the living and the dead; whose dominion has no end." *Saints' Herald*, February 1, 1968, page 17-20).

Having shown the original statement at the beginning of the chapter, it is not necessary to comment on what has been written as substitutes, but should be left to the reader to form his own conclusions. However, the similarity to the confusion that existed in the early church councils, such as the Nicene and others, seems to be apparent in these new statements being presented by the Reorganization. The trend towards 'protestant' thinking seems to be emerging and is of deep concern to the author.

It has always been a problem to understand why the Reorganization has felt it necessary to prepare something other than that which was given to the church by the Prophet. Is it due to a loss of confidence in the Prophet and his writings, or is it because of the use to which the Mormon Church had made of them? Is it possible that the unwillingness on the part of the Reorganization to use the original statement, may indicate to some, they had lost full confidence in the Prophet? This was referred to in the chapter on attitudes of the church toward Joseph Smith.

It might have been more appropriate if the Reorganization could have had someone capable of doing so, prepare a study outline of the original statement in book form for use of the membership that desired greater knowledge on the basic beliefs. This was done by the Mormon Church when James E. Talmadge wrote a book under the title of *Articles of Faith.* This book contains a very comprehensive exposition of the statement published by the prophet.

Several different versions have been prepared by individuals of the Reorganized Church but at no time have any of them been accepted or adopted officially by the church. The printing in the *Church Member's Manual* should not be construed as the official position of the church. This booklet is published primarily as a guide to the responsibilities of the members and is advisory only.

CHAPTER XXVI

GOD

"We believe in God the Eternal Father, and in his son Jesus Christ, and in the Holy Ghost." (First statement of the Epitome of Faith.)

It is strange that, out of a statement as simple as the one above, such a divergent concept of God can arise as that which exists between the two churches. Because so many books have been written by members of both churches, in an endeavor to justify their individual positions, the author will not attempt to treat this question exhaustively, but will give whatever scripture is necessary to show the position of the early church.

The first scripture is from the New Testament:

"And this is life eternal, that they might know thee the *only true God*, and Jesus Christ, whom thou hast sent." (John 17:3 I V)

The next quotation is taken from the Old Testament of the Inspired Version of the Bible:

"Ye are my witnesses, saith the Lord, and my servant whom I have chosen; that ye may know and believe me, and understand that I am he; *before me there was no god formed, neither shall there be after me.*" (Isaiah 43:10 I.V.).

Another quotation from the revelation to the church by Joseph Smith, is also from the Inspired Version; it also appears in the *Pearl of Great Price* of the Mormon Church. It reads:

". . . for I am *without beginning of days or end of years; and is not this endless?*" (Preface of I. V. page 7; P of GP, Moses 1:3).

From the Book of Mormon is another very interesting quotation:

"And Zeezrom said unto him, Thou sayest there is a true and living God? And Amulek said, Yea, there is a true and living God. Now Zeezrom said, Is there more than one God? and he answereth no. Now Zeezrom said unto him again, How knowest thou these things? and he said, An angel hath made them known to me." (Mormon B of M, Alma 11:26-31; RLDS B of M, Alma 8:79-84).

The above quotations establish the fact there is only one God and that he is without beginning or end. We also need to prove that he is unchangeable and to do this, we must rely upon scripture that has been revealed. The first reference is from the Old Testament:

"My covenant will I not break, nor alter the thing that is gone out of my lips." (Psalms 89:34).

Another from the same source:

"I am the Lord, I change not." (Malachi 3:6).

From the New Testament:

"Every good gift and every perfect gift is from above, and cometh down from the Father of lights, with whom is no variableness, neither shadow of turning." (James 1:17).

Going to the Book of Mormon for this statement:

"And behold, I say unto you, He changeth not; if so, he would cease to be God." (Mormon B of M, Mormon 9:19; RLDS B of M, Mormon 4:82).

And now from modern scripture given to the church through the Prophet Joseph Smith:

"He is the same God yesterday, today, and forever." (Mormon D&C 20:12; RLDS D&C 17:2).
"Listen to the voice of the Lord your God, even Alpha and Omega, the beginning and the end, whose course is one eternal round, the same today as yesterday, and forever." (Mormon D&C 35:1; RLDS D&C 34:1).

It may appear to some that the above quotations would be sufficient to prove the unchangeability of God, but in spite of them, there has arisen a doctrine within the Mormon Church that denies all of the above quotations. This doctrine is based upon the theory of Eternal Progression. This theory does not come from scriptural instructions as found in any of the standard books of scripture, but is based upon theories that have developed since the death of the Prophet Joseph Smith. It is practically impossible to locate the real source of the theories and just why they were developed to the extent they now exist within the church. The thought that man will continue to progress in intelligence and experience, is extremely appealing to our present day thinking and especially so, in light of the tremendous advancement in science and research that has developed in the last hundred years.

The first writings that indicated the possibility of plurality of Gods was in the publication in the *Times and Seasons* of the translation of the Book of Abraham, from the papyrus manuscripts described in a previous chapter. It should be remembered by the reader, that this translation was not given to the church as scripture by the Prophet, but was later made a part of the *Pearl of Great Price* that was adopted by the Mormon Church in 1880, as one of the standard books.

At times, a sermon preached by the Prophet shortly before his death, and known as the King Follet funeral sermon, is used as evidence that the Prophet taught the plurality of Gods. According to a statement made to the author by Richard P. Howard, historian for the Reorganized Church,

"The King Follet sermon was first published, apparently from a scribe's notes in August, 1844. This was later greatly expanded and revised as published in "Joseph Smith History" in the *Millennial Star* in 1863, and even further revised when it was published in 1902 in the six volume format." (Letter to author, June 29, 1967.)

It has been previously stated, and at this point will bear repeating, that a prophet of God is a prophet only when God, through his spirit, uses him for that purpose. It should not be presumed that every time he speaks he does so under the direction of God. It should not be assumed that every time he preaches a sermon it should become scripture to the church. A group or organization should not be held accountable for statements made by individuals unless especially authorized to do so. The Mormon Church has suffered much because of sermons preached by individuals expressing personal beliefs not fully in harmony with the beliefs of the church. Many of the early leaders and officers of the church are quoted in issues of the *Journal of Discourses* that have proven an embarrassment in later years. Both churches have been victims of unauthorized statements reflecting upon them and their beliefs.

Along with the introduction of the purported revelation on polygamy or celestial marriage, the theory of eternal progression also grew and resulted in a belief in the plurality of gods. It all evolved from various statements in this 'revelation.' In fact, because of the many statements contradictory to previous statements on doctrine given to the church, this 'revelation' is now one of the major sources of differences between the churches.

The position of the Mormon Church in reference to God at the present time is best expressed in a statement made by Lorenzo Snow, which he attributed to Joseph Smith and which is quoted: "As man is, God once was; as God is, man may become." No evidence has ever been produced to prove the Prophet was the author of this statement.

In a book written by Doctor John A. Widtsoe, a former member of the Quorum of Twelve Apostles, titled *Rational Theology*, we find the position of the Mormon Church well stated. He writes a great deal on the theory and philosophy of Eternal Progression. One of the very interesting statements made by Doctor Widtsoe in this book reads as follows:

"God, the supreme power, can not conceivably originate matter; he can only organize matter" (*Rational Theology*, p. 11).

Another quotation that is of interest:

"Why God is God. To determine this relationship between God and man it is necessary to discuss, first, the conditions under which God became God. As already said, God is the supreme intelligent Being in the universe, who has the greatest knowledge and the most perfect will, and who, therefore, possesses infinite power over the forces of the universe. However, IF the great law of progression is accepted, God must have been engaged in progressive development, and, infinite as God is, he must have been less powerful in the past than he is today." *Rational Theology*, p. 23)

"We may be certain that through self-effort, the inherent and innate powers of God have been developed to a godlike degree. Thus, he has become God." (*Ibid.*, p. 24)

To continue the advancement of the above stated theories, Dr. Widtsoe states:

"During the onward march of the Supreme Being, other intelligent beings were likewise engaged, though less vigorously in acquiring power over forces of the universe. Among many intelligent beings thus moving onward, there is little probability of any two attaining exactly the same place at the same time. There is rather the probability of infinite gradation from the lowest to the highest development. Next to God, there may be, therefore, other intelligent beings so nearly approaching his power as to be co-equal with him in all things so far as our finite understanding can perceive. These beings may be immeasurably far above us mortal men on earth. Such intelligent beings are as Gods to us. Under this definition there may be a great number of intelligent beings who possess to a greater or lesser degree the quality of Godhood." (*Ibid.*, p. 24)

The above quotations outline to some extent, the philosophy of the Mormon Church about God. It should be pointed out that there is no scripture justifying this position except that which has been adopted by the Mormon Church after the death of the Prophet and is subject to serious question. The scriptures referred to are the *Pearl of Great Price* (Book of Abraham), the purported revelation on polygamy and celestial marriage, and the changes made in the book of Doctrine and Covenants as outlined in previous chapters.

Based upon the theory as explained by Doctor Widtsoe, is the belief in the Mormon Church that every man, who becomes worthy by adhering to the requirements of the Church, will have the opportunity to progress to the ultimate and become a God in his own right. Included in the requirement is the necessity that he have sufficient posterity to be in a position to father the population of a new planet in the

214

same manner as Adam and Eve. To aid them in securing this posterity, the doctrine of polygamy was introduced and justified by them. Their belief also includes a conviction that the procreation of children or spirits, will continue after this life. It is also necessary that the parents go to the temple and have their children sealed to them in view of this future and to a part of the father's celestial state.

This doctrine and practice is the source of some complicated questions, especially if the father should have a number of sons in his posterity, that also strive to achieve the same goals as the father. They may have large families and meet all of the church's requirements, and have their children sealed to them. In the hereafter, will they be subjects of their father, or will they be independent of him? If the son is as successful as the father, will the father be deprived of those who have been sealed to him, or does the first sealing supercede any future sealings? These questions have never been satisfactorily answered for the author.

The doctrine of Eternal Progression is an attractive theory, especially to those who are never satisfied with the status quo, who are continuously seeking to learn. A static condition is not appealing to most people with ambition and a strong desire to be continually seeking to serve God. When a man comes to a belief in God, it will be based upon his personal experience, knowledge or understanding. It is not possible for any man to give a conviction or belief in God to any individual. He can be helpful and assist, but the real conviction must come from God through his Spirit to the person. His testimony can be of great assistance but can never be transferred to another. The greatest confusion that ever arose in the history of Christianity was at the time a group of men endeavored to describe God and his attributes, and to make them into dogmatic creeds. This has continued from the time of Christ and it is continuing at the present time.

The Mormon Church has endeavored to put at rest much of the speculation that now exists throughout the Christian World with this introduction of Eternal Progression. They have also set up definite statements describing God and his attributes as a progressive being. This makes it easy for the individual that does not seek his own answers, to accept and promulgate. This is another illustration of unquestioned acceptance of the leadership and what they teach. When it is remembered that the above theories are not based upon scripture given to the church during the lifetime of the Prophet, but were introduced afterwards and yet attributed to him, it is not difficult to understand why the confusion exists.

The Reorganized Church has never projected any such theories about God, nor have they officially endeavored to describe him or his attributes. They have accepted the story of the Prophet Joseph Smith, and the description of his first vision. It is in this vision that he claimed that two personages appeared to him. To quote from his statement:

> ". . . When the light rested upon me I saw *two personages*, (whose brightness and glory defy all description), standing above me in the air. One of them spake unto me, calling me by name, and said, pointing to the other—'This is my Beloved Son, hear him.' " (RLDS Ch. Hist. Vol. 1, p. 9)

Based upon this statement by the Prophet, the church recognizes that God is a personage and so is Christ. This is in harmony with the initial statement at the beginning of the chapter. Whether or not the Holy Ghost is a personage, in the sense claimed by the Mormon Church, that is a personage of spirit, is subject to much speculation and has always been so from the time of Christ.

Because most churches and the scriptures contained in the Bible, use the term Holy Spirit and Holy Ghost interchangeably, there has arisen a belief that they are one and the same. This belief creates considerable confusion due to the separate and distinct functions of each. However, to believe in a Trinity, it becomes necessary to agree with the above.

At this point, the author wishes to project an explanation that both appeals to him and satisfies his desire to know. This theory is in no way an official position of either church, but is strictly personal and is presented only for consideration. The theory comes from an acceptance of the story of the first vision to the Prophet. Especially in the fact that *two personages* appeared.

Scriptures, both old and new, present the functioning of two different spirits, such as the Holy Spirit or the Spirit of God. According to scripture, the Spirit of God is that which constantly strives with all mankind, to direct them to God and love, regardless of where they are or whom they may be. There is another spirit that is conferred upon man by the act

216

of confirmation after baptism, and this is called the Holy Ghost. It is this spirit that testifies and gives knowledge of Jesus Christ. It is this spirit that gives to man, his testimony and understanding of the mission of Christ. No attempt is being made to quote scriptures relative to this subject but, a suggestion to those reading or studying scripture, keep in mind what is being suggested here.

Recognizing that two personages appeared in the vision, it is only normal to assume that each of the personages has a spirit of its own, in the same manner that every individual has a spirit. If God and Christ appeared to the Prophet in the vision, it is therefore, reasonable to assume that each has a spirit of his own. Scripture informs us that Christ advised his disciples that after he was gone, he would send them a Comforter (Holy Ghost). It is also known that while he was with the disciples on earth, they had no need for this Comforter. It was after his ascension to heaven and on the day of Pentecost, that we read of the bestowing of the Holy Ghost. On the basis of this knowledge, is it not reasonable to believe that the function of the Spirit of Christ or Holy Ghost, will be as outlined above? Is not the gift that brings to man, a knowledge and understanding of Christ, his own Spirit? To the knowledge of the author, there is no scripture that truly controverts the above projection.

CHAPTER XXVII

THE NEGRO

With the rise of racial problems in the United States, the position of the Restoration has come into focus, primarily so from the position taken by the Mormon Church. When there arose a potentiality of a prominent member of the Mormon Church seeking the highest office the nation can give, a great deal of attention was focused on the church and its beliefs relative to the Negro.

In the early history of the church, no official position was taken as to the eligibility of the colored race in the church. There is record of Negroes joining the church and having been ordained to the priesthood. However, they were not numerous which is understandable, when it is remembered that most colored people of that period, were still slaves and had no free-will or choice. The real problem of the church's position relative to the colored, is one that has arisen since the death of the Prophet.

To understand the position of the Mormon Church, a statement in a book written by Bruce R. McConkie, published in 1958 in Salt Lake City, Utah, makes the following statement:

"In the pre-existent eternity various degrees of valiance and devotion to the truth were exhibited by different groups of our Father's spirit offspring. One-third of the spirit hosts of heaven came out in open rebellion and were cast out without bodies, becoming the devil and his angels. (D & C 29:36; Rev. 12:3-9). The other two-thirds stood affirmatively for Christ; there were no neutrals. To stand neutral in the midst of war is a philosophical impossibility. The Lord said, 'He that is not with me is against me; and he that gathereth not with me scattereth abroad.' (Matt. 12:30). Of the two-thirds who followed Christ, however, some were more valiant than others. . . . Those who were less valiant in the pre-existence and who thereby had certain spiritual restrictions imposed upon them during mortality are known to us as Negroes. Such spirits are sent to earth through the lineage of Cain.

Negroes in this life are denied the priesthood; under no circumstances can they hold this delegation of authority from the Almighty. (Abra. 1:20-27). The gospel message of salvation is not carried affirmatively to them (Moses 7:8, 12, 22), although sometimes Negroes search out the truth, join the church, and become by righteous living heirs of the celestial kingdom of heaven. President Brigham Young and others have taught that in the future eternity worthy and qualified Negroes will receive the priesthood and every gospel blessing available to any man."(Mormon Doctrine, pages 476-477)

The scriptural references shown in the above quotation are taken from the Book of Abraham and Moses as they appear in the *Pearl of Great Price.*

According to the Mormon belief, the curse of Cain, which is a black skin, was transmitted through Noah's grandson, Canaan, who married Egyptus, an Egyptian woman and from this union sprang the black race. Another portion of scripture used to support this theory is taken from the Bible and, quoting from the Inspired Version:

"And Noah began to till the earth, and he was an husbandman; and he planted a vineyard and he drank of the wine, and was drunken; and he was uncovered within his tent; And Ham, the father of Canaan, saw the nakedness of his father, and told his brethren without; and Shem and Japheth, took a garment and laid upon both their shoulders, and went backward and covered the nakedness of their father, and they saw not their father's nakedness. And Noah awoke from his wine, and knew what his youngest son had done unto him, and he said, Cursed be Canaan; a servant of servants shall he be unto his brethren." (Gen. 9:27-29 I.V.)

When analyzing the above scripture, several things should be noted. In the first place, God had no part in the act. The first defense that will be made to this statement is, that Noah was a prophet of God. Again the question should be asked, was he a prophet while intoxicated, and as he arose from this drunken stupor? Another unexplained portion of this story that the curse, made by a man in a drunken condition, cursed an innocent party and not the man who committed the offense. Canaan was the son of Ham, who was the guilty party.

It is inconceivable that a loving God would be a party to such an unjust action. Especially so when the purported curse would be so far-reaching as to condemn a race of people he had created. God did *not* curse Canaan but Noah did. It would be almost incomprehensible to love and worship a God with proclivities of this kind.

The scriptures used by the Mormon Church to justify their position in denying the right of priesthood is taken from the *Pearl of Great Price* and is found in the highly controversial Book of Abraham (refer to chapter XV).

"Behold, Potiphar's Hill was in the land of Ur, of Chaldea. And the Lord broke down the altar of Eljenah, and of the gods of the land, and utterly destroyed them, and smote the priest that he died; and there was great mourning of Chaldea, and also in the court of Pharoah; which Pharoah signifies king of royal blood. Now this king of Egypt was a descendant from the loins of Ham, and was a partaker of the blood of the Canaanites by birth. From this descent sprang all the Egyptians, and thus the blood of the Canaanites was preserved in the land. The Land of Egypt being first discovered by a woman, who was the daughter of Ham, and the daughter of Egyptus, which in Chaldean signifies Egypt, which signifies that which is forbidden. When this woman discovered the land it was under water, who afterward settled her sons in it; and thus, from Ham, sprang that race which preserved the curse in the land. Now the first government of Egypt was established by Pharoah, the eldest son of Egyptus, the daughter of Ham, and it was after the manner of the government of Ham, which is patriarchal. Pharoah, being a righteous man, established his kingdom and judged his people wisely and justly all his days, seeking earnestly to imitate that order established by the fathers in the first generations, in the days of the first patriarchal reign, even in the reign of Adam, and also Noah, his father, who blessed him with the blessings of the earth, and with the blessings of wisdom, but cursed him as pertaining to the priesthood. Now, Pharoah being of the lineage by which he could not have the right of priesthood, notwithstanding the Pharoahs would fain claim it from Noah, through Ham, therefore my father was led away by their idolatry." (Book of Abraham, 1:20-27)

It is from the above quotation and from statements made by some of the leaders of the church, that the policy of the Mormon Church refusing the priesthood to the colored race and especially the Negroes. This ban is so stringent that it denies the priesthood to anyone that may have a trace of Negro blood in his veins.

This doctrine, in recent months, has been the source of many articles appearing in magazines and newspapers throughout the country. In the Sunday issue of the *Los Angeles Times* of August 27, 1967, there appeared an article under the following headline: "Race Discrimination Becoming Hot Issue in Mormon Church." In this article quotations of Secretary of the Interior Stewart L. Udall are given. Mr. Udall is a member of the Mormon Church and writes his article as a member. Most of the statements by Secretary Udall were made in a letter to *Dialogue*, a publication sponsored by a group of educators and others who are members of the church. The magazine is not an official publication of the church nor is it approved by the church. In the Summer Issue of 1967, Vol. II, No. 2, the letter written by Secretary Udall was first published. Some of the interesting statements by him are as follows:

"At an earlier impasse, the Church, unable to escape history, wisely abandoned the deeply imbedded practice of plural marriage and thereby resolved a crisis of its own conscience and courageously faced the moral judgment of the American people. In 1890 for most Church leaders polygamy was a precious principle—a practice that lay at the very heart of Mormonism. Its proscription took genuine courage, but our leaders were equal to the task. By comparison, the restriction now imposed on Negro fellowship is a social and institutional practice having no real sanction in essential Mormon thought. It is clearly contradictory to our most cherished spiritual and moral ideals. Every Mormon knows that his church teaches that the day will come when the Negro will be given full fellowship. Surely that day has come. All around us the Negro is proving his worth when accepted into the society of free men. All around us are the signs that he needs and must have a genuine brotherhood with Mormons, Catholics, Methodists, and Jews. Surely God is speaking to us now, telling us that the time is here."

Many of the letters to *Dialogue* in reply to Mr. Udall's letter have been critical of his position and, in most cases, did not question the truthfulness of what he said, but more or less questioned his standing as a member of the church, or his right to say what he did.

In the Winter issue of *Dialogue* of 1967, Vol. II, No. 4, is another article of great interest and it is written by Armand L. Mauss, who recently became an Associate Professor of Sociology at Utah State University after five years of teaching at Diablo Valley College in California, and is now completing a doctoral dissertation on "Mormonism and Urbanism" for the University of California at Berkeley. He has been a counselor in the bishopric of the Walnut Creek Ward and is presently the general secretary for Aaronic Priesthood-Adult in the Logan Fourth Ward. In this article, Mr. Mauss discusses the scriptural material available on the Church's position and makes the following summation:

"So far, then, I think I have demonstrated that three of the most widespread 'explanations' in the Church for the denial of the Priesthood to Negroes are unsupported in the scriptures of the Church and should therefore be regarded as speculation, or even folklore; these are: (a) the War-in-Heaven theory; (b) the Curse-on-Ham theory; and (c) the mark of Cain theory. Whatever discomfiture we Mormons may feel at the lack of explanation for the Church's doctrine and practice relating to Negroes, we should once and for all disabuse ourselves and our Church friends of these folktales. Not only do they lack theoretical viability, but they add an encumbrance of ridiculousness and superstition to a Church policy that is otherwise enigmatic. Furthermore, and perhaps more seriously, these unscriptural tales may provide a pretext for those among us who are given to civil bigotry to rationalize it." (*Dialogue*, Winter 1967, Vol. II, No. 4, page 28)

Following the above quotation, Mr. Mauss then proceeds to prove that the doctrine of denying the priesthood to Negroes, does not necessarily, lead to civil rights violations. Having written previous articles and conducted research on this question, he claims there is no more violation of the Negro's civil rights in Utah than in any other state. In his conclusion he makes the following statement:

222

"Whenever change comes, however, it must come in the Mormon way; that is, the integrity of the principle of continuous revelation must be maintained. Without this, and without the charisma of the 'prophet, seer, and revelator.' Mormonism would be without its most vital distinguishing attribute. Any perceived threat to the 'due process' implied in the doctrine of continuous revelation will be resisted not only by the Church leadership, but also by the overwhelming majority of the rank and file." (*Ibid.*, p. 39)

An interesting statement of the position of the Mormon Church was made in an address by Brigham Young to the territorial legislature and is quoted from Wilford Woodruff's journal:

"President Young felt it, however, to be his duty to make plain the attitude of the Mormon people in Utah on the subject (slavery). In an address to the legislature he said: 'The Lord said I will not kill Cain, but I will put a mark upon him, and that mark will be seen upon the face of every negro upon the face of the earth; and it is the decree of God that that mark shall remain upon the seed of Cain until the seed of Abel shall be redeemed, and Cain shall not receive the priesthood, until the time of the redemption. Any man having one drop of the seed of Cain in him cannot receive the priesthood; but the day will come when all that race will be redeemed and possess all the blessings which we now have. I am opposed to the present system of slavery." (*Wilford Woodruff* by Matthias Cowley, page 351)

The above documentation should be sufficient to present the position of the Mormon Church and the trends that are developing within the organization.

The Reorganization is not completely innocent of indicating an anti-Negro attitude within the church. However, there has never been an official pronouncement indicating prejudice. Most of this sentiment has been shown, not in what the church has said, but in what has not been stated and in action that has not been taken by them. No real effort has ever been made to proselyte among the colored race in the United States. Recently efforts have been started for the development of a mission in Africa.

223

The only official statement, outside of resolutions passed by their conferences, is found in the Doctrine and Covenants and it reads:

". . . It is my will that my gospel shall be preached to all nations in every land, and that men of every tongue shall minister before me: Therefore it is expedient in me that you ordain priests unto me, of every race who receive the teachings of my law, and become heirs according to the promise. . . . Be not hasty in ordaining men of the Negro race to offices in my church, for verily I say unto you, all are not acceptable unto me as servants, nevertheless, I will that all may be saved, but every man in his own order, and there are some who are chosen instruments to be ministers to their own race. Be ye content, I the Lord have spoken it." (RLDS D&C 116:1-4)

This revelation was given to the Reorganized Church by Joseph Smith III, son of the martyr, on May 4, 1865. This was at the conclusion of the Civil War. It is very understandable why the Negroes who had been in slavery all their lives, and had been deprived of proper schooling, would be unfit for ordination at that time. As the Negro has progressed in schooling and living standards, many have joined the Reorganized Church and some have been ordained and are ministering to their congregations. The Reorganization does not accept the philosophy of a cursed race that is doomed to be the servants of others.

CHAPTER XXVIII

MISCELLANEOUS

When writing a book such as is attempted here, and doing it on a topical basis, it is not always possible to include personal experiences in a specific chapter. The author wished to present comparisons other than those of the specific subjects that have been covered. These will be primarily personal experiences that have occurred during his membership in both organizations. The first of these will be in reference to the teaching and training he received as a child, and comparing it with that training received by his children in like circumstances.

Having spent his childhood in the Mormon Church, and having been baptized at the age of eight, he does recall that he had been taught the Articles of Faith and was able to repeat them at the time of baptism. The Mormon Church, through its Sunday School and Primary Association, combined in their efforts to prepare children for baptism and membership prior to the important event. The instructions had included much about the activities of the Prophet Joseph Smith, especially of his athletic prowess, which is always very appealing to young boys. The Bible stories were not neglected because the teaching period was not confined to one hour a week. During this early period, they also had the children attend what was known at the time as Religion Class. This activity is now a part of the seminaries that are being conducted by the church. This resulted in at least three separate hours each week for instruction on the beliefs of the church. It is not difficult to understand that after a child has been through this type of program, he is ready for the important day of baptism.

After joining the Reorganized Church in Salt Lake City, the author became very active in the local congregation and was soon ordained to the priesthood. He had the privilege of spending some time in the missionary field before he moved to Independence, Missouri. Here he had the happy privilege of meeting and marrying a young lady who was a member of the church. To this marriage, six children were born. It is in

225

the teaching and training of these children that a comparison is to be made. The author does not overlook the fact that the direct responsibility for the training of children rests upon the parents, and is a task that cannot be avoided. What should be emphasized in this comparison is the responsibility resting upon the Church, should the parents fail in their obligation to teach the children. The author acknowledges that he failed in doing the task as it should have been done. His failure to do so can possibly be traced to his early training, which was mostly received from the church. It was not due to a failure to attend church services and Sunday School. He has constantly attended services, taking his children with him, and has been very active in the affairs of the congregations attended, especially in the field of teaching. He relied greatly upon the church school to teach the children what they should know. It was not until the oldest daughter was thirteen that she posed a question, "Who was Joseph Smith?" It was at this point that the author began an investigation in the curricula of the Sunday School. Letters were written to the leaders of the religious education department and several discussions were held. It was continually stressed by the leaders that the Church was relying upon the parents to shoulder their responsibility in the teaching of their children. They did not wish to assume any of the obligation involved in the teaching of children.

From the investigation made, it was learned that most of the material used in the Sunday School, and especially in the children's division, was centered in Bible stories and teachings. They had also developed a program that when a child approached the age for baptism, they would then start conducting special prebaptism classes and, in this way, attempted to meet the needs of the children not trained in the home.

As a result of this experience, the author was made aware of the tremendous inadequacy of trying to train our children on the basis of one hour a week in a Sunday School. There is great need for more extended instruction and additional class periods. How this is to be achieved is a problem that confronts the church.

A few words in an attempt to more or less justify the author in his reliance upon the church for the specific training of his children. It must be remembered that many of the church members are converts from other religious organizations, and they enter the church with many preconceived ideas and beliefs, especially so when the children are in-

226

volved. If the Sunday School is to achieve successfully the teaching of the children, it must be from a standard curriculum that will present the church in its truest form, even though it might be contrary to the preconceived ideas of the parents. By leaving the training to the home, it is not difficult to visualize the many different approaches that will be made unless a unified program is developed to aid the parents in their task.

In the early church, especially during the lifetime of the Prophet Joseph Smith, the use of the Cross as the emblem or standard of Christianity did not occur. The reason for this was the belief that the mission of Christ was one of life and life-giving teachings and therefore the Cross, which is an emblem of death and suffering and a means for the execution of criminals, was not a true symbol of Christ. Also, when it is recalled that the first emblem used by the early Christians was the Fish and that the use of the Cross did not occur until the days of Constantine, about three hundred years after Christ's death, the Cross cannot truly represent the real mission of Christ any more than could a hangman's noose, or an electric chair.

The Mormon Church has continued the policy of the early church in not making use of the cross as an emblem of the church. It will not be found in or on the church buildings.

The Reorganized Church followed the same policy for many years, and at the general conference of April 6, 1874, the church adopted the official Seal of the Church which appears on practically all of the literature and also appears on many of the buildings erected by the church. The design of the seal is: "Reorganized Church of Jesus Christ of Latter Day Saints. Emblem: a Lion and a Lamb lying down to rest. Motto: Peace. Incorporated 1872." No official action has ever been taken by the church discouraging the use of the cross, but it has been left to the discretion of individuals or congregations. In the past twenty-five years, there has developed a trend in the Reorganization to make use of the Cross as an emblem. It can now be found in the church, usually showing over the speaker's rostrum, as ornaments on the outside of the church building, and they now have some buildings with a huge cross erected in front of the church in the same manner as is being done by most of the Protestant churches. It is getting more and more difficult to distinguish a Reorganized church from any of the Protestant groups.

It is the opinion of the author that this is another of the

trends, within the Reorganization, that raises the concern that it is becoming more and more 'protestantized' as an organization, and becoming less and less distinctive as a church of the Restoration.

The lack of interchange of literature, music, etc., has been of some concern to the author, because it demonstrates the existence of an animosity toward one another that is not compatible with a Christian attitude. When it is remembered that both churches had the same origin, and that their basic beliefs are from the same books, there will be a great deal of research information done by each that could be utilized by either. This is especially true in reference to the archaeological research that is being done by both churches. Because of their financial capability, the Mormon Church has done much in research, both on the coming forth of the Book of Mormon and the archaeological findings, and much has been written in dissertations by students in various universities that is extremely valuable to scholars investigating and doing research.

As an illustration of what the author has in mind, a reference is made to a recent article in the *Saints' Herald* of the Reorganized Church. It was an article on the church and the social order. This is subject matter that has always been of great importance to the beliefs of the Restoration. Accompanying the article was an extensive bibliography for research. On checking the sources of the books that were in this bibliography, they were all from primarily Protestant church writers. Not one reference to any book written by a believer in the Restoration, whether it was from the Reorganized Church or the Mormon Church.

The same attitude exists between the churches in reference to music and hymns that have been written by members of either church. There is no interchange between them and as a result, many beautiful hymns are unknown to both groups. Both churches have in their hymnals songs written for the Restoration by devout members which are suitable to be sung in either church because they are not controversial. However, the deep animosity that exists stands in the way of any interchange and, as a result, both organizations lose much in spite of having had a common origin. A prayer should constantly ascend to God, by members of both organizations, that God will remove from their hearts the blinding and deleterious effect of such animosity, and that greater efforts be made to understand and appreciate each other.

228

CHAPTER XXIX

CONCLUSIONS

It is impossible to make a study of the many things written in this book and not arrive at some conclusions. This extensive study was, in many ways, forced upon the author when he was called upon to defend his position, and to justify his reasons for changing from one organization to another. It must be remembered that any conclusion reached by an individual is strictly personal, and is based upon his understanding of that which is written, plus his own personal experiences and studies. It is extremely important, when forming conclusions, that the subject be approached with an open mind and a sincere desire to know what is true and that which is false. All previous biases or prejudices should be forgotten if possible, in order that the reader will honestly approach the study to be made.

The author is also well aware that his tolerant attitude to the Mormon Church has not been fully appreciated by those with whom he has been associated, and in a large measure this has devaluated his services to the Reorganized Church. However, it is far better for one to live up to the principles of his knowledge and belief than to sacrifice them for position or any other consideration. The author does have great appreciation for the patience and kindness shown him over the years, in spite of the differences of opinion, by the many friends and fellow members of the priesthood.

The first major and possibly the most important, in its impact upon the Mormon Church, conclusion to be reached by the author is the doctrine of unquestioning obedience to the leaders of the church, to accept them as "living oracles" when the matter of doctrine is considered. It was because of this teaching by the leaders that many of the new and questionable doctrines were introduced into the Church. It has been justified by some Mormons because of the adoration and respect in which the Prophet Joseph Smith was held, especially during the latter years of his life. It is not difficult to realize that the thinking and ideas of Joseph Smith became very important to his followers, so much so that he ultimately became the final word to his adherents. This was not because of his desire to have it so, but was a result of close association and a desire to recognize his prophetic mission. Since the death of the Prophet, this admiration has grown until it has practically attained the point of infallibility among many of the members of the Mormon Church. This feeling of infallibility is now being passed on to other leaders of the church, including the present heads of the organization.

After the death of the Prophet, it was very necessary for the leaders that took over the supervision of the church to secure their position, and this could best be accomplished by utilizing the admiration and reverence in which the Prophet was held. This is demonstrated by the wholesale elimination of those in prominent position who did not go along with them in their thinking. Many were excommunicated and complete obedience was required of the followers. They were taught that so long as the people had men of God (living oracles) leading the church, all that was necessary was to obey. This philosophy is still deeply ingrained in the membership of the church and has left them extremely vulnerable to the introduction of new doctrine and procedures. Acceptance of this philosophy by the membership permits the altering of revelations given by another prophet, or what is stated in other words as "amendatory rights." This, of course, is in support of a changeable God implying that what has been given previously may be amended or changed. Under conditions like this, anything can be done. This same doctrine is what led to so many changes that took place in the Roman Catholic Church, which accepted the infallibility of the Pope.

It is the contention of the author that all of the differences between the two churches are based on doctrines and ideas that were introduced into the church after the Prophet's death and under the circumstances outlined above.

There can be no question of the success of the Mormon Church, especially in matters of organization. They have proven to the world that, by following the teachings of the Prophet in matter of organization, the church can be so mechanically perfect that the teachings of Christ could be spread throughout the world, fulfilling the commandment of Christ, "Go ye into all the world." When it is realized the principles of this organization were given to the Prophet by revelation, it is a further testimony of his divine mission.

230

In the field of education and teaching, the Mormon Church cannot be surpassed. The Brigham Young University at Provo, Utah, is reputed to be the largest wholly church-owned university in the United States. The church's teaching influence upon its members, and especially its youth, is one of the most outstanding achievements to be seen anywhere. To so train and teach the young men and women to a point where they are willing to give a portion of their life to the church, and at their own expense, is unequalled anywhere. Yet it is through the efforts of these young people that the church receives its greatest growth, in the field of baptisms and new converts. It has been of real interest to note that, in the past years, the church has had an annual growth rate of 7.6 percent, which is more than double the growth rate of various other church organizations which is an annual 3.09 percent.

To live among or to be closely associated with the members of the Mormon Church, one cannot but appreciate the devotion of these people to their church. The author has had the privilege and opportunity, because of many relatives in the church, to visit among them and to learn, at first hand, how these people feel about their church. Their adherence to the Word of Wisdom is highly commendable and is probably one of the reasons for the longevity of the lives of their leaders this being one of the promises to those who will heed this divine instruction.

Another interesting feature, and an additional indication of their devotion to the church, is the way they financially support the organization. Because they have been so taught from early childhood, it is never necessary for the church to pass collection plates during a service. The Mormon Church has never found it necessary to follow the general practice as carried on in other churches, either in the type of service or procedures. They have maintained a very distinctive type of organization of great self-reliance. This is especially true when it is realized that all of their activities are under the guidance of an unpaid ministry. Service to the church is considered among the highest of opportunities and becomes one of the utmost satisfactions to those who serve. This is one of the finest demonstrations that real devotion can never be purchased. In the opinion of the author, this is the genius of the Restoration Movement.

While the attitude of the Mormon Church about marriage, not referring to the belief in polygamy which was stopped by federal action, is one of the major differences between the two churches, it is well to have some knowledge of its effect on members of the church. The philosophy of Celestial Marriage, or marriage for time and eternity, is what is being considered. In a search for statistics relative to marriage and divorce, we have learned that there is one divorce in every fifty-five temple marriages. When this is compared to the national average, which is one divorce to every four marriages, it does have a very salutary effect. It does indicate that marriage is taken more seriously among the membership of the church than is usually found on the outside.

Another proof of the devotion of the members of the Mormon Church has been demonstrated in the development of their Welfare Program, and the great concern they have had as an organization for the needy members of the church. In this field, they have done more than any other organization in the world to fulfill the admonition given by Christ, both in the early church and then through the Prophet Joseph Smith, to be constantly aware of and care for the needs of the poor and afflicted.

An overall view of the Mormon Church is best shown by the fact that here is an organization which has suffered a great deal of oppression, and has been looked upon with disgust for some of its teachings, has been sneered at by many, and has suffered many indignities; yet it has reached a point where one of its members was being considered for the highest office in the land. For many years they have had members of the church in the Presidential Cabinet at Washington, D.C. This stature has not been a result of compromise with other churches or doctrines but in spite of this. They have never made it a practice to join ministerial alliances or participate in any ecumenical movements. It has been done by a firm conviction of what they believe and a great deal of self-reliance.

The Reorganized Church, in the opinion of the author, has adhered doctrinely more closely to the church as founded by the Prophet Joseph Smith. It has not participated in the introduction of false doctrine and peculiar beliefs, and has not suffered from the doctrine of complete obedience to the leadership, though at times it would have been to members' advantage had they done so. They have never endeavored to have the membership accept any doctrine that is not in the Doctrine and Covenants, Bible, or Book of Mormon. They have tried to raise the level of spirituality of the church and its members. The extent to which they have been successful can only be measured by the devotion and conviction of the individual member.

The major weaknesses of the Reorganization are found in its mechanical functioning and its willingness to compromise on procedures. Please remember the author did not say compromise on doctrine. Were it not for the very deep concern of the author about the trends indicated in the Reorganization, this book would never have been written. It is at this point that writing becomes extremely difficult, because it is so close to the heart of the author. Early in life, it was found necessary to give up some of the more pleasant things of life for a principle, and it has always been a very important part of his thinking over the years that honest conviction of principle is not to be compromised or sacrificed for any reason other than the truth.

Recently there appeared an article in *Time* magazine about the Reorganized Church that has added greatly to the author's concern. This article appeared a short time after the World Conference of April, 1966, held at Independence, Missouri, and was commented upon by one of the editors of the *Saints' Herald* of July 15, 1966. Knowing that the article is not readily available to the reader, and to avoid the charge of taking thoughts out of context, the entire article is quoted. It is taken from the April 29, 1966, issue of *Time*:

"THE OTHER SAINTS:
After Mormon Prophet Joseph Smith, Jr. was killed by an Illinois lynch mob in 1844, Brigham Young led 10,000 of his followers on the great westward trek to the land of Zion that became Utah. Not all of the new religionists went with him. Denouncing Young as a usurper, a little band of Smith's disciples stayed in the Midwest to form the Reorganized Church of Jesus Christ of Latter Day Saints, which last week opened its biennial world conference at its dome-topped headquarters in Independence, Missouri.

TRUE HEIRS. By comparison with the 2,396,000 thriving, mission-minded Utah Mormons, the Reorganized Saints appear to be a fossilized, forgotten sect: their membership is only 191,400, mostly in California and the Midwest, and the church's growth rate is a modest 5,000 a year. Nonetheless, the Reorganized Saints steadfastly maintain that they are the true spiritual heirs of Joseph Smith, and they have plenty of his progeny to bolster the claim. Although the Utah Mormons claim only one direct descendant of Smith, at least 190 are Reorganized Saints, and their President, W. Wallace Smith, 65, is the prophet's grandson. The Reorganized Saints hold to the belief that Joseph Smith, before his death, anointed his eldest son, Joseph III, to succeed him as the sect's leader. Young Joseph became President of the Reorganized Church in 1860, ruled it for 54 years, and was followed by three of his sons in succession.

The Reorganized Saints do not call themselves Mormon, and differ with the Utah church on a number of doctrinal lines. They have never practiced polygamy, and admit Negroes to the priesthood—although only a few hundred belong to the church. Both churches accept the Book of Mormon as inspired scripture along with the Bible, and both believe that God provides continuous revelation through the church President. Last week Wallace Smith told the 20,000 delegates and visitors at Independence that his newest guidance calls for a replacement of certain officers in the hierarchy and for an expanded new program of evangelism. The delegates responded by approving a record budget of $8,200,000 for the next two years.

WARMER TOWARD UTAH. Smith also suggested that the Reorganized Saints should, without compromising their beliefs, take more of an interest in the Christian ecumenical movement. *As it happens, the Reorganized Saints feel more akin to other church groups—such as Methodists—than they do to the Utah Mormons*, even though relations between the two denominations are warmer than they used to be. Members of the Reorganized Saints district in Utah are no longer shunned as apostates by Mormons, while spokesmen for the two churches now politely refer to their differences as problems of doctrinal interpretation rather than of heresy."
(Italics by author for emphasis.)

The real value of an article such as the above is in the objectivity of the writer as an outside observer, not bound by any ties to either organization. We realize also that articles of this type, while not always free from prejudice, enable us to have a glimpse of the view of others so far as we are concerned. We cannot vouch for the accuracy of the writer of the article's statistics or his interpretation of them, but we have emphasized a portion of the statement that appears to confirm the author's thinking relative to the Reorganization's position.

Referring to the statistics shown in the article relative to the annual growth of the Reorganization which is shown as 5,000: The writer of the article used the annual baptism figure, which is not a true gauge of its annual growth. We checked the statistical department of the Reorganization and learned that the annual growth rate for the church in 1960 was 1.75 percent. The most recent information was that at the close of 1967, the growth rate had dropped to 1.3 percent. This figure is causing a great deal of concern in the Reorganization because it is less than half of the annual growth rate of all other churches, which is 3.09 percent as a national average. When the growth rate figure of 1.3 percent is compared to the 7.6 percent of the Mormon Church, the concern is well understood. It is an indication that somewhere or somehow, the Reorganization is not reaching the people to the extent it should.

When it is realized that the main missionary arm of the Reorganization is comprised of church appointees, functioning on a full-time basis and securing their livelihood from the church, and then compare the results of their efforts with those of the Mormon Church who are in the field voluntarily and unpaid as ministers, many very serious questions arise. The author has been greatly concerned for many years that the Reorganization was becoming much too professionalized in their activities, which can only result in the development of a division between the standing ministry of the local priesthood and the professional or appointee ministry in the church. This has grown to the point that every key position in the church is now held by appointees and none by the local or standing ministry. This has obviously resulted in making administrators of most of the appointees, and therefore, reduced the actual missionary activities to practically nil. In the opinion of the author, the Reorganization is wasting its resources on unproductive manpower. There are some minor local areas or districts that are supervised by local standing ministers, but none are the major key, policy-making positions. In some areas the appointee serves as pastor or presiding elder of the congregation.

As a result of this policy, many questions arise such as, Is it possible that this development of professional ministers is in any way, responsible for the church's failure to grow? Will not this reliance upon appointees in filling the key positions in the church tend to downgrade the need for relying upon the local men of the priesthood, and this, in turn, tend to diminish the feeling of responsibility by the local men?

A very good illustration has arisen in one of the center stakes. It is being contemplated by the stake to employ a professional marriage counselor. Over the years and by the intent of God, this function has been one of the important callings of the Elders of the Melchisedec priesthood. Would it not have been much more in line with the will of God to have been training this priesthood over the years, to qualify in this field? In another stake, they have recently employed a full-time youth leader. Will the church always be in a position to hire men to do the work that should be done? When it is realized that most of the income to the church is disbursed for manpower that should be building up the membership, and we look at the growth statistics, questions do arise as to the efficiency of the policy.

It has been an observation of the author over the years that the use of appointees, particularly in local capacity, tends to remove from the local priesthood a sense of responsibility, and as a result they have become more and more reluctant to fulfill their obligations. This and the failure of the church to follow through with priesthood quorum organization, which was given to the church by revelation, has resulted in a lack of enthusiasm, devotion, and a sense of responsibility among many of the local priesthood. There is a feeling of a lack of confidence in them by the general church authorities. Leadership is not developed and the men of the priesthood have come to rely upon the appointee to assume the work they should be called upon to do. It should be repeated that true devotion and conviction can never be purchased.

It should be very apparent to any observer that even though the church may have adhered more closely to the principles of the gospel, that with failure to properly implement the projection of those principles, all efforts will prove in vain. It is the opinion of the author that this is one of the major reasons why God had to restore his church.

The Reorganized Church has not been totally unaware of the trends and this is indicated in an article in the *Saints'*

Herald for January 7, 1954, and it is from writings of Presiding Patriarch Roy Cheville. The statement outlines some of the future alternatives of the church and is as follows:

"1. The institution may lose faith in itself as having a distinctive purpose for existing—and degenerate into nothingness.

2. Possibly, differences over distinctives can cause it to divide into two or more schisms.

3. It may merely "self-maintain" its membership totals and gradually increase with the general population growth and become immersed in society and lost as a conventional religious body.

4. It may seize upon a certain distinctive message or quality, emphasize and exploit it, and thereby stand out as an unusual church."

Most everyone who reads the above statements will immediately attempt to categorize the church and rightly so. Only by learning where we have been, where we are and where we are headed can we intelligently analyze our problems. Unless we know and understand those problems, we can never correct or solve them. We know that the leading officers of the church are very conscious of the situation, and have been meeting in council seeking solutions. They should be the recipients of the prayers of the membership for God to direct them in their deliberations.

Should there be a motive for the writing of this book, it should be attributed to the desire on the part of the author for a closer understanding between the two organizations endeavoring to represent the principles of the Restoration as given through the Prophet Joseph Smith. There is a very earnest desire that the animosity that exists in the hearts of many of the leaders on both sides be thoroughly eliminated and that the love for our fellow men should take its place. Only when that love exists is there an opportunity for an understanding; only when that love fills our hearts can we fully accomplish the work of the Lord and understand his will. If we will attribute to every man the sincerity that we feel is ours, then there is an opportunity for mutual understanding.

To close, I again wish to give my testimony of this great work—that I know it is of God, given through the instrumentality of Joseph Smith as a prophet of God. I know the Book of Mormon was translated by the power of God. I also know that God will continue to lead and guide his people when permitted to do so.